LEADING WITH PURPOSE: IGNITING SUCCESS, INSPIRING TEAMS, AND CREATING POSITIVE CHANGE

LEADING WITH PURPOSE: IGNITING SUCCESS, INSPIRING TEAMS, AND CREATING POSITIVE CHANGE

The Power of Visionary Leadership in the Digital Era

PANKAJ PRASOON

Leading with Purpose: Igniting Success, Inspiring Teams, and Creating Positive Change

First Edition

Paperback ISBN: 979-8-8229-1818-4

To my beloved wife, your unconditional love, enduring patience, and unwavering support have served as my beacon, crafting a life that exceeds our wildest dreams. Your companionship and understanding have been a cornerstone in our journey together.

To my dear son, your youthful enthusiasm, curiosity, and boundless joy have significantly reshaped my outlook on life, infusing it with a renewed sense of purpose. Your presence and constant evolution have contributed immensely to the man, husband, and father I am today.

Additionally, I extend my profound gratitude to my dear father and mother. Their unwavering love, timeless wisdom, and constant guidance have been a bedrock of support throughout my life, significantly shaping the person I have become.

This book, a testament to my love for all of you, bears the indelible imprint of your invaluable presence and influence in my life. Each page is a tribute to the family we have built together, a reflection of our shared experiences, and a chronicle of the journey we continue to embark on as a united front.

DISCLAIMER

This book, "Leading with Purpose: Igniting Success, Inspiring Teams, and Creating Positive Change," is intended to serve as an educational and informational resource for readers interested in leadership development. Please do not use it as a substitute for professional advice in business, management, or any other field.

The author's understanding and interpretation of the concepts and practices discussed form the basis for this book's examples and case studies. These interpretations are influenced by the author's personal experiences, knowledge, and perspectives. Therefore, individuals with different backgrounds or viewpoints may have different interpretations or opinions regarding the situations or individuals portrayed in these examples.

The leadership traits, strategies, and practices described in this book are not one-size-fits-all solutions. Leadership is a complex and multi-faceted discipline that varies significantly depending on various factors, including individual personality traits, team dynamics, organizational culture, and broader societal and market trends. Therefore, readers are encouraged to critically evaluate and adapt the information to their unique contexts and needs.

We have made every effort to ensure the accuracy and completeness of the information contained in this book. However, we provide it "as is" without any warranty, express or implied. The author assumes no responsibility for errors, omissions, or actions relying on the information.

The views and opinions expressed in this book are those of the author and do not necessarily reflect the official policy or position of any other agency, organization, employer, or company. Readers are encouraged to seek professional advice for their specific circumstances.

This book may reference third-party trademarks, service marks, and logos. All such trademarks are the property of their respective owners, and their use in this book does not imply any affiliation with or endorsement by them.

"Leading with Purpose: Igniting Success, Inspiring Teams, and Creating Positive Change" is a tool intended to stimulate thought and discussion about leadership. It aims to inspire readers to reflect on their leadership styles and practices and to consider new perspectives and approaches. However, the responsibility for applying this information lies with each reader. As with any resource, the value derived from this book will depend on the reader's engagement, openness, and willingness to adapt the insights to their unique situations.

BACKGROUND AND MESSAGE TO THE READERS

"Leading with Purpose: Igniting Success, Inspiring Teams, and Creating Positive Change" is crafted with real-life examples of leaders and a comprehensive guide for aspiring and experienced leaders who yearn to weave purpose into the very fabric of their management style. In a rapidly changing world where countless organizations battle for the hearts and minds of customers and employees alike, what truly sets apart the extraordinary from the ordinary? The answer lies in purpose-driven leadership – the art of leading with a deep-rooted sense of purpose that transcends the mundane aspects of everyday business.

Think of the most exceptional leader you've ever encountered – the kind of leader who inspires followership and leaves a lasting, transformative impact. What qualities set them apart? Beyond their technical understanding and strategic prowess, these luminaries possess an unwavering sense of purpose that drives every decision, action, and interaction. This book aims to unlock the secrets of purpose-driven leadership, shedding light on the benefits of a purposeful approach to leaders, teams, and organizations.

Why do we need purpose-driven leadership in the first place, you may ask? In a world of challenges and distractions, a strong sense of purpose is a light ray guiding teams toward a shared vision and common goal. Moreover, it fosters engagement, motivates employees, and imbues a sense of belonging – all critical ingredients for a thriving organization.

The journey towards purpose-driven leadership begins with a deep dive into understanding purpose. Like a master potter shaping a lump of clay into a vessel that carries meaning, the book molds the abstract concept of purpose into a tangible, actionable framework for leaders. Next, it dissects the difference between personal and organizational purpose. Finally, it elucidates the powerful constructive collaboration that emerges when these two intertwine.

So, how does one go about developing their leadership purpose? First, the book serves as a roadmap, guiding leaders through introspection and self-reflection to unearth their core values and aspirations. It helps leaders align their purpose with organizational values, creating a harmonious marriage that inspires commitment and loyalty.

But how can leaders communicate this purpose to their teams? The book unravels the art of storytelling and the power of metaphor to illuminate the path for leaders to share their purpose and vision with their team members. It also encourages leaders to create an environment where team members can find their sense of purpose, fostering a culture where everyone is empowered to contribute meaningfully.

Imagine a team where each member is aligned with the organization's purpose and inspired and motivated to achieve great things. The book delves into the techniques leaders can use to create such an environment, from leading by example to recognizing and rewarding purpose-driven behavior. It emphasizes the importance of fostering a growth mindset, transforming teams into vibrant ecosystems where learning and growth are the norms rather than exceptions.

However, the path to purpose-driven leadership is not without obstacles. The book delves into the challenges leaders may face, such as resistance to change, balancing purpose with performance, and navigating ethical dilemmas. Like a skilled navigator plotting a course through treacherous waters, it equips leaders with the tools and strategies needed to overcome these obstacles and emerge stronger on the other side.

How do we know that purpose-driven leadership truly makes a difference? The book addresses this question by exploring methods for measuring the impact of purpose-driven leadership on team engagement, satisfaction, and performance. In addition, it empowers leaders to evaluate the long-term benefits of leading with purpose, painting a compelling picture of a brighter future for organizations that embrace this approach.

As you turn the pages of this inspiring narrative, envision yourself as the protagonist of this story – a leader poised to make a difference in the lives of your team members and the trajectory of your organization. Every chapter will equip you with new insights, tools, and strategies to hone your leadership skills and bring purpose to the forefront of your management style.

What if you could be the leader who inspires people to go above and beyond, spark change, and foster a culture of innovation and growth? By embracing the principles of purpose-driven leadership, you can become that leader – a catalyst for positive change and a beacon of inspiration for your team.

This book is a call to action, inviting individuals to take the first step on their purpose-driven leadership journey. It's time to step out of the shadows of mediocrity and into the light of greatness. Are you ready to lead purposefully, inspire your team, and create a legacy? The answers lie within the pages of "Leading with Purpose: Igniting Success, Inspiring Teams, and Creating Positive Change."

As we get ready to explore the exciting world of leadership focused on a clear purpose, opening new paths for ourselves, our teams, and our organizations, I want to share some personal experiences. These are times when I was lucky enough to see this kind of leadership up close. The impact of these moments has profoundly shaped my way of leading.

I've learned from various experiences, like watching a mentor stay strong in difficult times, a boss who understood my feelings during a job change, and a leader in the industry with a clear plan for the future. All these stories are different, but they're all inspiring. Each one is full of lessons, showing the great power that purposeful leadership can have.

So, as we start this exciting journey together, I hope you'll dive into these stories with an open mind and heart. Think about them, question them, and see what feels true to you. How might these stories change the way you lead? How might they help you transform your methods, your team's work, or your organization's path?

I genuinely believe that my personal experiences with purposeful leadership will give you valuable insights. I'm excited to share these stories because they've changed my life. They will inspire you just as much, making you rethink and reshape your leadership style.

So, let's get started. Let's step into the world of purposeful leadership, guided by the bright light of these powerful stories. Let's discover the considerable potential each of us has, waiting to be sparked by the power of purpose.

THE BLUEPRINT OF LEGACY : WEAVING PURPOSE INTO EVERY LINE OF MY LIFE

Our story starts in my childhood home, a simple place where my wise and humble dad taught me about leadership with a clear purpose.

My dad worked hard in the heart of a busy city filled with machine noises and bright lights. He was an engineer, always coming up with new ideas and never giving up, which was inspiring. He worked in a world of technical drawings and industry sounds but saw it with an artist's eyes and a thinker's mind.

Looking back, I remember seeing my dad working at his desk, his pen moving over the complicated blueprints. His work filled the room with sounds - the scratch of his pen, the sound of paper, and the clicking of his tools.

Yet, I carry the most profound memory unencapsulated within his work's tangible elements. However, instead, it resides within the unseen realm of his ethos. My father was not simply an engineer but a purposeful leader, his every action underscored by a relentless commitment to his craft and team. His career is abundant with inspirational stories, yet one in particular truly shines through. It transpired during his tenure at an offshore location situated amid the ocean. Amidst his assignment, a disastrous incident occurred, resulting in him sustaining significant burn injuries.

Rather than letting concern for his well-being overshadow his duties, he concentrated on controlling the raging flames and safeguarding his colleagues. His undeterred commitment to his responsibilities and extraordinary respect for his team's safety, even in the face of personal danger, exemplify professional dedication and selflessness.

So, what was it that set my father apart, transforming him from an engineer into a purposeful leader? First, let's uncover the threads of his leadership style, each strand woven with the distinctive traits of purposeful leadership.

- Strong Commitment: My dad believed sincerely in the power of engineering. He saw his job not just as a way to earn a living but as a way to improve society. This purpose fueled his dedication, driving him to relentlessly strive for excellence, even in the face of adversity.
- Caring Mentorship: My dad's clear purpose guided his actions and helped others. He was a real mentor, helping his team members grow with understanding, patience, and belief in their abilities. This caring leadership created a team culture of respect, teamwork, and constant learning.
- Vision for Innovation: My dad believed in the power of new ideas, not just for the sake of being different, but to make a real change. He constantly challenged the usual way of doing things, encouraging his team to think creatively and solve problems. His leadership went beyond just managing tasks; he grew the next generation of innovative thinkers.

- Moral Integrity: My dad was a man of the highest ethical standards. He and his team always did what was right, no matter what. It earned him the trust and respect of his team, clients, and colleagues, a crucial part of being a successful leader.

Thinking about my dad's legacy, I remember something he used to say: "An engineer is like a weaver, creating the fabric of our society. Each thing we make is a solution, a connection, a way forward. And as we create, we need to remember - it's not just about what we make today, but how it lasts and helps the society of tomorrow."

His words echo in my mind, constantly reminding me of the transformative power of purposeful leadership. He did not merely etch his legacy in his engineering work but also in the values he instilled within his team and me. His leadership narrative, underpinned by purpose, empathy, innovation, and integrity, continues to guide my journey, inspiring me to weave my unique leadership grace.

Lessons in Leadership and Innovation: An Unforgettable Encounter with Infosys Founder NRN Murthy

After earning my computer science and engineering degree in 2006, I started my career at Infosys. I had no idea that this job would bring me face-to-face with NRN Murthy, the founder of Infosys. One day, I got an email inviting me to meet him. I was one of the lucky few chosen for this. But just before this, I had surgery and couldn't walk well. How was I going to meet the man who started this great company?

Despite feeling nervous and in pain, I went home to get some formal shoes, hoping they would help me walk better. Even though it hurt,

I was determined to go to the meeting. As I got closer, excitement and nerves filled my mind.

Excitement filled the room as we waited for NRN Murthy. When he walked in, you could feel his importance. Then, he started talking and asked us to explain semaphores in simple terms.

I felt nervous but knew I could answer. I slowly raised my hand and started explaining. "Semaphores in operating systems are like traffic signals on our roads," I said. "They help keep everything together, ensuring only one process can use a shared resource. It avoids conflicts and keeps everything running smoothly. For example, suppose two processes want to write to the same file. In that case, a semaphore allows only one to do it simultaneously. It keeps the data safe."

Murthy smiled, showing he was happy with my answer. "Good job," he said kindly. "As engineers, we need to make complex things easy to understand. Sit down."

As I sat down, I listened to Murthy share his thoughts on developing new ideas and adapting to changes. He emphasized that continuous innovation and adapting to market changes and new technology are critical to long-term growth and success in a constantly changing business world. Because of his commitment to innovation, Infosys became a global leader in the IT industry.

During that meeting, NRN Murthy, a true leader, shared his wisdom on innovation, adaptability, purpose, service, values, and authenticity. He gave us deep insights and examples that left a lasting impression.

"Have a clear goal," said Murthy with much confidence. "Let me take you back to the early days of Infosys. Our goal was straightforward

- we wanted to build a top-notch company that provided excellent services and helped society progress. The idea of changing lives with technology drove us. This goal guided us, keeping us focused on our mission even when times got tough."

Murthy told us to be clear about who we were helping. " At Infosys, we understood that our success was linked to our client's success," he said with a steady look. "We worked hard to understand their needs, problems, and dreams. It helped us design solutions that fit their desires because we could see things from their perspective. Our focus on clients helped us build strong, long-lasting relationships based on trust and mutual growth."

Murthy also talked about the importance of values. "Values are like the pillars that hold up a company's character," he said with conviction. "Here's an example to explain this. In the early years, we had to make a tough decision. We turned down a profitable deal because it went against our ethics. That moment showed our commitment to honesty, transparency, and fairness. By sticking to our values, we earned respect and laid the groundwork for a strong, principled company."

Lastly, Murthy encouraged us to be genuine. "Being authentic is the key to real connections," he said, looking sincere. "Here's a personal story. Once, I had to talk to a big group of employees. I stood in front of them, simple and open. I spoke from the heart, not hiding my flaws and worries. This honesty struck a chord with the team, creating an atmosphere of trust, open communication, and teamwork. Leaders can inspire and motivate their teams by being authentic and uniting them towards a shared goal."

Reflecting on the essential lessons from NRN Murthy, I realize their power to change things. Having a clear goal, knowing whom you're serving, sticking to your values, and being authentic aren't just buzzwords. They're the building blocks of outstanding leadership. With these insights from Murthy, I set out on my journey with a clear goal, a focus on serving, grounded in my values, and committed to authenticity.

A Personal Account of Innovation and Empowerment Under CEO Vishal Sikka

On the first day of November 2016, we received an invitation that excited me and my team. The invitation was to attend a distinctive event called "Greet Great Minds," hosted by our CEO, Dr. Vishal Sikka, at his Palo Alto, USA office. The invitees were carefully selected from across the company, comprising individuals and teams who had pushed the boundaries of innovation and harnessed the power of technology to drive transformation on a grand scale.

For my team and me, it was like meeting a superstar. Sikka wasn't just our CEO but also a role model and a pioneer in the tech field. We were lucky to be working on a product showcasing his creativity as SAP's ex-Chief Technology Officer. Although we had met Sikka before, the excitement was still fresh. I remember a past meeting where he closely checked our program code and gave us helpful feedback. His hands-on style left a strong impression on me.

On the day of the event, the mood was buzzing. We made sure we had a good view of what was going on. During the event, Sikka started talking to me. "What is your role, and what new idea have you come up with?" he asked. I took a moment to gather my thoughts. Then I told him about our journey and how we leveraged the product he and his team had designed to solve a problem for a customer. Because of this, we made processes more efficient, solved compliance issues, and saved money. I could see he was excited when he realized the impact of our work.

As the event went on, something unexpected happened. Sikka was addressing the innovators when he suddenly turned to me. He asked me to tell everyone our story, explaining how we found the problem, identified who would benefit from the solution, and used technology to provide real value for our client. It took me by surprise, but I was ready for it. I felt nervous but excited and proud as I took his microphone. I felt pride and passion as I shared our project's journey with my respected peers.

That day is a clear memory, reminding me of the power of new ideas, strong leadership, and using technology to overcome challenges. It also taught me that intelligent people can create solutions that change things with the right tools and the freedom to be creative. During that unforgettable event, I noticed several things about Vishal Sikka that showed he was a great leader. Promoting Innovation: His commitment to fostering innovation was undeniable. By hosting the "Greet Great Minds" event, he recognized and celebrated our use of technology to transform business. In addition, his interest in understanding our project and its impact showed me how much he valued innovation.

- Engagement and Communication: Dr. Sikka's engagement and open communication level were remarkable. He took the time to engage with us personally, showing genuine interest in our work and its effect on our clients. His openness and attentiveness made me feel truly appreciated.
- Empowerment: I realized I was empowered when Dr. Sikka asked me to share our story with the group. He provided me with a platform to validate our work and express our accomplishments. This empowerment made me feel recognized and further motivated to innovate.

- Inspirational & Motivational – Dr. Sikka's inspirational motivation was palpable. As the former Chief Technology Officer of SAP and CEO of Infosys, his work has always inspired us. His presence and interest in our work fueled our desire to innovate and excel.
- Promoting Learning and Growth: Sikka encouraged a learning and growth culture by inviting me to share our project's journey. This opportunity to share our process and problem-solving techniques was a testament to his commitment to knowledge-sharing and collaboration.

I realized that Dr. Vishal Sikka's approach to leadership was not just inspiring but also purposeful. He created an environment that fostered innovation, engagement, empowerment, and continuous learning, all crucial for our organization's success.

Unyielding Conviction: Bonnie Titone's Masterclass in Leadership

2016, I returned to the USA to spearhead a crucial data center migration project. Previous attempts to shift the workload have been unsuccessful, leading to growing concerns within our customer base. The company entrusted me with this mission-critical project. I led a diverse team of professionals, many boasting longer tenures in the field. This project was paramount as the systems in question-powered vital processes for our customers.

This endeavor marked a pivotal point in my professional journey. It significantly influenced my personal growth and subsequent decision to pursue further studies. The program once perceived my short two-day absence as the top risk. Despite the challenging environment, I recognized the gravity of my responsibilities. I dedicated myself to the task, working tirelessly around the clock. I rallied our teams around a unified vision and ensured everyone aligned with our overarching goal. Though we faced numerous unforeseen challenges, I remained steadfast, ensuring a solid contingency plan was in place. But internally, I harbored an unwavering conviction: there was no turning back. We had to succeed.

Two critical instances come to mind:

- Securing business approval for system downtime and post-migration testing.
- Addressing a pivotal setback post-migration when a key functionality malfunctioned, giving us a narrow window of just three hours to rectify the issue or resort to our backup plan.

Bonnie Titone, then the Head of Business Systems at the Northern California Utility company (now the CIO at Duke), soon became a beacon of guidance. Known for her robust leadership acumen, Bonnie played a pivotal role in ensuring the project's success, emphasizing the imperative nature of our program, and demonstrating unwavering support in critical times.

Always an astute listener and observer, Bonnie gave invaluable feedback upon reviewing our proposal. She emphasized the need for client-centricity, ensured our approach resonated with a spectrum of user needs, and removed potential barriers to a smooth migration. She offered a crystal-clear vision, steering us towards maintaining business continuity for our clients during this critical transition.

Guided by Bonnie's insights, we further honed our strategy over subsequent weeks. This phase instilled profound insights into client expectations, the essence of collaborative endeavors, and the significance of innovation in driving tangible outcomes.

From the incident above, we can extract several traits of purposeful Leadership exhibited by Bonnie Titone. Here they are in bullet points, followed by explanations:

- Visionary Leadership: - She offered the team a clear and unambiguous direction. She emphasized the imperativeness of the program and ensured everyone understood its gravity.
- Unwavering Support in Critical Times: In moments of crisis, such as when a key functionality malfunctioned, Bonnie's unwavering support gave the team the motivation and confidence to persevere.
- Astute Listening and Observation: Bonnie's ability to listen attentively and observe the nuances of the project allowed her to give valuable feedback. This trait is essential for leaders to understand their teams' challenges and needs.
- Emphasis on Collaboration and Unity - Steering the team towards a unified vision and ensuring everyone was on the same page highlighted Bonnie's emphasis on the power of collaborative efforts.
- Proactive Problem Solving - Securing business approval for system downtime and post-migration testing and addressing pivotal setbacks showcased her proactive approach to potential issues.

These traits reflect the holistic leadership approach Bonnie Titone took to guide a project to its successful completion and mentor, empower, and drive the personal and professional growth of those working under her Leadership.

Lessons from a President's Visionary and Client-Centric Approach – Ravi Kumar S

In the middle of 2018, an unexpected message began a transformative journey: "Ravi Kumar S, President at Infosys, wants to speak to you." Known for his exceptional leadership and deep industry expertise, Ravi has been instrumental in steering Infosys to its current stature as a global digital solutions and services leader. He is the CEO of Cognizant now. Fresh from a high-level leadership conference where he'd gathered insights from other industry executives, Ravi presented us with a challenge that would shape the future of our organization.

The task was straightforward in its ask yet intricate in its execution: we were to recalibrate our strategy to accelerate industry growth, catalyze transformation, foster a culture of innovation, and position ourselves in the leaders' quadrant for the exemplary customer-centric work we were already doing. This endeavor necessitated a meticulously coordinated, cross-functional effort to conceive a unique proposition in terms of positioning and execution.

Spearheading a dedicated team of over 20 professionals, we rose to the challenge. After three weeks of relentless collaboration, we had the blueprint for our revamped go-to-market strategy. This preliminary strategy encapsulated a feasibility study and an initial assessment of the investment and operational implications.

Upon reviewing our initial proposal, Ravi, an attentive listener, he offered his candid feedback. He urged us to revisit our approach to make it more client-centric, formulate solutions that resonate across various industries, and eliminate barriers to innovation and transformation. He provided us with a clear vision and purpose, guiding us towards becoming trusted partners for our clients on their digital transformation journeys and leading the charge in embracing technological advancements and emerging trends.

Over the next three weeks, under Ravi's guidance, we refined our strategy, with him reviewing our progress and steering us toward his envisioned goal. Throughout this process, I absorbed invaluable lessons on recognizing and profoundly understanding client needs and challenges. I also learned how to cultivate a culture of collaboration and innovation, driving tangible business outcomes through tailored solutions.

This period of strategic recalibration, guided by a leader like Ravi Kumar S, was a watershed moment in our journey. It elevated our strategic thinking and redefined our approach to client engagement, setting the stage for Infosys's continued success in the ever-evolving digital landscape.

Reflecting on my interaction with Ravi during this crucial period, a few key traits of purposeful leadership were apparent:

- Visionary Leadership: Ravi demonstrated a clear vision for our company's growth, including our positioning in the industry and how we should serve our clients. His ability to articulate this vision gave us a clear direction and purpose, hallmarks of a purposeful leader.
- Promotion of Collaboration and Innovation: He urged us to foster a culture of collaboration within our team and across different stakeholders. Moreover, he emphasized the importance of innovation, insisting that we remove any barriers to it. It demonstrated his commitment to the principles of shared leadership and collective problem-solving.

- Client-Centric Approach: The President's feedback on our initial strategy centered on being more client-centric. He wanted us to develop solutions catering to various industries and help our clients in their digital transformation journeys. His focus on the client's needs underscored his importance of serving our stakeholders effectively, an essential aspect of purposeful leadership.
- Active Engagement and Guidance: Ravi didn't just provide feedback and left us with it. Instead, he continuously engaged with us, reviewed our work, and offered guidance. His active participation ensured that our strategy aligned with his vision and fostered a sense of ownership and empowerment in our team.
- Emphasis on Learning and Adaptability: Ravi's approach pushed us to think differently, to learn, and adapt our strategies. He encouraged us to deeply understand our client's needs and develop tailored solutions. This commitment to learning and adaptability is a defining characteristic of purposeful leadership.
- Building Trust and Open Communication: Ravi's candid feedback and ongoing dialogue with us fostered an environment of trust and open communication. It allowed us to feel comfortable sharing our ideas and concerns, facilitating better problem-solving and decision-making.

Reflecting on these traits, I can see how Ravi's purposeful leadership shaped our strategy development process, leading us to create a more effective, client-centric strategy. In addition, his leadership style served as a powerful example for me and my team influencing our approach to our work and interactions with each other and our clients.

How Empathy and Adaptability Shape Successful Leadership – Ashley Gaare

June of 2021 was a month of significant crossroads in both my personal and professional life. An important moment was fast approaching on the horizon of my personal life as my partner, and I eagerly anticipated the arrival of our first child. Simultaneously, my professional life was gearing up for evolution. Finally, I was ready to join Microsoft, a titan in the technology landscape that every tech enthusiast dream of being a part of.

Not long before, I had taken up the mantle of Vice President at SoftwareONE, embarking on a mission to steer the company into a new digital transformation era. We had begun crafting a compelling narrative for the industry, making strides in our journey, when an enticing opportunity from Microsoft came knocking. It presented a fascinating alignment with my future aspirations, ability to make larger impact. So after much contemplation, I decided to seize it.

I recall the conversation with Ashley Gaare, President of North America at SoftwareONE, where I revealed my intentions. As I disclosed my aspirations to join Microsoft, I could discern a subtle cloud of disappointment shadowing her. A moment of pause and in a soft, earnest voice, she asked, "Is there anything I could do to hold you back and reconsider?" She expressed her reluctance to lose the momentum we had built and, more importantly, to lose me from the team. Despite the sentiment, my resolution to embark on the new journey was unwavering, and I tendered my notice.

In a serendipitous twist of fate, during my notice period, our little bundle of joy made the entrance. With the pandemic adding another layer of complexity, I found myself in a predicament, needing to conclude my tenure at SoftwareONE a week earlier than planned, potentially disrupting the transition process.

With a hesitant heart, I reached out to the President, explicating my situation and requesting an early release. Her response was nothing short of heartwarming. "Go ahead," she encouraged, her voice imbued with empathy, "this is the most important deal in your life. Work can wait, and we will work out a way."

Her generous response, underscored by empathy and understanding, cemented a bond that has endured beyond professional confines. To this day, we maintain contact, a testament to her empathic nature's profound impression on me. It was a emotional reminder that amidst the relentless pursuit of professional milestones, moments of human connection and understanding truly define our journeys. The incidence reminds of traits as follows.

- Empathy: Ashley showed a deep sense of compassion in understanding my situation. When I had to leave earlier than planned due to the arrival of my child during the pandemic, she didn't hesitate to let me prioritize my family over work. It is an essential aspect of purposeful leadership as it recognizes the holistic well-being of employees beyond their professional roles.
- Flexibility: She demonstrated flexibility when she accepted my request to end my tenure earlier than planned. Despite the potential disruption to the transition process, she was willing to adapt and find alternative solutions. This trait is crucial in purposeful leadership as it illustrates the ability to adapt to unexpected changes and situations.
- Respect for Individual Aspirations: When I shared my intent to join Microsoft, Ashely respectfully acknowledged my decision, despite her disappointment. It shows her affection

for individual growth and aspirations, a key characteristic of purposeful leadership as it fosters a culture where individuals feel valued and motivated.

- Long-term Relationship Building: The fact that she and I have stayed in touch demonstrates her commitment to building long-term relationships, even beyond professional interactions. It is a significant aspect of purposeful leadership as it emphasizes the importance of nurturing lasting connections based on trust and mutual respect.
- Prioritizing People over Profit: By allowing me to leave early for personal reasons, she demonstrated that she prioritizes people over profit or business objectives. It is a core tenet of purposeful leadership, as it cultivates a supportive and caring work environment, contributing to higher employee satisfaction and loyalty.

These actions by Ashley exemplify the principles of purposeful leadership, where leaders seek to impact their employees' lives professionally and personally positively. In addition, it helps build a positive work culture and promotes individual growth and development.

As you embark on this journey further with exemplary purpose-driven business and world leaders, the transformative power of leading with purpose will become evident. 'Leading with Purpose: Igniting Success, Inspiring Teams, and Creating Positive Change' is an indispensable guide, providing practical strategies and real-world instances that help you unlock your team's utmost potential. This book illuminates the path towards a nurturing work environment, precise goal setting, and cultivating creativity and innovation while navigating hurdles that come your way.

Whether you are an experienced leader or a newcomer entering the realm of leadership, this book aims to ignite your desire to lead with purpose and significantly influence the individuals under your guidance. The challenge is indeed immense, but the rewards are immeasurable. So let this book steer you on your journey to becoming a remarkable leader who inspires, energizes, and leaves a lasting imprint on the world.

Are you ready to take the leap and become the leader you have always envisioned? The moment is here, and the decision is in your hands. It is your opportunity to transform the narrative of leadership. Are you prepared to seize it? Let's begin"

TABLE OF CONTENTS

I. INTRODUCTION

"True leadership sparks not from authority, but purpose. Ignite success, inspire teams, and create change: your journey starts with a single, purposeful step"

LEADERSHIP IS FREQUENTLY employed in business and extensively explored in numerous books, articles, and seminars. However, what exactly is leadership? And what does it take to be a great leader in today's world? What sets great leaders apart from average ones? It's not just their skills or experience but something more profound - a sense of purpose.

Purpose-driven leadership is a philosophy that emphasizes the importance of aligning personal and organizational purpose with actions and decisions. At its core, purpose-driven leadership is about creating meaning and positively impacting the world. In addition, it's about leading with integrity, empathy, and vision and inspiring others to do the same.

Purpose-driven leadership is not a new concept, but it has gained renewed attention recently as organizations and leaders seek to create more meaningful and sustainable businesses. It's about aligning personal and organizational purpose with actions and decisions and positively impacting the world. Purpose-driven leadership has increased employee motivation, engagement, and well-being while driving innovation, growth, and profitability.

In this book, we will explore the power of purpose-driven leadership and provide insights and strategies for leading with purpose, inspiring and motivating teams, and creating positive change in the world. We will examine the science of purpose, the paradox of purpose and profit, and the importance of balancing purpose and profit in leadership. We will provide practical guidance and advice for defining and communicating a clear purpose, inspiring creativity, and innovation, providing opportunities for growth and development, setting clear goals and expectations, recognizing and rewarding team members, and fostering a positive work environment.

The science of purpose suggests that people with a strong sense of purpose are happier, more engaged, and more resilient. For example, a study published in the Journal of Positive Psychology found that people who reported a strong sense of purpose had better mental and physical health and were likelier to engage in healthy behaviors. Another study published in the Journal of Organizational Behavior found that employees who reported feeling a sense of purpose in their work were more engaged, more satisfied with their jobs, and less likely to leave their organizations.

Purpose-driven leadership can also have benefits for organizations. A study by Deloitte[1] found that purpose-driven companies tend to outperform their peers in areas such as financial performance, innovation, and employee engagement. Purpose-driven companies also tend to be more resilient during times of crisis, as their employees are more committed to the organization's purpose and mission.

To understand the power of purpose-driven leadership, let's take the example of the multinational technology giant Microsoft. Satya Nadella[2], the CEO of Microsoft, took over the company in 2014 when it struggled to keep up with its competitors. He introduced a new mission statement for Microsoft - "empower every person and every organization on the planet to achieve more" - and emphasized innovation and collaboration more. This purpose-driven approach paid off, as Microsoft became the most valuable company in the world in 2019, surpassing Apple and Amazon.

But purpose-driven leadership isn't just about profits - it's also about positively impacting the world. Under the leadership of former CEO Paul Polman, Unilever adopted the Unilever Sustainable Living Plan (USLP) in 2010, an ambitious set of goals aimed at reducing the environmental impact of its products, improving the health and well-being of people, and enhancing the livelihoods of those in its value chain. By 2025, the company aims to have all its plastic packaging reusable, recyclable, or compostable.

Unilever's purpose-driven approach has led to creating of sustainable, eco-friendly products and the implementation of ethical sourcing practices. Furthermore, the company has invested in community development programs and initiatives that address social and environmental issues. By leading purposefully, Unilever has driven significant business growth and contributed positively to the world.

Unilever's commitment to purpose-driven leadership serves as an example for organizations worldwide. The company's dedication to sustainability, social responsibility, and ethical practices demonstrates the powerful impact of purposeful leadership on business performance and the broader community.

Another example of purpose-driven leadership is Starbucks, the global coffee company. Starbucks' mission statement is "To inspire and nurture the human spirit – one person, one cup, and one neighborhood at a time." This purpose has led Starbucks to prioritize sustainability, ethical sourcing, and community engagement. Starbucks has also invested in employee training and development and has been recognized for its commitment to diversity and inclusion.

Purpose-driven leadership extends beyond the corporate world, as seen in the example of Tata Group, an Indian multinational conglomerate. Founded in 1868, Tata Group has become one of India's largest and most respected business entities. Its purpose, "To improve the quality of life of the communities we serve globally through long-term stakeholder value creation based on Leadership with Trust," is reflected in its operations and business practices. Tata Steel's commitment to sustainability and social responsibility, and Tata Motors' focus on safety and sustainability, are prime examples of this purpose-driven approach.

Tata Group's dedication to purpose-driven leadership extends to its corporate governance practices, establishing various committees and policies to ensure transparency, accountability, and ethical behavior. In 2019, the group announced an ambitious new sustainability framework, aiming to become a 100% sustainable company by 2025 and achieving carbon neutrality by 2030. Tata Group is an excellent example of purpose-driven leadership in the Indian context. The group aligns its purpose with a commitment to sustainability, social responsibility, and ethical behavior. As a result, it has helped it to create long-term stakeholder value.

While purpose-driven leadership can lead to many benefits, it has challenges. Leaders must navigate the tension between purpose and profit, deal with setbacks and failures, manage conflict, and stay committed to goals over time. In addition, it requires resilience, perseverance, and a willingness to learn and grow as a leader.

Throughout this book, we will use examples from purpose-driven organizations and leaders to illustrate the principles and strategies of purpose-driven leadership. We will discover how purpose-driven leaders have created positive change in their organizations and communities and how readers can apply these principles and techniques in their lives and work. For example, we will look at how Indra Nooyi, the former CEO of PepsiCo, led with purpose by emphasizing sustainability, diversity, and healthy living.

In addition to these real-life examples, this book will provide practical guidance and advice for cultivating purpose-driven leadership. For instance, we will see how to define and communicate a clear purpose, inspire creativity and innovation, provide opportunities for growth and development, set clear goals and expectations, recognize and reward team members, and foster a positive work environment. We will also offer strategies for overcoming common challenges of purpose-driven leadership, such as dealing with setbacks and failures, managing conflict, and staying committed to purpose over time.

As we embark on this journey of purpose-driven leadership, let us remember that it is about achieving success in our careers and positively impacting the world. Purpose-driven leadership requires us to look beyond ourselves and our immediate goals and consider the needs of our communities and the world.

Today's challenges are immense - from climate change to social injustice to economic inequality. But purpose-driven leadership gives us hope to create a better world for all. It empowers us to use our skills, talents, and resources to make a positive difference and to inspire others to do the same.

So let us embrace purpose-driven leadership with open hearts and minds and strive to lead with integrity, empathy, and vision. Let us cultivate a culture of purpose in our organizations and communities and inspire others to join us in this critical journey.

In the following pages, we will examine purpose-driven leadership principles and strategies. First, we will provide practical guidance and advice for leading with purpose, inspiring and motivating teams, and creating positive change in the world. Next, we will examine the science of purpose, the paradox of purpose and profit, and the importance of balancing purpose and profit in leadership. Finally, we will use real-life examples to illustrate the power of purpose-driven leadership and provide strategies for overcoming common challenges.

We hope this book will inspire and empower you to lead purposefully and create a better world for all. So let us begin this journey together and positively impact the world through purpose-driven leadership. By the end of this book, readers will have a deep understanding of the power of purpose-driven leadership and the strategies for cultivating it. Consequently, they will find inspiration to lead with purpose, positively impact their organizations and communities, and contribute towards creating a better world for everyone. Whether you are a seasoned leader or just starting your career, this book will provide the knowledge, tools, and inspiration to lead with purpose and make a lasting impact.

Remember that the accurate measure of success lies in our professional achievements and the positive impact we create worldwide. The following pages will challenge you to ponder the immense possibilities when individuals and organizations harness the power of purpose. We invite you to join us on this transformative journey, and as you turn each page, consider how leading with purpose could reshape not only your life but the very fabric of our society.

The Power of Purpose: Why Purpose-Driven Leadership is Essential for Success

"Purpose fuels the heart of leadership; it's the compass that guides us to success. When purpose drives the leader, the path to triumph becomes inevitable."

The need for purpose-driven leadership has never been more crucial. As we witness trailblazing companies like Microsoft and Unilever redefine the essence of success, it becomes increasingly evident that leading with purpose is commendable and essential. "The Power of Purpose: Why Purpose-Driven Leadership is Essential for Success" delves deep into the compelling narrative of how purpose-driven leaders are transforming the business landscape and altering the course of history. Embrace the power of purpose and discover how it can catapult your leadership to unparalleled heights.

Purpose-driven leadership is not just a trendy buzzword - it is a fundamental principle that is essential for success in today's world. The most successful organizations and leaders are those who have a clear sense of purpose and align their actions and decisions with that purpose. Therefore, exploring the science behind purpose-driven leadership, the benefits of leading with purpose, and the paradox of purpose and profit is essential.

What is the Science of Purpose? - At its core, the purpose is finding meaning and direction in life. Research has shown that people with a strong sense of purpose are happier, more engaged, and more resilient. They also tend to have better mental and physical health outcomes.

A study published in the Journal of Positive Psychology found that people who reported a strong sense of purpose had better mental and physical health and were likelier to engage in healthy behaviors. Another study published in the Journal of Organizational Behavior found that employees who reported feeling a sense of purpose in their work were more engaged, more satisfied with their jobs, and less likely to leave their organizations.

In addition to individual benefits, purpose-driven leadership can also benefit organizations. A study by Deloitte found that purpose-driven companies tend to outperform their peers in areas such as financial performance, innovation, and employee engagement. Purpose-driven companies also tend to be more resilient during times of crisis, as their employees are more committed to the organization's purpose and mission.

The Paradox of Purpose and Profit - One of the challenges of purpose-driven leadership is the tension between purpose and profit. Many leaders believe that to achieve their goals, they must sacrifice profitability. However, research has demonstrated that purpose and profit can mutually reinforce each other.

A study by Harvard Business Review found that purpose-driven companies tend to have higher levels of customer loyalty and employee engagement, which can lead to higher profits. Purpose-driven companies also tend to have a more innovative and adaptive culture, which can lead to increased competitiveness and growth.

Take the example of Patagonia, the outdoor clothing and gear company. Patagonia's mission statement is "We're in business to save our home planet." This purpose has led Patagonia to take bold actions, such as donating 100% of their Black Friday sales to environmental causes and suing the Trump administration over its decision to reduce the size of two national monuments in Utah. By leading purposefully, Patagonia has created a successful and sustainable business that significantly impacted protecting the environment.

Purpose-driven leadership is more than a theoretical idea; it's a fundamental key to success. It prioritizes creating meaning and making a positive difference, not just achieving financial performance. Such leaders are motivated by a deep sense of purpose and passion, which they use to inspire their teams.

Leading with integrity, empathy, and vision, purpose-driven leaders don't solely focus on monetary success but on their impact on the world. As a result, this approach boosts financial performance, innovation, and employee engagement, outperforming other leadership styles.

Research validates the effectiveness of purpose-driven leadership. These leaders demonstrate resilience during crises, primarily due to the commitment of their employees to the organization's purpose and mission. Purpose-driven leadership cultivates successful individuals and organizations, even in challenging times.

To be a purpose-driven leader, you must first define your purpose and communicate it to your team and stakeholders. Then, you must lead by example, encourage creativity and innovation, and provide opportunities for growth and development. You must also set clear goals and expectations, provide recognition and rewards, and foster a positive work environment.

To be a purpose-driven leader, you must first define your purpose. It involves identifying your personal and organizational values and vision and aligning your actions and decisions with these values. It also involves communicating your intention to your team and stakeholders.

Defining your purpose can be challenging, but it is essential for success. It requires self-reflection, introspection, and a willingness to be vulnerable. It also requires a willingness to change course if your purpose no longer aligns with your values or vision.

Communicating Your Purpose - Once you have defined your purpose, sharing it with your team and stakeholders is essential. It involves articulating your intention clearly and compellingly and aligning your actions and decisions with that purpose.

Effective communication is vital to purpose-driven leadership. It requires transparency, authenticity, and a willingness to listen to feedback. It also requires a willingness to be vulnerable and admit when you have made mistakes.

Purpose-driven leadership defines and communicates a clear purpose and inspires and motivates your team. It involves leading by example, encouraging creativity and innovation, and providing opportunities for growth and development.

Leading by example is essential for purpose-driven leadership. As a leader, you must model the behaviors and values that you want to see in your team. It means being accountable, ethical, and empathetic. It also means being open to feedback and willing to admit when you have made mistakes.

Encouraging creativity and innovation is another critical aspect of purpose-driven leadership. Purpose-driven leaders understand that innovation is essential for growth and success and create a culture of experimentation and risk-taking. It involves providing resources and support for new ideas and creating a safe space for team members to share their thoughts and opinions.

Providing opportunities for growth and development is also essential for purpose-driven leadership. Purpose-driven leaders understand that their team members are not just employees but individuals with goals and aspirations. Therefore, they provide opportunities for learning and development and support their team members in pursuing their purpose and vision.

Motivating your team is another essential aspect of purpose-driven leadership. It involves setting clear goals and expectations, providing recognition and rewards, and fostering a positive work environment. Setting clear goals and expectations is essential for keeping your team focused and motivated, defining specific, measurable, and achievable goals, and providing regular feedback on progress. It also means being flexible and adaptable in the face of changing circumstances.

Providing recognition and rewards is also essential for motivating your team. Purpose-driven leaders understand the importance of acknowledging and rewarding team members for their hard work and achievements. It can take many forms, from public recognition to bonuses to opportunities for career advancement.

Fostering a positive work environment is another critical aspect of purpose-driven leadership. Purpose-driven leaders acknowledge that their team members are not to be exploited as mere assets but as individuals with their own needs and aspirations. Therefore, they create a culture of respect, trust, and collaboration and support their team members in achieving a healthy work-life balance.

Leading with purpose is not always easy, but it is essential for creating a better world for all. Embracing purpose-driven leadership can positively impact our organizations and communities and create a better world for future generations.

As you continue reading this book, you will discover the principles and strategies of purpose-driven leadership in more depth. You will learn how to cultivate a culture of purpose in your organization, inspire and motivate your team, and overcome common challenges. You will also learn from real-life examples of purpose-driven leaders who have positively impacted the world.

But leading with purpose is not just about following rules or strategies but about embracing a mindset and way of life. It is about finding meaning and direction and aligning your actions and decisions with that purpose. Finally, it is about recognizing the interconnectedness of all beings and working towards a common good.

So, as you embark on this journey of purpose-driven leadership, let us remember that it is not just about achieving success in our careers but about making a positive impact in the world. Let us cultivate a culture of purpose in our organizations and communities and inspire others to do the same. Let us lead with integrity, empathy, and vision and create a better world.

As we reach the culmination of our exploration into the power of purpose, purpose-driven leadership is not merely a fleeting trend but an enduring force that has the potential to reshape our world. Let this knowledge serve as a beacon, guiding your actions and decisions and inspiring you to lead with unwavering conviction. The closing pages of "The Power of Purpose: Why Purpose-Driven Leadership is Essential for Success" leave you with an undeniable truth – that the legacy you forge as a leader is not solely determined by the wealth you accumulate or the accolades you receive but by the indelible mark, you leave on the hearts and minds of those whose lives you touch through purposeful leadership.

The Benefits of Purpose-Driven Leadership for Individuals and Organizations

In an ever-changing world marked by rapid advancements in technology, shifting societal values, and the urgent need to address global challenges, the role of leadership has evolved significantly. The success stories of purpose-driven businesses like Patagonia, Microsoft, and Starbucks, as well as political leaders like Jacinda Ardern and Emmanuel Macron, highlight purpose-driven leadership's profound impact on individuals and organizations. It has become abundantly clear that purpose is no longer a mere buzzword or moral imperative but a powerful driving force for navigating today's complex landscape. It is also an intelligent business strategy. Purpose-driven leaders recognize that they do not measure their success solely based on financial performance.

As you immerse yourself in these inspiring stories, you will uncover the undeniable truth that leading with purpose is not only about achieving personal and organizational success but also about making a meaningful impact in the world.

With each turn of the page, you will gain a deeper understanding of the myriad benefits that purpose-driven leadership brings to individuals and organizations – from increased motivation, engagement, and well-being among employees to improved innovation, growth, and profitability. This compelling narrative will challenge your preconceptions of success, urging you to reconsider how you lead and inspire you to embark on a transformative journey toward purpose-driven leadership.

As you delve into the world of purpose-driven leadership, remember that the potential to create a positive and lasting impact lies within each of us. As leaders, we are responsible for harnessing this potential, inspiring and empowering those around us, and forging a brighter future for ourselves and our organizations. "The Benefits of Purpose-Driven Leadership for Individuals and Organizations" offers an invaluable guide to unlocking the true power of purpose and the extraordinary possibilities that await when we lead with conviction, compassion, and a clear sense of purpose.

Leading with purpose has many benefits for individuals, including increased happiness, engagement, and resilience. In addition, when individuals have a clear sense of purpose, they tend to be more focused, motivated, and fulfilled. Purpose also provides a sense of direction and meaning, which can help individuals navigate challenges and setbacks.

Research has shown that purpose is associated with many positive outcomes, including better mental and physical health, increased job satisfaction, and improved relationships. For example, a study published in the Journal of Positive Psychology found that people who reported a strong sense of purpose had better mental and physical health and were likelier to engage in healthy behaviors. Another study published in the Journal of Organizational Behavior found that employees who reported feeling a sense of purpose in their work were more engaged, more satisfied with their jobs, and less likely to leave their organizations.

But what exactly is the purpose? One can define purpose as a sense of direction and meaning that extends beyond oneself. It involves understanding one's unique talents and strengths and using them to serve the greater good. Purpose can come from many sources, including religion, family, community, or personal values.

Purpose-driven leaders appreciate the value of purpose for their well-being and proactively inspire their team members to identify their sense of purpose. They cultivate a culture of learning and development, allowing team members ample opportunities to delve into their purpose and vision.

One such example from the business world is Richard Branson, the founder of the Virgin Group. Branson's purpose has always been to challenge the status quo and create positive change in various industries. This purpose-driven mindset established numerous innovative and disruptive companies under the Virgin brand, such as Virgin Galactic, aiming to make space tourism a reality.

In the realm of world leaders, we can look to Nelson Mandela, the first Black president of South Africa. Mandela's purpose was to dismantle apartheid and create a society where people of all races could live together in harmony. As a purpose-driven leader, he pursued this goal relentlessly, even spending 27 years in prison for his beliefs. Nevertheless, his unwavering dedication to his purpose eventually led to the end of apartheid and the establishment of a new, democratic South Africa.

Warby Parker's eyewear company aims to "offer designer eyewear at a revolutionary price while leading the way for socially conscious businesses." This purpose has led Warby Parker to take bold actions, such as partnering with non-profits to provide free eyewear to people in need and investing in sustainability initiatives to reduce its environmental impact. By leading with purpose, Warby Parker has not only created a successful business but also made a significant impact in promoting social and ecological sustainability.

Purpose-driven leadership is also essential for the success of organizations. Purpose-driven organizations outperform their peers in financial performance, innovation, and employee engagement. Purpose-driven organizations also tend to be more resilient during times of crisis, as their employees are more committed to the organization's purpose and mission. Purpose-driven companies also tend to have a more innovative and adaptive culture, which can lead to increased competitiveness and growth.

The Body Shop, the beauty and cosmetics company's purpose is to "enrich our products, people, and planet. We are proud to be part of a global community of people and organizations working towards a sustainable future." This purpose has led The Body Shop to take bold actions, such as becoming one of the first companies to ban animal testing and launching a Community Trade program to support fair trade and community empowerment. By leading with purpose, The Body Shop has not only created a successful business but also made a significant impact in promoting social and environmental sustainability.

Consider the example of Tesla in the business realm, led by Elon Musk. Tesla aims to "accelerate the world's transition to sustainable energy." This purpose has driven Tesla to innovate and develop electric vehicles and renewable energy solutions. By leading purposefully, Tesla has built a successful enterprise and significantly impacted environmental sustainability and technological advancement.

When we look at world leaders, the example of Angela Merkel, the former Chancellor of Germany, illustrates the power of purpose-driven leadership. Merkel's administration focused on fostering a stable and prosperous European Union, promoting multilateralism, and addressing global challenges such as climate change. Her steadfast commitment to these goals led to significant economic and diplomatic successes in Germany and beyond. Merkel's purpose-driven approach to leadership has not only improved the lives of German citizens but also left a legacy on the global stage.

Purpose-driven leaders also understand the importance of stakeholder engagement. They recognize that their organizations do not exist in a vacuum but are part of a larger ecosystem that includes customers, suppliers, employees, and the environment. Purpose-driven leaders work to create value for all stakeholders, not just shareholders. They develop a transparency, authenticity, and accountability culture and prioritize long-term sustainability over short-term profits.

But what exactly are the benefits of purpose-driven leadership for organizations? Let's study in more detail:

1. **Financial Performance**: Purpose-driven organizations tend to outperform their peers in economic performance. According to a study by EY Beacon Institute, purpose-driven companies outperformed the S&P 500 by a factor of 10 between 1996 and 2011. Purpose-driven companies also tend to have higher market valuations, lower risk profiles, and stronger brand reputations. For example, the clothing and home goods retailer, IKEA, is committed to creating a better everyday life for its customers. This purpose has led to the development of innovative and affordable products that appeal to a wide range of consumers, resulting in substantial financial performance. In 2019, IKEA reported revenues of €41.3 billion, an increase of 6% from the previous year.
2. **Innovation**: Purpose-driven organizations tend to be more innovative and adaptive. By aligning their purpose with their business strategy, purpose-driven leaders can create a culture of innovation that fosters creativity, experimentation, and risk-taking. Purpose-driven organizations also tend to be more open to new ideas and perspectives, which can lead to breakthrough innovations. For example, Tesla's electric car company is committed to accelerating the world's transition to sustainable energy. This purpose has led to the

development of innovative, high-performance electric vehicles that have disrupted the automotive industry. In addition, Tesla's innovative approach to product development and manufacturing has also led to innovations in battery technology and renewable energy.

3. **Employee Engagement**: Purpose-driven organizations have higher employee engagement and retention levels. Employees who feel their work is meaningful and aligned with their values are more committed, motivated, and loyal. Purpose-driven leaders also tend to invest in their employees' growth and development, which can lead to higher levels of job satisfaction and performance. For example, the technology company, Salesforce, is committed to creating a more equitable and sustainable world. This purpose has led to the development a strong company culture that emphasizes social responsibility and employee engagement. In addition, Salesforce offers a range of employee benefits and programs that promote work-life balance, professional development, and community service, which has resulted in high levels of employee satisfaction and retention.
4. **Customer Loyalty:** Purpose-driven organizations have higher customer loyalty and advocacy levels. When customers feel that a company's purpose aligns with their values and beliefs, they tend to be more loyal and willing to pay a premium for its products and services. Purpose-driven leaders also tend to prioritize customer satisfaction and experience, which can lead to higher levels of loyalty and advocacy. For example, the outdoor gear company, REI, is committed to promoting outdoor recreation and environmental sustainability. This purpose has led to the developing of high-quality and sustainable outdoor gear that appeals to a loyal customer base. In addition, REI's focus on customer service and community

engagement has also led to a strong brand reputation and high levels of customer loyalty and advocacy.

5. **Social Impact**: Purpose-driven organizations have the potential to make a significant positive impact on the world. By aligning their purpose with their business strategy, purpose-driven leaders can create a social responsibility and sustainability culture that promotes positive change. Purpose-driven organizations can also inspire and mobilize other organizations and individuals to join them in their mission. For example, TOMS's shoe and apparel company is committed to improving lives through business. This purpose has led to the development of a "One for One" model, where for every product purchased, TOMS donates a pair of shoes to a child in need. In addition, TOMS has expanded its impact to include initiatives supporting safe water, eye care, and mental health. This social impact has resulted in a strong brand reputation and inspired other companies to adopt similar business models.

Purpose-driven leadership has numerous benefits for individuals and organizations. From increased happiness and engagement to financial performance and social impact, purpose-driven leadership is essential for success in today's world.

Purpose-driven leadership is not just about achieving success - it's also about positively impacting the world. Purpose-driven leaders understand that their organizations are part of a larger ecosystem that includes customers, employees, suppliers, and the environment. They work to create value for all stakeholders, not just shareholders. They are visionary leaders who see beyond the short-term and focus on the long-term impact of their actions. They understand that purpose is not just a buzzword - it's a powerful force that can inspire and motivate people to achieve their full potential.

Purpose-driven leadership is more critical than ever in today's fast-paced and complex world. As we face challenges such as climate change, social inequality, and technological disruption, purpose-driven leaders are needed to guide us toward a more sustainable and equitable future.

The benefits of purpose-driven leadership for individuals and organizations are both far-reaching and profound. As we have seen through the powerful examples of visionary business and world leaders, the power of purpose can elevate individuals to reach their full potential and transform organizations into forces for positive change. Such leadership's ripple effects can permeate communities, industries, and nations. As we move forward in an increasingly complex and interconnected world, it is the responsibility of each of us to reflect on our sense of purpose and to ask ourselves not only what we can achieve but how we can make a difference. Through purpose-driven leadership, we will unlock the potential to create a brighter, more equitable, and more sustainable future for all.

To become a truly impactful, purpose-driven leader, define your purpose and integrate it into your team's culture. This alignment will inspire and empower your team to reach their highest potential. Living your purpose daily, leading by example, and fostering an environment that nurtures growth, creativity, and positivity are crucial steps. Finally, embrace your role as a purpose-driven leader, and together with your team, make a meaningful difference in the world. The time to embark on this transformative journey is now.

The Impact of Inspired and Motivated Teams

The power of inspired and motivated teams cannot be understated; they can drive organizations to new heights and change the world. Exceptional leaders, like the late Steve Jobs at Apple or Angela

Merkel in German politics, can revolutionize industries and shape the course of nations with their energy and determination. These leaders recognize that empowering their teams with a shared vision ignites passion, spurring innovation and resilience. As we delve into the impact of inspired and motivated teams, we will study the transformative potential of purpose-driven leadership in various fields. It is a journey into what makes teams thrive and how that energy reverberates worldwide.

Purpose-driven leadership is essential for creating a sense of direction and purpose for individuals and organizations. However, purpose alone is not enough to drive success. Thought Leadership is not just about setting goals and delegating tasks - it's about inspiring and motivating your team to achieve their full potential. The inspired and motivated individuals within the organization can bring that purpose to life and achieve the organization's goals. Inspired and motivated teams are essential for organizations to achieve their purpose and mission. When individuals feel inspired and motivated, they infuse their work with energy, creativity, and passion, resulting in higher performance. It, in turn, leads to significant innovation, productivity, and success, creating an impact that reverberates throughout the entire organization.

Inspired and motivated individuals tend to be more engaged, focused, and productive. They also tend to be happier and more fulfilled in their work. In addition, research has shown that inspired and motivated individuals experience a range of positive outcomes, including improved job performance, greater job satisfaction, and better mental and physical health.

Both inspiration and motivation are crucial in enabling individuals to perform at their best. Inspiration, a feeling of enthusiasm and excitement from within, fuels their inner drive. On the other hand, motivation, defined as the drive to achieve goals or fulfill needs, propels them forward.

Inspired and motivated individuals have a clear sense of purpose and direction. They understand how their work contributes to the organization's goals and feel a sense of ownership and responsibility. They also tend to have a growth mindset, meaning they are open to new challenges and opportunities for learning and development.

At Pixar, the animation studio renowned for its culture of creativity and innovation, employees find inspiration and motivation to create groundbreaking films that captivate and inspire audiences worldwide. By fostering a culture of inspiration and motivation, Pixar has created some of the most successful animated films of all time, including Toy Story, Finding Nemo, and The Incredibles.

When we look at Salesforce, the cloud-based software company, it has a culture of innovation and customer success, and its employees are inspired and motivated to create products and services that help businesses grow and succeed. By fostering a culture of inspiration and motivation, Salesforce has achieved remarkable success, including being named the World's Most Innovative Company by Forbes for four years.

Inspired and motivated teams also tend to be more collaborative and supportive. When team members feel inspired and motivated, they tend to be more willing to help and support each other, leading to stronger relationships and a more positive work environment.

But how can leaders inspire and motivate their teams? Let's investigate in more detail:

1. **Leading by Example:** Leaders who are inspired and motivated tend to inspire and motivate their teams. By leading

by example and demonstrating a clear sense of purpose and passion for their work, leaders can inspire and motivate their teams to do the same. Leading by Example: Leaders who are inspired and motivated tend to inspire and motivate their teams. By leading by example and demonstrating a clear sense of purpose and passion for their work, leaders can inspire and motivate their teams to do the same. For example, Indra Nooyi, the former CEO of PepsiCo, was known for her leadership style that emphasized purpose and ethics. Nooyi inspired and motivated her team by demonstrating her commitment to the company's values and purpose. She encouraged her team to do the same.

2. **Encouraging Creativity and Innovation**: Teams encouraged to be creative and innovative tend to be more inspired and motivated. Leaders can promote creativity and innovation by creating a culture of experimentation, providing resources and support for new ideas, and recognizing and rewarding creativity and innovation. A culture of innovation and creativity can inspire and motivate teams to reach new heights. Leaders can encourage innovation by creating an environment that supports experimentation, providing resources and support for new ideas, and recognizing and rewarding creativity and innovation. 3M is known for its innovative culture and commitment to encouraging creativity and innovation. The company provides its employees with the resources and support they need to pursue their ideas. In addition, it rewards creativity and innovation through programs such as its "15% Time" program, allowing employees to spend 15% of their work time pursuing projects.
3. **Providing Opportunities for Growth and Development**: Teams with opportunities for growth and development tend to be more inspired and motivated. Leaders can provide opportunities for growth and development by offering training

and development programs, mentoring and coaching, and stretch assignments that challenge team members to learn new skills and take on new responsibilities. For example, Salesforce provides its employees with various training and development programs, including its "Trailhead" program, which offers online courses and certifications in different technical and business skills.

4. **Fostering a Positive Work Environment**: Teams that work in a positive and supportive environment tend to be more inspired and motivated. Leaders can foster a positive work environment by creating a culture of respect and trust, recognizing and rewarding good work, and providing a sense of work-life balance. A positive work environment can inspire and motivate teams to perform at their best. Leaders can foster a positive work environment by creating a culture of respect and trust, recognizing and rewarding good work, and providing a sense of work-life balance. For example, Airbnb is known for its commitment to creating a positive work environment. The company offers a variety of perks and benefits to its employees, including unlimited vacation time and free travel credits.
5. **Setting Clear Goals and Expectations**: Teams with clear goals and expectations tend to be more inspired and motivated. Leaders can set clear goals and expectations by communicating the organization's mission and vision, providing clear and measurable objectives, and outlining the expectations for performance and behavior. Leaders can set clear goals and expectations by communicating the organization's mission and vision, providing clear and measurable objectives, and outlining the expectations for performance and behavior. For example, Microsoft sets clear goals and expectations for its employees through its "One Microsoft" initiative, which aims to align its goals and values across all its divisions and teams. The

initiative provides clear guidance on achieving the company's mission and vision. In addition, it sets clear expectations for employee performance and behavior.

We cannot overstate the impact of inspired and motivated teams. Individuals who feel inspired and motivated tend to elevate their performance, and organizations with such teams often surpass their peers regarding achievements and outcomes. Leaders who understand the importance of inspiration and motivation can create a culture that fosters these qualities, leading to increased productivity, innovation, and success. We will examine the impact of inspired and motivated teams on the benefits of purpose-driven leadership.

- **Improved Job Performance** - Inspired and motivated individuals tend to be more engaged in their work, which leads to better job performance. When individuals feel a sense of purpose and direction, they are more likely to be focused and productive. This focus and productivity can improve job performance, benefiting individuals and organizations. In addition, inspired and motivated individuals tend to be more willing to take on new challenges and responsibilities. They are more likely to step outside their comfort zones and try new things, which can lead to new opportunities for growth and development. Take the example of Google, the multinational technology company. Google aims to organize the world's information and make it universally accessible and helpful. Google's employees are inspired and motivated to create products and services that achieve this purpose, such as Google Search and Google Maps. Google has performed remarkable success and improved job performance by fostering a culture of inspiration and motivation.
- **Greater Job Satisfaction** - Inspired and motivated individuals tend to have greater job satisfaction. When individuals

feel a sense of purpose and direction, they are more likely to be satisfied with their work. This satisfaction can lead to excellent retention rates, which benefits individuals and organizations. In addition, inspired and motivated individuals tend to have a positive attitude toward their work. As a result, they are more likely to feel fulfilled and engaged in their work, which can lead to a more positive work environment and greater overall satisfaction. Take the example of Patagonia, the outdoor clothing company. Patagonia's purpose is to build the best product, cause no unnecessary harm, and use business to inspire and implement solutions to the environmental crisis. As a result, Patagonia's employees are encouraged and motivated to create products and services that achieve this purpose, such as environmentally friendly clothing and gear. As a result, Patagonia has achieved greater job satisfaction among its employees by fostering a culture of inspiration and motivation.

- **Better Mental and Physical Health -** Inspired and motivated individuals experience better mental and physical health. When individuals feel a sense of purpose and direction, they are less likely to experience stress and burnout. It can improve mental and physical health, benefiting individuals and organizations. In addition, inspired and motivated individuals tend to have a greater sense of well-being. They are more likely to feel fulfilled and satisfied with their work, which can lead to greater overall well-being. Take the example of Zappos, an online shoe and clothing company. Zappos aims to deliver happiness to customers, employees, and vendors. Zappos' employees are inspired and motivated to create a positive customer experience that achieves this purpose. Zappos has improved its employees' mental and physical health by fostering a culture of inspiration and motivation.

- **Improved Financial Performance** - Inspired and motivated teams can significantly impact an organization's financial performance. When teams are inspired and motivated, they tend to be more innovative, productive, and adaptive. As a result, it can improve the organization's financial performance. Inspired and motivated teams tend to be more innovative and creative. They are more likely to develop new ideas and solutions to problems, which can lead to new products and services that drive revenue growth. For example, Apple's inspired and motivated team was responsible for developing the iPhone, which has been a significant source of revenue growth for the company. In addition, inspired and motivated teams tend to be more productive. They are more likely to be focused and efficient in their work, which can lead to increased output and revenue. For example, Southwest Airlines inspired and motivated team is known for its efficiency and productivity, which has helped the company maintain profitability even during difficult economic times.

  Furthermore, inspired and motivated teams tend to be more adaptive and resilient. As a result, they possess enhanced capabilities to navigate change and uncertainty, ultimately leading to long-term improvements in financial performance. For example, Amazon's inspired and motivated team has adapted to changing market conditions and remained an e-commerce industry leader.
- **Greater Innovation and Creativity** - Inspired and motivated teams tend to be more innovative and creative. As a result, they are more likely to develop new ideas and solutions to problems, which can lead to improved products and services. In addition, when inspired and motivated, teams tend to think outside the box and take risks, which can lead to breakthrough innovations, take the example of Tesla, the electric vehicle and clean energy company. Tesla's purpose is to accelerate the world's transition to

sustainable energy. Tesla's inspired and motivated team has been responsible for developing new products and technologies, such as the Model S and the Powerwall, which have transformed the automotive and energy industries.

- **More substantial Commitment to the Organization's Goals and Mission -** Inspired and motivated teams tend to be more committed to the organization's goals and mission. When teams feel a sense of purpose and direction, they are more likely to be invested in the organization's success. This commitment can lead to more extraordinary dedication and loyalty among team members. Take the example of The Coca-Cola Company's purpose is to refresh the world and make a difference. Coca-Cola's inspired and motivated team is committed to achieving this purpose. In addition, it actively engages in various philanthropic efforts, such as supporting clean water initiatives and promoting recycling. By fostering a culture of inspiration and motivation, Coca-Cola has built a strong commitment to its purpose among its team members.

  The impact of inspired and motivated teams on the benefits of purpose-driven leadership is undeniable. When teams feel a sense of purpose and direction, they are more likely to be engaged, productive, and innovative. In addition, they bring energy, creativity, and passion to their work, leading to tremendous success for individuals and organizations.

The examples we have explored show how inspired and motivated teams can achieve remarkable success and positively impact the world. From Google to Coca-Cola, from Zappos to Tesla, these organizations have harnessed the power of inspired and motivated teams to achieve their purpose and mission.

But it's not just about achieving success for the sake of victory. Purpose-driven leadership and inspired and motivated teams can also positively impact the world. Whether improving the environment, delivering happiness to customers, or improving lives through business, these organizations make a difference in the world through their purpose and mission.

Their influence extends far beyond the organizations they serve. The ripple effect of their passion, drive, and commitment can reshape industries, redefine societal norms, and create lasting positive change. Just as Elon Musk's SpaceX has revolutionized space exploration or Malala Yousafzai's advocacy for girls' education has inspired millions, a single motivated team's power can send tremors worldwide. Our collective responsibility as leaders, team members, and citizens is to harness this potential, nurturing the fires of inspiration and motivation within our teams. For we forge the future within those flames, and we hold the power to shape that future for the betterment of all.

As we forge ahead in a world teeming with rapid change and uncertainty, the significance of purpose-driven leadership, coupled with inspired and motivated teams, takes on paramount importance. Confronting challenges like climate change and social inequality requires audacious ideas and ground-breaking solutions. Only through the synergy of purpose-driven leadership and passionate, motivated teams can we attain the level of success and influence our world desperately needs.

Let us ignite inspiration within ourselves and kindle it in others. Let us uncover our purpose and aid others in discovering theirs. Let us construct organizations that prosper and leave an indelible positive mark on the world. The immense power of purpose-driven leadership and inspired, motivated teams lie within our reach. Let us grasp it firmly and pave the way for a brighter, more equitable future for all.

The Paradox of Purpose: How to Navigate the Tension Between Purpose and Profit

"The delicate dance between purpose and profit is a test of true leadership. Embrace the paradox: it's not about the tension, but how we orchestrate a harmony for sustainable success."

Business and political leaders often find themselves walking a tightrope in the delicate dance between purpose and profit. Consider the example of Elon Musk, whose ambitious vision for a sustainable future led to the creation of Tesla and SpaceX, or Angela Merkel, who championed the need for renewable energy during her tenure as Germany's Chancellor.

As leaders, we face a complex, ever-changing landscape of challenges and opportunities. One of the most pressing challenges is navigating the tension between purpose and profit - the paradox of purpose. For we forge the future within those flames, and we hold the power to shape that future for the betterment of all. Yet, on the other hand, we are driven by a sense of purpose and a desire to impact the world positively. Unfortunately, these two goals can often seem at odds, creating a tension that is difficult to navigate. The paradox of purpose lies in the tension between pursuing a higher calling and generating profits, a balancing act that can either propel an organization to new heights or lead to its downfall.

Pursuing purpose and the desire for profit have long been seen as forces pulling in opposite directions. As if locked in a cosmic struggle, they vie for the soul of every business and political leader, each seeking to dominate the other. On one side, purpose sets the stage—an noble aspiration to make a lasting impact on the world. Conversely, profit emerges—a practical need for resources to fuel and sustain those aspirations. So how can a leader embrace both contradictory forces without being torn asunder? How can they navigate the narrow, treacherous path separating a company's vision from its bottom line?

Imagine standing on the precipice of a mountain with a chasm of uncertainty gaping beneath your feet. You are the tightrope walker, poised to take the first step onto a wire strung taut between the twin peaks of purpose and profit. Can I maintain my balance, traversing the line between the noble aspiration of making a difference and the cold reality of financial necessity?

"The Paradox of Purpose" delves into the intricacies of navigating this complex relationship, shedding light on how leaders can marry their ideals with the reality of financial sustainability. The paradox of purpose is not new, but it has become increasingly relevant in today's business environment.

Take, for instance, the story of Richard Branson, the entrepreneurial genius behind the Virgin Group, who managed to infuse purpose into his business empire while maintaining a keen eye on the balance sheet. During the COVID-19 pandemic, Ravi Kumar S showed great leadership in rapidly transitioning most of Infosys's workforce to remote work. In addition, he prioritized the health and well-being of employees while ensuring business continuity, showcasing a commitment to people over profit.Or consider the legacy of Aung San Suu Kyi, the once-celebrated leader of Myanmar who, in her quest for democracy and human rights, eventually found herself facing accusations of complacency in the face of atrocities committed against the Rohingya minority. How did these leaders navigate the paradox of purpose, and what can we learn from their successes and failures?

Consumers, investors, and employees increasingly demand that companies demonstrate a commitment to social and environmental responsibility, and leaders are under pressure to deliver both financial results and social impact. For decades, companies have pursued profit at the expense of social and environmental responsibility. However, this approach is no longer sustainable. Consumers are becoming more aware of their purchases' impact on the world, demanding that companies demonstrate a commitment to social and environmental responsibility.

The tension between purpose and profit is not an easy one to resolve. Many leaders feel caught in a bind, forced to choose between what suits the organization and what is suitable for society. However, purpose-driven leaders understand that the two goals are not mutually exclusive - they can be mutually reinforcing. Furthermore, purpose-driven leaders recognize that creating shared values that benefit the organization and society is the key to achieving sustainable success.

Fortunately, purpose-driven leadership has emerged as a solution to the paradox of purpose. Purpose-driven leaders prioritize creating shared value that benefits the organization and society over short-term financial gains. Moreover, purpose-driven leaders recognize that economic success and social impact are not mutually exclusive but can be mutually reinforcing.

Industry leaders such as Unilever and Danone have embraced purpose-driven leadership and demonstrated this approach's potential to create value for the organization and society. For example, Unilever's Sustainable Living Plan has helped the company achieve double-digit growth while reducing its environmental impact. Likewise, Danone's commitment to social responsibility has helped the company attract and retain talent and win over socially conscious consumers.

Navigating the tension between purpose and profit is difficult, but purpose-driven leadership provides a roadmap for success. Leaders can create financially successful and socially responsible organizations by prioritizing shared value, authenticity, and transparency.

Navigating the tension between purpose and profit is not an easy task. Numerous challenges associated with purpose-driven leadership include balancing short-term and long-term objectives, navigating stakeholder expectations, and measuring the impact of social initiatives.

Moreover, there is a need for purpose-driven leadership to be authentic and transparent. Unfortunately, purpose-washing has become increasingly prevalent in recent years - using purpose as a marketing tool without following through on social and environmental commitments. It has led to skepticism from consumers, investors, and employees. On the other hand, it has highlighted the importance of authenticity and transparency in purpose-driven leadership. We will illuminate how leaders can marry their ideals with the reality of financial sustainability. We will confront the hard questions and reveal the hidden truths at this paradox's heart.

Can a leader truly serve both purpose and profit without losing their way? Can they create a future where purpose and profit walk together, forging a path that benefits their organization and the world? We will understand the challenges and opportunities of purpose-driven leadership and provide insights and strategies for navigating the tension between purpose and profit and unravel the Paradox of Purpose and reveal the keys to unlocking the potential that lies at the heart of every organization, every leader, and every individual who dares to dream of a better tomorrow.

The Importance of Balancing Purpose and Profit in Leadership

Successful leadership demands finding the proper equilibrium between purpose and profit in today's complex world, where stakeholders place growing value on corporate social responsibility and stakeholder capitalism. For example, Warren Buffett, Chairman and CEO of Berkshire Hathaway, has shown that businesses can achieve remarkable financial success while adhering to a long-term vision and strong ethical principles, as evident in his philanthropic endeavors and value-based investment strategy. Similarly, Justin Trudeau, the Prime Minister of Canada, has demonstrated how prioritizing social welfare, inclusivity, and environmental responsibility can strengthen a nation's economic prosperity and global standing. Conversely, the perils of disregarding this balance are evident in cases like the 2008 financial crisis and the Boeing 737 MAX tragedies, where the pursuit of profit precedes ethical considerations. By examining these compelling examples, we gain a deeper understanding of the importance of harmonizing purpose and profit and its influence on shaping exceptional leadership in the 21st century.

As purpose-driven leadership gains traction in business, leaders face the increasing challenge of balancing purpose and profit. Purpose-driven leaders are motivated to positively impact the world while ensuring their organizations remain financially sustainable. We will look at the importance of balancing purpose and profit in leadership, including the benefits of purpose-driven leadership, the challenges of balancing purpose and profit, and strategies for achieving this balance.

Purpose-driven leadership involves aligning an organization's mission, values, and purpose with its business strategy and operations. This approach emphasizes creating shared value for all stakeholders, including customers, employees, shareholders, and society. In addition, purpose-driven leaders prioritize impact and sustainability over short-term financial gains, recognizing that a strong sense of purpose can drive long-term success and profitability.

The Benefits of Purpose-Driven Leadership

Before we delve into the challenges of balancing purpose and profit, it is vital to understand the benefits of purpose-driven leadership. Purpose-driven leaders desire to positively impact the world and create a sense of meaning and fulfillment in their work. This sense of purpose can have a powerful impact on their organizations, inspiring employees to work harder, innovate more, and stay loyal to the company.

Purpose-driven leadership can also be a powerful driver of financial performance. Research has shown that purpose-driven companies outperform their peers regarding revenue growth and profitability. For example, a study by Harvard Business Review found that companies with a strong sense of purpose outperformed the S&P 500 by a factor of 12 between 1996 and 2011. Some other benefits include the following.

- **Increased Customer Loyalty and Engagement** - Purpose-driven leadership can increase customer loyalty and engagement. When a company's values and purpose align with its customers, it can create a powerful emotional connection beyond the transactional relationship. For instance, the cosmetics company Lush has a solid commitment to ethical sourcing and animal welfare, which has resonated with its customers. As a result, it has increased customer loyalty, brand advocacy, and higher sales and profitability.

- **Improved Employee Engagement and Satisfaction** - Purpose-driven leadership can also enhance employee engagement and satisfaction. Employees who feel their work is meaningful and aligned with their values are more likely to be motivated and committed to their jobs. It can lead to higher levels of productivity, creativity, and innovation, as well as reduced turnover and absenteeism. For example, the pharmaceutical company Novo Nordisk is strongly committed to improving global health. It has implemented various initiatives to engage employees in its purpose-driven mission.
- **Enhanced Reputation and Brand Image** - Purpose-driven leadership can enhance an organization's reputation and brand image. When a company's values and purpose align with its stakeholders, it can create a positive perception in the marketplace. It can increase customer loyalty and advocacy and improve relationships with regulators, investors, and other stakeholders. For example, outdoor gear company REI is firmly committed to environmental sustainability. Demonstrating responsible business practices has earned recognition and bolstered its reputation, brand image, and financial performance.

In all three cases, purpose-driven leadership can result in a win-win situation where the company benefits financially while positively impacting society and the environment. By aligning purpose with profitability, companies can create a sustainable and profitable business model that helps all stakeholders involved.

The Risks of Prioritizing Profit over Purpose

While profit is essential for the sustainability of any organization, prioritizing profit over purpose can have serious consequences.

When leaders prioritize short-term financial gains over long-term impact and purpose, they risk damaging their organization's reputation, losing the trust and loyalty of employees and customers, and ultimately hurting their bottom line.

For example, Wells Fargo's aggressive sales tactics in the early 2000s prioritized profit over purpose, ultimately leading to a scandal that cost the company billions of dollars in fines and lost business, resulting in significant repercussions for the organization. Similarly, Volkswagen's prioritization of profit over environmental impact led to the "Dieselgate" scandal, which cost the company billions of dollars in fines and lost business.

Strategies for Balancing Purpose and Profit

So how can leaders balance purpose and profit to benefit their organizations and the world? One key strategy is to focus on creating shared value or finding ways to create value for the organization and society. It can involve investing in initiatives that benefit the organization and the community, such as sustainability efforts, employee volunteer programs, or partnerships with local nonprofits.

Another strategy is to prioritize transparency and authenticity. Leaders can build trust and credibility with employees, customers, and other stakeholders by being open and honest about their organization's purpose and values. It can help to mitigate the risks of prioritizing profit over purpose and ensure that the organization remains accountable to its mission and values.

- **Embed Purpose into Business Strategy** - Purpose-driven leaders must embed purpose into their business strategy to balance purpose and profit. It involves identifying the organization's mission, values, and purpose and aligning these with its strategic objectives and operations. In addition, it can help to ensure that purpose remains a priority, even in the face of short-term financial pressures. For example, Unilever has successfully embedded purpose into its business strategy. The company's goal is to make sustainable living commonplace, and it has aligned all its business practices, from sustainable sourcing to reducing environmental impact to social responsibility, with this purpose.

- **Create a Culture of Purpose** - Creating a culture of purpose is also essential for balancing ambition and profit. It involves fostering a sense of shared purpose and values among employees and aligning their work with the organization's mission and purpose. Leaders can create a culture of purpose by communicating the organization's purpose and values, recognizing and rewarding purpose-driven behavior, and providing opportunities for employees to engage in purpose-driven initiatives. A company that has created a strong culture of purpose is Warby Parker. The eyewear company's mission is to provide affordable, stylish eyewear while giving back to those in need. The company has built a culture around this purpose, with employees passionate about the company's social impact initiatives and regularly participating in volunteer events.
- **Measure and Communicate Impact** - Measuring and communicating the impact of purpose-driven initiatives is also critical for balancing purpose and profit. Leaders must develop metrics that capture purpose-driven initiatives' social, environmental, and financial implications and communicate this impact to stakeholders. It can help justify investments in purpose-driven initiatives and build stakeholder support. Danone has excelled in measuring and communicating impact. The food and beverage company has a dual mission

of making healthy food accessible while promoting sustainability. It has developed a comprehensive set of sustainability metrics measuring carbon emissions and water usage. It communicates its progress toward sustainability goals regularly to stakeholders.

- **Lead with Authenticity** - Finally, purpose-driven leaders must lead with authenticity. It involves demonstrating a clear commitment to purpose and values and leading by example. Authentic and transparent leaders, in their purpose-driven leadership, are more likely to inspire and motivate their teams and build trust and credibility among stakeholders. Paul Polman, the former CEO of Unilever, is a purpose-driven leader who leads authentically. Polman was a vocal advocate for the company's purpose-driven mission and led by example, acting on issues such as climate change and sustainable sourcing. His leadership helped to embed purpose into Unilever's business strategy and create a culture of purpose among employees.

Balancing purpose and profit is a critical challenge for purpose-driven leaders. However, leaders can balance purpose and profit that drives long-term success and sustainability by embedding purpose into business strategy, creating a culture of purpose, measuring, communicating impact, and leading with authenticity. Purpose-driven leadership is not only good for the world, but it is also suitable for business. By prioritizing purpose over profit, leaders can create sustainable organizations that create value for all stakeholders, including shareholders, employees, customers, and society. Companies such as Unilever, Warby Parker, Danone, and Unilever have successfully integrated purpose into their business strategy, created a purpose culture, measured, communicated impact, and led authentically, driving long-term success and sustainability.

The delicate dance between purpose and profit in leadership reveals itself as a powerful force for shaping our world. As we navigate the complexities and challenges of our modern era, stories of leaders who have boldly pursued financial success and a higher calling remind us that there is a way to marry ambition with compassion, innovation with sustainability, and profitability with responsibility. As the sun sets on the era of persistent profit-seeking, a new dawn breaks, illuminating a path for leaders to enrich themselves and the communities and environments surrounding them. The tales of those who have embraced this approach shines as a beacon, guiding us toward a future where the pursuit of success harmoniously intertwines with the well-being of our planet and its inhabitants.

It is essential to reflect upon the profound influence of leaders who have successfully struck this balance and ponder the potential ripple effect of our actions. May their narratives resonate within us and inspire us to transcend the confines of our own goals and ambitions, look beyond the horizon, and envision a world where purpose and profit unite to cultivate a more just, equitable, and sustainable future.

Essential to remember the power of combining purpose with profit, for it is within this harmonious intersection that the most significant potential for lasting impact lies. Only then can we genuinely rise to the challenges of our time and leave a legacy that stands the test of time, both in the realm of material success and in the hearts and minds of those whose lives we touch.

The Challenges and Opportunities of Purpose-Driven Leadership

As the tides of modern society shift, purpose-driven leadership emerges as a lighthouse of hope in a world fraught with challenges and opportunities. Guided by a moral compass, these leaders, such as Tony Hsieh of Zappos and Mother Teresa, demonstrate how the pursuit of a higher calling can inspire transformative change on a global scale. By placing the well-being of people and the planet at the core of their mission, they are redefining success metrics, transcending traditional boundaries, and inviting us to reimagine what leadership could be. Yet, navigating the complex landscape of purpose-driven leadership presents unique challenges and opportunities as leaders grapple with balancing their ethical convictions and the competitive marketplace demands. By examining these leaders and their triumphs and tribulations, we can better understand the potential at the heart of purpose-driven leadership.

Leadership stands as the bedrock of success in any organization, and purpose-driven leadership has risen to prominence as a catalyst for positive transformation in today's dynamic business environment. Purpose-driven leaders, driven by a higher calling such as social or environmental impact, prioritize this over financial gain, galvanizing their teams to rally around a shared vision and aligning business strategies with core values and missions.

In an age where social and environmental concerns increasingly demand attention, the significance of purpose-driven leadership becomes ever more pronounced. These leaders possess the potential to instigate meaningful change globally and propel innovation and growth within their organizations. Nevertheless, purpose-driven administration presents challenges, including navigating the delicate balance between purpose and profit, managing short-term financial performance alongside long-term sustainability, and overcoming resistance to change.

Yet, despite these hurdles, purpose-driven leadership offers immense opportunities for leaders to foster innovation, enhance employee engagement and retention, and bolster an organization's reputation and brand. By leading with transparency and authenticity, cultivating a culture of purpose, and engaging stakeholders, these leaders can surmount the challenges and harness the opportunities intrinsic to purpose-driven leadership.

Our exploration of purpose-driven leadership will delve into the challenges and opportunities, providing strategies to navigate these complexities while maintaining a balance between purpose and profit. First, we will analyze the intricacies of purpose-driven leadership, considering financial pressures, resistance to change, and impact measurement. Furthermore, we will uncover the opportunities that await, encompassing innovation, employee engagement and retention, and reputation enhancement. Lastly, we will offer strategies for surmounting challenges and seizing opportunities, including stakeholder engagement, metric development, transparent and authentic leadership, and fostering a culture of purpose.

The Challenge of Defining Purpose

Striking the delicate balance between short-term financial goals and long-term impact and purpose is a significant challenge for purpose-driven leadership. Succumbing to the temptation of prioritizing profit over purpose may be enticing in the face of financial pressures or market volatility. However, leaders who emphasize long-term impact and purpose are more likely to build sustainable organizations resilient to economic and market fluctuations. Consider Patagonia, an outdoor clothing company with a robust commitment to environmental sustainability. By incorporating recycled materials in its products and adopting sustainable manufacturing practices, Patagonia has positioned itself as a leader in sustainable fashion, garnering a devoted following of environmentally conscious customers, despite not generating immediate financial returns.

The Challenge of Financial Pressures

The tension between purpose and profit presents a critical challenge for purpose-driven leaders. Pressure from investors and stakeholders to prioritize financial returns over social or environmental impact may lead to conflict between short-term financial performance and long-term sustainability. For instance, take the example of the fashion industry, known for its significant environmental effects. Many purpose-driven leaders in this industry advocate for sustainable practices, such as using eco-friendly materials and reducing waste. However, they also face pressure to maintain financial performance and profitability, which can create a challenge in balancing purpose and profit. For example, Elon Musk, CEO of Tesla and SpaceX, frequently faces scrutiny and criticism for prioritizing sustainable energy solutions and space exploration over immediate profitability. Despite facing financial pressures, his dedication to long-term impact drives innovation in the automotive and space industries.

The Challenge of Resistance to Change

Purpose-driven leaders may encounter resistance to change from employees, customers, or other stakeholders who do not share their values and mission. This resistance can create tension and undermine the effectiveness of purpose-driven initiatives. For example, former Starbucks CEO Howard Schultz, a proponent of social responsibility and sustainability, faced initial skepticism when implementing ethically sourced coffee and waste reduction programs. Nevertheless, his perseverance resulted in a transformed company culture and an enhanced reputation for Starbucks.

The Challenge of Measuring Impact

Measuring the impact of purpose-driven initiatives is also a challenge for leaders. While financial metrics are relatively easy to measure, the social and environmental result is more difficult to quantify. It can make it difficult to justify investments in purpose-driven initiatives and communicate their value to stakeholders. For instance, purpose-driven leaders in the food industry who advocate for sustainable agriculture practices may struggle to measure the impact of these initiatives on the environment and society. They may need to develop new metrics and measurement tools to communicate these initiatives' value to stakeholders effectively. Leaders like Paul Polman, former Unilever CEO, have pushed for innovative methods to measure the impact of purpose-driven initiatives on the environment and society. For example, Unilever's Sustainable Living Plan, aimed at improving health and well-being, reducing environmental impact, and enhancing livelihoods, has necessitated the development of new metrics to communicate its value effectively to stakeholders.

The Opportunity for Innovation and Creativity

Purpose-driven leadership can also create opportunities for innovation and creativity. By prioritizing purpose over profit, leaders can encourage their teams to think outside the box and find new ways to create value for the organization and society. It can lead to breakthrough innovations, increased employee engagement and satisfaction, and improved financial performance.

Microsoft's CEO Satya Nadella, focusing on creating a positive societal impact through technology, has driven innovation within the company, resulting in breakthroughs like AI for Earth, which aim to address global environmental challenges.

The Opportunity to Attract and Retain Top Talent

Purpose-driven leadership can also be a powerful tool for attracting and retaining top talent. In today's competitive job market, many employees are looking for more than just a paycheck - they want to work for organizations that align with their values and offer a sense of purpose and meaning. By prioritizing purpose and creating a positive work environment, leaders can attract and retain top talent motivated to impact the world positively.

By prioritizing equality, sustainability, and social responsibility, Salesforce's CEO, Marc Benioff, has fostered a positive work environment that attracts and retains motivated employees.

The Opportunity for Reputation and Brand

Purpose-driven leadership can also enhance an organization's reputation and brand. When an organization aligns with a higher purpose, it fosters the ability to build stakeholder trust and credibility. Purpose-driven leaders can improve their reputation and brand by communicating the organization's purpose and values, measuring and communicating the impact of purpose-driven initiatives, and demonstrating a commitment to purpose-driven leadership. A great example is Unilever, one of the world's largest consumer goods companies, whose purpose is to make sustainable living commonplace. They have enhanced their reputation and brand by aligning their business strategies. They have also built trust and credibility with stakeholders by communicating their purpose and values, measuring and communicating the impact of their purpose-driven initiatives, and demonstrating a commitment to purpose-driven leadership.

Unilever's commitment to purpose-driven leadership has enhanced its reputation and brand and driven innovation and growth in its business. By prioritizing sustainability and social impact, they have differentiated themselves from their competitors and attracted customers who value these principles. They have also engaged and retained their employees, motivated by the company's purpose and values.

Strategies for Overcoming Challenges and Leveraging Opportunities

The challenges of purpose-driven leadership can be daunting, but the opportunities for positive impact are limitless. Purpose-driven leaders face a delicate balancing act between prioritizing financial performance and pursuing a higher purpose, such as social or environmental impact. The tension between purpose and profit can create obstacles that may seem insurmountable. However, with the right strategies, purpose-driven leaders can overcome these challenges and leverage opportunities to drive positive change.

- **An engaging stakeholder** is a critical strategy for overcoming challenges and leveraging opportunities of purpose-driven leadership. Purpose-driven leaders must engage stakeholders to overcome the challenges of purpose-driven leadership and leverage the opportunities. It involves communicating the organization's purpose and values, building stakeholder relationships, and listening to feedback. For example, a multinational tech corporation engages its stakeholders, including customers, employees, and suppliers, in its purpose-driven initiatives. The corporation utilizes various channels, such as its website, social media, and in-person meetings, to ensure its stakeholders understand its values and purpose well.

The corporation also regularly solicits stakeholder feedback on its initiatives and incorporates it into its decision-making processes.

- **Developing** metrics for measuring the impact of purpose-driven initiatives is another essential strategy. For instance, a global manufacturing company measures the environmental impact of its products through its sustainable production program. This program provides detailed information about the environmental impact of the company's products, including the amount of water and energy used in production, the amount of waste generated, and the carbon footprint. By providing transparent metrics, the company enables stakeholders to assess the impact of its purpose-driven initiatives and hold the company accountable for its environmental performance.
- **Leading with transparency and authenticity** is another critical strategy for purpose-driven leadership. For example, a major retail chain has a purpose-driven mission to improve the well-being of its customers and employees. As a result, the company is transparent about its social impact, sharing its social responsibility report publicly on its website. In addition, the company partners with various charitable organizations and encourages its employees to participate in community service activities. By leading with transparency and authenticity, the company demonstrates its commitment to purpose and values and builds trust with its stakeholders.
- **Creating a culture of purpose** is the final strategy for purpose-driven leadership. For instance, a healthcare organization has a purpose-driven mission to provide quality healthcare to underserved communities. The organization has created a culture of purpose by aligning its employee work with its purpose and values. For example, the organization implements a program that donates a portion of the proceeds for

every patient served, supporting community health initiatives. The organization also encourages its employees to engage in purpose-driven initiatives by offering volunteer opportunities and resources for personal and professional development. By creating a culture of purpose, the healthcare organization fosters a sense of community and purpose among its employees and stakeholders.

Despite these challenges, purpose-driven leadership offers significant opportunities for leaders. Purpose-driven leadership can drive innovation, enhance employee engagement and retention, and enhance an organization's reputation and brand. Purpose-driven leaders leveraging these opportunities can create significant value for their organizations and society.

The journey of purpose-driven leadership is ongoing and requires a commitment to continuous learning and improvement. Purpose-driven leaders must remain open to feedback and must be willing to adapt their strategies as they encounter new challenges and opportunities. Ultimately, purpose-driven leadership is about creating a better world for us and future generations. As purpose-driven leaders, we are responsible for using our leadership to positively impact the world and inspire and motivate others to do the same.

Navigating the tumultuous waters of the 21st century, purpose-driven leadership emerges as a beacon of hope, steering organizations toward a sustainable, prosperous future. The challenges and opportunities that define this paradigm shift beckon leaders to continuously learn and adapt their strategies to drive innovation, enhance employee engagement, and bolster their reputation and brand. The visionary tales of leaders like Patagonia's Yvon Chouinard, Tesla's Elon Musk, and Microsoft's Satya Nadella resonate across generations, igniting the flame of purpose in the hearts of future trailblazers.

As you embark on your odyssey of purpose-driven leadership, take a moment to ponder the intricate interplay between purpose and profit. When purpose drives innovation and profit aligns adeptly with the values shaping our world, your leadership can create an impact that ripples through the ages, forging a sustainable, equitable, and just future.

As the dusk of today's world gives way to the dawn of a new era in leadership, stand steadfast in your pursuit of purpose. Embrace this journey, for the echoes of your actions will reverberate in generations to come, immortalizing your leadership in the annals of history. Allow the guiding light of purpose to illuminate your path, leaving an indelible imprint on the world, and forge a legacy that stands the test of time.

II. DEFINING YOUR PURPOSE

"Success is not a destination but a journey defined by your own values. Carve your own path, for the true measure of success is the footprint of our unique purpose."

THINK OF A conductor standing before an orchestra, weaving a harmonious symphony from an ensemble of diverse instruments. Now, envision a leader amid a constantly changing world, orchestrating their team's strengths to create a collective masterpiece. What do these two images have in common? Purpose. A clear, unwavering purpose forms the foundation for extraordinary achievements.

Why do some leaders excel in adversity while others falter? What enables a few visionaries to inspire and galvanize their team while others struggle to elicit commitment and loyalty? The answer lies in purpose – a driving force transcending the realms of the tangible, forging an undeniable connection between leaders and those they serve. Purpose, akin to the baton of a maestro, aligns the actions and decisions of a leader, harmonizing them with the team's collective vision.

Consider the entrepreneurial odyssey of Mukesh Ambani, the Chairman and CEO of Reliance Industries, who transformed his father's small-scale textile business into a global conglomerate spanning diverse sectors. What guides him as he navigates the complexities of global markets, fostering innovation and collaboration at every turn? Or contemplate the resolute spirit of Narendra Modi, the Prime Minister of India, who, despite humble beginnings, has risen to become a leader of one of the world's largest democracies. What drives him to pursue development and progress for his nation relentlessly? Again, one finds a common thread at the core of their respective narratives: a clearly defined purpose, transcending the bounds of personal ambition and leaving an indelible mark on the world.

So, how does one forge this essential element that lends resilience to leaders and captures the imagination of those who follow them? How do you unearth the essence of your leadership purpose, transforming it into a harmonious melody that guides you and your team through the symphony of life's challenges?

The purpose is a powerful force that drives individuals and organizations to greatness. It is the driving force behind innovation, progress, and success. Purpose-driven leaders understand the importance of defining and communicating their purpose to their teams to inspire and motivate them to achieve their goals.

Defining your purpose as an individual or organization requires a deep understanding of what drives you, what you value, and what you hope to achieve. It involves asking difficult questions, reflecting on past experiences, and envisioning a better future. This process can be challenging, but the rewards are great.

When you have a clear purpose, you can better make decisions that align with your values and goals. You are also better able to inspire and motivate your team to achieve their full potential. Purpose-driven leaders understand the importance of communicating their purpose to their teams concisely and compellingly.

In the following pages, we embark on a journey to the heart of purpose-driven leadership, unraveling the intricate composition of values, vision, and impact that defines an exceptional leader. We delve into leaders' minds who have orchestrated extraordinary transformations in the world around them, examining the roots of their unwavering commitment to their cause. By probing the depths of their stories and unlocking the secrets that lie within, we aspire to craft a blueprint for your leadership journey –guided by the harmonious melody of purpose, steering your ensemble toward success, fulfillment, and lasting change.

Remember, dear reader, as you traverse the path of purpose-driven leadership, the journey is as unique as the individual. Your purpose, the symphony you compose, is a product of your experiences, values, and aspirations. By embarking on this odyssey of self-discovery, you can create a legacy that transcends the limitations of time and space, forever echoing through the annals of history. So, let us begin, and may the harmonious melody of purpose conduct your orchestra toward the crescendo of greatness.

Understanding Your Personal and Organizational Purpose

"Unearthing your purpose is like finding your North Star - it guides your journey, aligning personal passion with organizational progress. Embrace it, for it is the foundation of transformational leadership."

A tree rooted deeply in the earth reaches for the sky, an emblem of purpose and growth. Like this tree, every leader embarks on a journey guided by their personal and organizational purpose. For example, Steve Jobs transformed the world of technology, driven by his relentless pursuit of innovation. At the same time, Malala Yousafzai's dedication to education and gender equality has made her an inspiring advocate for millions. The secret to their success lies in the fusion of personal and organizational purpose, creating a powerful synergy that resonates through their actions and decisions.

The purpose is a powerful force that drives individuals and organizations to greatness. It is the driving force behind innovation, progress, and success. Defining your purpose is a crucial step toward effective leadership. To lead purposefully, you must understand what drives you, your team, and your organization. Purpose-driven leaders understand the importance of defining and communicating their purpose to their teams to inspire and motivate them to achieve their goals.

Defining your purpose as an individual or organization requires a deep understanding of what drives you, what you value, and what you hope to achieve. It involves asking difficult questions, reflecting on past experiences, and envisioning a better future. This process can be challenging, but the rewards are great.

When you have a clear purpose, you can better make decisions that align with your values and goals. You are also better able to inspire and motivate your team to achieve their full potential. Purpose-driven leaders understand the importance of communicating their purpose to their teams concisely and compellingly.

Personal purpose is the underlying reason why individuals do what they do. The driving force motivates them to pursue their goals and aspirations. Various factors shape personal purpose, including upbringing, education, life experiences, and values.

To understand personal purpose, leaders must first take the time to reflect on their values, passions, and motivations. They must also be willing to listen to feedback and learn from their experiences. Personal purpose is not static and can change as individuals grow and evolve.

Leaders who understand their purpose are better equipped to make decisions that align with their values and beliefs. They are also more effective at motivating their teams, as they can communicate a clear sense of purpose that resonates with team members.

Organizational purposes are the reason why a company exists. It is the larger mission or vision that guides decision-making and strategy development. The organizational purpose is shaped by various factors, including the company's history, culture, and values.

Leaders play a critical role in defining and communicating their organization's purpose. They must ensure alignment of the purpose with the needs of stakeholders, including employees, customers, and shareholders. They must also provide a meaningful and inspiring purpose to their teams.

Leaders who understand their organization's purpose are better equipped to make decisions that align with the larger mission and vision. They are also more effective at motivating their teams, as they can communicate a clear sense of purpose aligned with the organization's goals and objectives.

Numerous examples of purpose-driven leaders have successfully aligned personal and organizational purposes to achieve extraordinary results. For instance, Oprah Winfrey aims to empower and inspire others. So she founded OWN, the Oprah Winfrey Network, to provide programming that encourages people to live their best lives.

Satya Nadella, the CEO of Microsoft, aims to empower people and organizations to achieve more. Under his leadership, Microsoft has shifted its focus to cloud computing and artificial intelligence to enable individuals and organizations to achieve more.

Understanding personal and organizational purpose is essential for effective leadership. Leaders aligned with their purpose are better equipped to make decisions that align with their values and beliefs. They are also more effective at motivating their teams, as they can communicate a clear sense of purpose that resonates with team members.

Leaders who understand their organization's purpose are better equipped to make decisions that align with the larger mission and vision. They are also more effective at motivating their teams, as they can communicate a clear sense of purpose aligned with the organization's goals and objectives.

It is essential to define your purpose as an individual or organization. The benefits of having a clear and defined purpose, as well as the challenges that come with the process of defining your purpose, are significant. We will also understand strategies for communicating your purpose to your team in a way that inspires and motivates them to achieve their goals.

By the end of this chapter, you will have a better understanding of what it means to define your purpose and the benefits that come with it. You will also have practical strategies for communicating your purpose to your team in a way that inspires and motivates them to achieve their full potential. So, let's dive in and look at the power of purpose.

Why Purpose Matters in Life and Work

As dawn broke, casting its first light on the bustling city below, Muhammad Yunus contemplated the immense power of a simple idea that changed millions of lives: microcredit. Like other visionary leaders throughout history, Yunus understood the unparalleled impact of a purpose-driven life that transcended personal ambitions to create lasting change. "Why Purpose Matters in Life and Work" delves into the fascinating stories of transformative leaders, from the unwavering determination of Rosa Parks in her fight for civil rights to the innovative spirit of Thomas Edison, who illuminated the world with his inventions. These captivating tales showcase the boundless potential of purpose to transform lives, disrupt industries, and shape history.

This riveting narrative investigates the intricate tapestry that intertwines purpose and passion, molding the human experience. We witness the undeniable influence of purposeful leadership, not only in the realms of the corporate world, where visionaries like Bill Gates and Indra Nooyi left their indelible mark, but also on the global stage, where trailblazers like Aung San Suu Kyi and Mother Teresa inspired social change. This exploration casts light on the inextricable connection between our sense of purpose and the overarching trajectory of our careers and lives.

Imagine a world without purpose—where people wander without direction or intention. Where organizations exist solely for profit, with no sense of responsibility to society or the environment, it's a bleak and uninspired world that lacks the creativity, innovation, and progress that come with a sense of purpose.

The purpose is the foundation of a meaningful and fulfilling life, personally and professionally. It provides direction, motivation, and a sense of belonging. Without it, individuals and organizations are adrift, lacking the clarity and focus necessary to achieve their goals and positively impact the world.

The importance of purpose in life and work has become increasingly apparent in recent years. The purpose has become a buzzword from the personal development industry to the business world. This concept is constantly talked about but often poorly understood. However, the benefits of purpose are real and tangible, and those who embrace it stand to gain a significant competitive advantage.

This captivating journey, filled with real-world examples, illuminates purpose's essential role in our personal and professional lives and challenges us to find our own North Star as we strive for meaningful change. We must delve into the science behind purpose, examine examples of purpose-driven individuals and organizations, and provide practical strategies for discovering and embracing our sense of purpose.

Through this exploration, you'll understand the importance of purpose in personal and professional contexts and discover how to harness its power to achieve your goals and create a meaningful, fulfilling life.

The Importance of Purpose in Life:

At its core, purpose is about finding meaning in life. It is about identifying what matters most and aligning our actions and behaviors with those values. People who have a clear sense of purpose in life are more likely to experience a sense of fulfillment and happiness. They are more resilient in the face of adversity and better able to cope with stress and uncertainty. In addition, research has shown that people with a strong sense of purpose are less likely to develop mental health issues such as depression and anxiety.

Moreover, having a sense of purpose has been linked to greater longevity. Studies have shown that people with a strong sense of purpose live longer than those without a clear purpose. Purpose gives us a reason to wake up and stay engaged with life. It motivates us to care for ourselves and pursue activities that bring us joy and fulfillment.

The Importance of Purpose in Work:

In addition to its importance in life, purpose is crucial in the workplace. Purpose-driven organizations have outperformed their peers regarding financial performance, customer satisfaction, and employee engagement. In addition, employees are more motivated, committed, and productive when they have a clear sense of purpose. They are also more likely to stay with their organizations long-term.

Moreover, purpose-driven organizations tend to attract and retain top talent. Employees today are looking for more than just a paycheck; they want to work for companies that align with their values and positively impact the world. Therefore, purpose-driven organizations that articulate their mission and values are more likely to attract and retain employees who share those values.

The Benefits of Purpose-Driven Leadership:

Purpose-driven leadership is about aligning personal and organizational values with a greater purpose. Purpose-driven leaders can inspire and motivate their teams to achieve great things. In addition, they can create a sense of meaning and purpose in their employees' work, which leads to greater engagement, commitment, and productivity.

Purpose-driven leaders are also better able to navigate the challenges and uncertainties of the business world. They can stay focused on their long-term vision and goals, despite short-term setbacks and failures. They can make tough decisions that are in the best interests of their employees and the organization.

We cannot overstate the importance of purpose in life and work. Purpose provides meaning, direction, and a sense of fulfillment. In addition, purpose-driven individuals and organizations tend to be more resilient, innovative, and successful in achieving their goals. From the examples of purpose-driven individuals like Emmanuel Macron and Reed Hastings to purpose-driven organizations like Patagonia and Google, the purpose is a powerful force that can drive us to achieve great things.

Research shows that purpose-driven individuals are likelier to be happy, healthy, and successful. For example, a study conducted by the Harvard Business Review found that purpose-driven employees are more likely to be engaged and committed to their work, leading to higher levels of productivity and job satisfaction. Similarly, purpose-driven organizations are more likely to attract and retain top talent, create a strong brand reputation, and achieve long-term success.

But the purpose is not just about individual and organizational success. It is also about making a positive impact on the world around us. Purpose-driven individuals and organizations have the power to create meaningful change and make a difference in the lives of others. From Bill Gates's work and philanthropic efforts to eradicate polio to the sustainable practices of companies like Tesla and IKEA, purpose-driven leaders leave a legacy far beyond their personal or organizational success.

So, as we reflect on the importance of purpose in life and work, let us remember that purpose is not just a lofty ideal or a buzzword. Instead, it is a powerful force that can drive us to achieve great things, positively impact the world, and ultimately, find meaning and fulfillment in our lives. By embracing purpose and living with intention, we can create a brighter future for ourselves, our organizations, and the world around us.

Techniques for Identifying Your Purpose and Values

As the room fell silent, a young Malala Yousafzai fearlessly took to the podium, her heart pounding with purpose and determination. Driven by her deeply rooted values of education and gender equality, she faced the United Nations to advocate for the rights of millions of girls worldwide. "Techniques for Identifying Your Purpose and Values" invites you on an introspective voyage, inspired by the courageous journey of Malala and other iconic leaders, to discover the core principles that steer our lives.

We all crave a sense of purpose and meaning in our lives. Yet, defining our purpose can be difficult and sometimes overwhelming for many of us. Whether we seek to understand our purpose or the purpose of our organization, the journey toward clarity and alignment can be challenging.

But why does purpose matter so much? It goes beyond just feeling fulfilled in our personal lives or being more productive in our work. Purpose is a fundamental driver of human behavior and an essential ingredient for success. Research has shown that people with a strong sense of purpose are more resilient, focused, and likely to achieve their goals. Organizations with a clear and meaningful purpose also tend to be more successful, as they attract and retain talented employees, build strong customer relationships, and positively impact the world.

Let us look at the techniques for identifying your purpose and values, both personally and as an organization, and delve into the science behind the purpose and its impact on our lives and work, as well as real-world examples of individuals and companies who have found their purpose and achieved remarkable success as a result. With this knowledge, we can begin to uncover our purpose and values and use them as a guide to making meaningful contributions to our lives, our organizations, and the world around us.

Techniques for Identifying Your Purpose and Values:

1. **Self-reflection**: Self-reflection is one of the most effective ways to identify your purpose and values. It involves taking the time to think deeply about your passions, strengths, and values. Reflecting on your life experiences, achievements, and challenges can help you gain insight into what truly matters to you. Take the case of Oprah Winfrey, known for her inspirational and impactful work in media and philanthropy. Oprah has said that her purpose is to use her platform to inspire and empower others. She has been able to do

so by reflecting on her life experiences and the impact she wants on the world.

2. **Visioning exercises** involve visualizing your ideal life or organization and what it would look like if you lived your purpose and values to the fullest. This technique helps you to gain clarity and focus on what truly matters to you. For example, Patagonia, the outdoor clothing company, has a clear purpose and values related to sustainability and environmental protection. The company's visioning exercises have helped them to align their business practices with their purpose, leading to tremendous success and impact.
3. **Feedback and assessments**: Feedback from others can be a valuable tool in identifying your purpose and values. Seeking feedback from colleagues, friends, or family can help you gain insight into how others perceive you and what strengths they see in you. There are also a variety of assessments, such as personality tests or strengths assessments, which can help you identify your unique strengths and values. For example, Zappos, the online shoe retailer, has a vital purpose related to delivering exceptional customer service. Therefore, they use customer feedback to continuously improve their processes and align their actions with their purpose.
4. **Experimentation:** Sometimes, the only way to honestly know if something aligns with your purpose and values is to try it out. Experimenting with different activities, hobbies, or projects can help you clarify what you are genuinely passionate about. For example, Maya Angelou, the renowned poet and author, experimented with various careers and hobbies before discovering her true passion for writing. Her experimentation allowed her to live a life aligned with her purpose and values and inspired millions worldwide.

Finding one's purpose is not a one-time event but a continuous journey. By using techniques such as reflection, visualization, and exploring your passions, you can begin to understand your personal and organizational purpose.

One important lesson is that external forces cannot impose your purpose on you but rather something from within. Yet, as we have seen through the examples of purpose-driven leaders such as Howard Schultz of Starbucks and Steve Jobs of Apple, a strong sense of purpose can drive transformative change and success.

However, it is not always easy to identify your purpose and values, and it can require a great deal of self-reflection and introspection. The journey to discovering your purpose may be uncertain, but it is worth taking.

Understanding your purpose and values can help you live a more fulfilling and meaningful life. By aligning your actions and decisions with your purpose, you can create a sense of direction and focus that can guide you through any challenge.

So, take the time to reflect on your values, passions, and strengths, and use these insights to guide your journey toward a purpose-driven life. And remember, as purpose-driven leaders such as Oprah Winfrey and Richard Branson have shown us, pursuing purpose is a never-ending journey filled with challenges and opportunities for growth and impact.

Communicating Your Purpose to Your Team

"Sharing your purpose isn't just about talking, it's about inspiring. Paint a vision so compelling that it not only speaks to minds, but resonates in hearts and kindles a shared ambition."

Underneath the pale glow of moonlight, as the rest of the world slept, Mahatma Gandhi meticulously penned his thoughts, preparing to share his powerful vision of a free India with his devoted followers. Just as Gandhi's unwavering purpose rallied millions around a shared dream, "Communicating Your Purpose to Your Team" delves into the art of conveying one's vision, igniting passion, and fostering unity within organizations and communities. In this captivating narrative, we discover the methods employed by transformational leaders, such as Martin Luther King Jr. and Oprah Winfrey, who have etched their visions into the collective consciousness of society, driving individuals to strive for a common goal.

In this mesmerizing journey, we examine the subtle nuances of effectively communicating purpose, weaving a tapestry of inspiration, motivation, and shared ambition. We bear witness to the significant impact of purposeful communication on the success of organizations, both large and small, as we traverse the halls of Google, where Larry Page and Sergey Brin instilled a culture of innovation, to the bustling kitchens of world-renowned chef Massimo Bottura, who cultivated an environment of culinary creativity. This exploration reveals the secrets of these exceptional communicators. Moreover, it offers valuable insights into how to harness their methods in our lives and careers.

Leadership is about more than just setting goals and delegating tasks. It's about inspiring and motivating your team to achieve those goals and share your vision for the future. One of the critical components of effective leadership is communication, particularly the ability to communicate your purpose to your team. When your team understands the purpose behind their work, they are more engaged, motivated, and committed to achieving their goals. Therefore, it is essential to discuss the need for effective communication, the challenges leaders face when communicating their purpose, and strategies for overcoming those challenges.

Understanding the Importance of Effective Communication:

Effective communication is a critical component of leadership. When you communicate your purpose to your team, you tell them what to do and inspire them to believe in something greater than themselves. You are creating a shared sense of purpose and vision, which can be incredibly powerful in motivating your team to achieve their goals.

However, effective communication can be challenging, mainly when communicating purpose. Purpose can be difficult to define and articulate, and finding the right words to express your vision in a way that resonates with your team can be difficult.

Challenges in Communicating Your Purpose:

One of the biggest challenges in communicating your purpose to your team is making it relevant to them. Your team members may have different backgrounds, experiences, and priorities, making creating a shared sense of purpose difficult. Additionally, your team members may be focused on their tasks and responsibilities, making it difficult to see how their work fits into the larger picture.

Another challenge is making your purpose tangible and actionable. Your purpose may be abstract or idealistic, making translating into specific goals and actions difficult. Your team members may resist change, mainly if your purpose requires them to change their habits or behaviors.

Strategies for Communicating Your Purpose:

Despite these challenges, there are strategies that you can use to communicate your purpose to your team effectively. One of the most important is to create a clear and compelling vision. Your vision should be simple, memorable, and relevant to your team members. It should inspire them to act and to believe in the potential for change.

Another strategy is to make your purpose tangible and actionable. It means breaking down your purpose into specific goals and actions your team members can take. It also means providing them with the necessary resources and support to achieve those goals.

Finally, it's essential to be consistent in your communication. Your purpose should be a constant theme in your conversations with your team members, and you should reinforce it through your actions and behaviors. It will help create a shared sense of purpose and vision to motivate your team to achieve their goals—some techniques for communicating your purpose to your team.

- **Start with Why -** One of the most effective ways to communicate your purpose to your team is to start with why. It means explaining why your organization exists and your team's work is essential. By starting with why, you can help your team connect emotionally with their work and inspire them to give their best effort. Simon Sinek's famous "Start with Why" book offers a powerful communication framework. Sinek argues that successful leaders start with why, then move on to how and what. It means starting with a clear sense of purpose, explaining how you will achieve your goals, and finally, what specific actions you will take.

- **Tell Stories** - Another powerful technique for communicating your purpose is to tell stories. Stories are a powerful way to convey your organization's values and mission. In addition, they can help your team connect emotionally with their work. When telling stories, highlight specific examples of how your organization has made a positive impact and how your team's work is contributing to the organization's success. For example, the CEO of Patagonia, Yvon Chouinard, often tells stories about the company's commitment to environmental sustainability. Chouinard can inspire his team and build a sense of purpose around the company's mission by sharing stories about how Patagonia works to protect the planet.
- **Use Visuals** - Visuals can be a powerful tool for communicating your purpose to your team. Images and graphics can help your team better understand your organization's mission and values. Visuals can also be an effective way to make complex ideas more accessible and engaging. For example, Zappos uses a "Culture Book" to communicate its purpose and values to its team. The book is filled with images and graphics that illustrate the company's culture and help new hires better understand the organization's mission.
- **Create a Shared Language** - Creating a shared language can also effectively communicate your purpose to your team. Using everyday language and terminology can help your

team feel more connected to the organization's mission and create a sense of community. For example, Airbnb uses the term "belong anywhere" to communicate its purpose. Using this term consistently across the organization allows Airbnb to create a shared language that helps its team better understand its mission.

- **Lead by Example** - Finally, leaders must lead by example when communicating their purpose to their team. By embodying your organization's values and mission in your behavior, you can inspire and motivate your team to do the same. For example, the founder of Toms, Blake Mycoskie, is known for his commitment to social responsibility. Mycoskie's daily practice of wearing Tom's shoes exemplifies the mission and values of the company.

Communicating your purpose to your team is crucial for aligning everyone towards a common goal and inspiring them to work towards a shared vision. It's not just about telling them what to do, and it's about inspiring them with a sense of purpose and empowering them to make a meaningful impact.

One of the most powerful examples of purpose-driven communication comes from Howard Schultz, the former CEO of Starbucks. When Schultz returned to the company in 2008, Starbucks was struggling. Schultz rallied his team by communicating a clear purpose: to create a "third place" between home and work, where people could connect over great coffee.

Schultz went on a cross-country tour to meet with baristas and hear their stories, and he shared those stories with the rest of the company to inspire them. He also invested in training and development programs to help his team understand the craft of coffee and develop a passion for it. As a result, Starbucks turned its fortunes around and became a beloved global brand.

Another example of purpose-driven communication comes from John Mackey, Whole Foods Market's co-founder and CEO. Mackey believes that a company's purpose should be at the center of everything it does, and he has made a point of communicating that purpose to his team and the world.

Mackey aims to "improve people's health, happiness, and well-being through high-quality food and great service." He communicates that purpose through his writing, public speaking, and interviews, and he has built a culture within Whole Foods that is passionate about healthy food and sustainable practices.

By communicating his purpose clearly and consistently, Mackey has inspired his team to share that passion and make a difference in the world. And by doing so, he has built one of the world's most successful and beloved companies.

Communicating your purpose to your team is not just telling them what to do. It's about inspiring them with a sense of purpose and empowering them to make a meaningful impact. By following the techniques discussed in this chapter and looking to purpose-driven leaders like Howard Schultz and John Mackey for inspiration, you can build a team that is passionate, committed, and aligned toward a common goal. And that, in turn, can lead to extraordinary results and a legacy.

As we conclude our exploration of purposeful communication, we cannot deny the truth that a shared vision has the potential to create ripples capable of transforming teams and entire societies. Much like the captivating speeches of Martin Luther King Jr., which stirred the hearts and minds of millions, the power of communicating one's purpose can become the catalyst for unprecedented change. So let this be a call to action for each of us: to discover our purpose and articulate it passionately, inspiring those around us to unite in our pursuit of a brighter tomorrow.

The Power of Purpose-Driven Communication

Effective communication is a critical component of successful leadership, and purpose-driven communication is the key to creating a lasting impact. Purpose-driven communication is communicating in a way that aligns with your values and your organization's purpose, and it can help you build trust, inspire action, and create positive change. It's about connecting with our audience on a deeper level, sharing our passion and values, and inspiring movement toward a shared goal. We will discover the power of purpose-driven communication and how it can drive engagement, build trust, and create meaningful change. Purpose-driven communication involves what you say and how you say it, and it requires a deep understanding of your audience and their needs.

Benefits of Purpose-Driven Communication:

- **Building Trust**: Purpose-driven communication helps build trust with your audience by demonstrating authenticity and commitment to your values. When you communicate purposefully, your audience can see that you are invested in your message and speaking from a place of integrity.
- **Inspiring Action**: Purpose-driven communication can inspire your audience to act by tapping into their emotions and values. By communicating aligning with your purpose, you can

create a sense of shared purpose with your audience and inspire them to support your goals.

- **Creating Positive Change**: Purpose-driven communication can help make positive change by bringing attention to important issues and inspiring action. By communicating with purpose, you can raise awareness of important social, environmental, or business issues and motivate your audience to take action to create change.

The Elements of Purpose-Driven Communication

Purpose-driven communication comprises several key elements, each essential in effectively conveying our message and inspiring action. These elements include:

- **Clarity:** To effectively communicate our purpose, we must be clear about what we stand for and hope to achieve. Transparency helps our audience understand our message and connect with our purpose more deeply.
- **Authenticity:** Authenticity is essential for building trust with our audience. By being genuine in our values, we can demonstrate our commitment to our purpose and inspire others to join us in our cause.
- **Passion:** Passion is contagious, and when we communicate with passion, we can inspire others to believe in our message and take action to support our cause.
- **Storytelling:** Stories are a powerful tool for communicating our purpose and engaging our audience. By sharing stories that illustrate our purpose and values, we can help our audience connect with our message on a deeper, more emotional level.
- **Action:** Purpose-driven communication is not just about words. It's also about action. Demonstrating our commitment

to our purpose through our actions can inspire others to act and support our cause.

Techniques for Purpose-Driven Communication:

- **Know Your Audience:** Understanding your audience is essential for effective communication. Take the time to research your audience's needs, values, and interests, and tailor your message accordingly. Consider their demographics, motivations, and communication preferences to ensure that your message resonates with them.
- **Be Authentic:** Authenticity is critical for purpose-driven communication. Your message should reflect your values and your organization's purpose genuinely and sincerely. Don't try to be someone you're not or use language that doesn't feel natural. Authenticity builds trust and credibility with your audience.
- **Use Storytelling:** Storytelling is a powerful tool for purpose-driven communication. Stories can help you connect with your audience emotionally and inspire them to action. Use personal anecdotes, case studies, or real-world examples to illustrate your points and make your message more memorable.
- **Use Clear and Concise Language:** Clarity and concision are essential for effective communication. Use simple language to ensure that your message is easily understood. Avoid jargon or technical terms that may be unfamiliar to your audience.
- **Use Visuals:** Visuals are an effective way to communicate complex ideas and engage your audience. Use graphs, charts, images, or videos to illustrate your message and make it more engaging.

We can observe purpose-driven communication, ranging from marketing campaigns to speeches and social media posts. Here are a few examples of purpose-driven communication in action:

Nike's "Just Do It" campaign: Nike's iconic "Just Do It" campaign is an excellent example of purpose-driven communication. By inspiring athletes to push themselves to their limits and never give up, Nike has built a loyal following of passionate customers who believe in its message.

The Body Shop's "Forever Against Animal Testing" campaign: The Body Shop, a cosmetics company, launched its "Forever Against Animal Testing" campaign in 2017 to raise awareness about the cruelty of animal testing in the cosmetics industry. The campaign encouraged customers to sign a petition and call on the United Nations to ban animal testing worldwide. By aligning its brand with a purpose-driven message, The Body Shop was able to increase customer loyalty and create a positive impact on society.

Effective communication is a crucial component of purpose-driven leadership. Leaders who articulate their organization's purpose clearly and compellingly can better inspire and motivate their teams, build strong relationships with stakeholders, and drive meaningful global change.

To illustrate this point, let's consider the example of Apple Inc., widely recognized as a leader in purpose-driven communication. From its iconic "Think Different" campaign to its focus on innovation and design, Apple has always been a company that is deeply committed to its purpose of empowering individuals to be creative and express themselves through technology.

Under the leadership of Steve Jobs, Apple's purpose was communicated in a way that was both simple and powerful, inspiring millions of people worldwide to become loyal customers and advocates of the brand. Today, Apple continues to use purpose-driven communication to build strong relationships with its customers, employees, and stakeholders, driving innovation and growth.

Purpose-driven communication is a powerful tool for leaders who want to change the world positively. Purpose-driven leaders can inspire and motivate their teams, build strong relationships with stakeholders, and drive meaningful change by being clear, concise, and compelling in their messaging. Whether you lead a small team or a global organization, you should not underestimate the power of purpose-driven communication.

Strategies for Aligning Communication with Purpose and Vision

As a purpose-driven leader, it is essential to communicate your purpose and vision effectively to your team and stakeholders. Without clear communication, your team may not understand the "why" behind their work, leading to disengagement, confusion, and a lack of alignment. Effective communication of your purpose and vision can help your team understand their role in achieving the organization's goals. In addition, it can inspire them to work towards a common purpose.

Understanding the Power of Language

Your language can significantly impact how others perceive your purpose and vision. Using language consistent with your purpose and values can help you build credibility and trust with your team and stakeholders. It can also help you communicate your message in a way that resonates with your audience.

For example, consider the difference between two mission statements:

"Our mission is to provide high-quality products to our customers."

"Our mission is to improve the lives of our customers through the products and services we provide."

The second mission statement is more purpose-driven and focused on the customer's experience. Using language that emphasizes their work's impact, the organization can inspire its team to focus on providing the best possible experience for their customers.

Below are the strategies for aligning communication with purpose and vision, including the importance of consistency, the power of storytelling, and the role of leadership in communicating meaning.

- **The clarity in Communication**: Clarity is vital when communicating purpose and vision. Leaders must clearly articulate their organization's purpose and vision in an understandable and meaningful way to their team, customers, and stakeholders. It requires a deep understanding of the organization's values, goals, and objectives and the needs and interests of those receiving the communication. Reed Hastings, CEO of Netflix, is a leader who has successfully communicated a clear purpose and vision. Hastings has stated that the purpose of Netflix is to "create a planet where people can belong anywhere and find entertainment they love." This purpose is clear, concise, and memorable, reflected in every aspect of the company's operations, from content selection to user experience.

- **The Importance of Consistency in Purpose-Driven Communication:** Consistency is vital in purpose-driven communication. Confusion and mistrust can arise if an organization's messaging is inconsistent across all communication channels. Therefore, it is essential to establish a consistent tone, voice, and message that aligns with the organization's purpose and vision. One should ensure that this consistency is reflected across all communication channels, encompassing internal and external communications, marketing and advertising efforts, and employee interactions. For example, when an organization aims to create a more sustainable world, its communication should consistently reflect this value, using language and imagery that supports this message. Tim Cook, CEO of Apple, a leader who has effectively maintained consistency in communication is. Cook has consistently communicated Apple's purpose and vision of creating innovative technology that enhances people's lives through all the company's communication channels. This consistency has helped to reinforce the brand's reputation and build a loyal customer base.
- **The Power of Storytelling in Purpose-Driven Communication:** Storytelling is a powerful tool for communicating purpose and vision. Stories can inspire and motivate people, helping them to connect emotionally with the organization's purpose. Stories can also help to illustrate the organization's impact on the world, making the goal tangible and real. In purpose-driven communication, stories should reinforce the organization's purpose and vision, providing examples of how it lives its values. Steve Jobs, the late co-founder of Apple, was a master of purpose-driven communication, often employing the power of storytelling to inspire, motivate,

and convey his vision. One of the most iconic examples of this was his commencement address at Stanford University in 2005. In that speech, Jobs shared three deeply personal stories from his life: his adoption, dropping out of college, and cancer diagnosis. These tales were emotionally resonant and woven with a central theme: following one's passion, embracing life's setbacks, and seizing every moment as an opportunity for growth. Jobs' ability to connect his personal experiences with the broader purpose of inspiring the graduating class to pursue their dreams demonstrated his mastery of storytelling in purpose-driven communication. His stories were not merely anecdotes but powerful tools that imparted valuable life lessons, creating an emotional connection with the audience and leaving an indelible impact. Through his words, Jobs not only solidified his legacy as a visionary leader but also sparked a flame in the hearts of countless individuals, inspiring them to chase their passions and pursue a purpose-driven life.

- **Authenticity in Communication:** Authenticity is critical when communicating purpose and vision. Stakeholders can quickly detect when communication is insincere or lacking in authenticity, which can erode trust and credibility. Therefore, leaders must be genuine and transparent in their communication. In addition, they must be willing to share successes and failures to build trust and engagement. Tony Hsieh, a former CEO of Zappos, is an example of a leader who has communicated authentically. Hsieh was known for his transparent communication style and willingness to share the company's successes and failures with his team and customers. This authenticity helped to build trust and engagement among stakeholders and contributed to the company's overall success.

- **The Role of Leadership in Communicating Purpose:** Leadership plays a critical role in communicating an organization's purpose and vision. Leaders must be committed to the purpose and vision and communicate it consistently and effectively to their teams. They must also lead by example, embodying the organization's purpose and values in their behavior and decision-making. When leaders are purpose-driven, their teams are more likely to be aligned with the organization's purpose and more motivated to achieve its goals. For example, Patagonia's founder, Yvon Chouinard, is a passionate advocate for environmental causes, and his leadership has helped to create a company culture that is deeply committed to sustainability.
- **Using Different Communication Channels**: Different communication channels can reach different audiences and effectively reinforce purpose and vision. Leaders must consider the needs and preferences of various stakeholders and tailor their communication accordingly. It may include using social media, email, video, or other channels to reach different audiences. For example, Jeff Bezos, CEO of Amazon, is a leader who has effectively used multiple communication channels. Bezos has used a variety of communication channels, including video messages, interviews, and shareholder letters, to communicate Amazon's purpose and vision to different audiences. As a result, it has helped reinforce the brand's reputation and build stakeholder engagement.
- **Leverage Technology**: In today's digital age, technology provides various tools and platforms to communicate with stakeholders. Purpose-driven leaders can leverage technology to communicate their purpose and vision creatively and engagingly. For example, they used social media platforms to share stories, created interactive websites to explore the organization's purpose and values, and used virtual reality to

immerse stakeholders in its mission. A purpose-driven leader who leveraged technology to make a significant impact is Jack Dorsey, the co-founder and former CEO of Twitter and the founder and CEO of Square. Jack Dorsey envisioned a world where everyone had a voice and information could be shared easily and quickly, breaking down barriers and fostering communication. Dorsey's purpose was to create a platform that would democratize the flow of information and empower individuals to express themselves, irrespective of their social status or geographical location. To achieve this goal, he co-founded Twitter in 2006, an online social networking service that allows users to post and interact with short messages called "tweets." By leveraging technology, Dorsey and his team designed Twitter to be a simple, user-friendly platform accessible through the internet and mobile devices, making it easy for people across the globe to share information, express their opinions, and engage in real-time conversations. The platform quickly gained traction and became essential for news dissemination, social activism, and public discourse. As a result of Jack Dorsey's purpose-driven leadership and innovative use of technology, Twitter has become one of the world's most influential social media platforms, boasting over 330 million active users as of 2021. The platform has given a voice to millions of individuals, allowed instant communication during critical events, and provided a space for global discussions, shaping how we consume and share information today.

- **Measure the Impact**: To ensure that communication efforts align with the organization's purpose and vision, purpose-driven leaders must actively measure the impact of their communication strategies. By measuring the effectiveness of communication efforts, leaders can identify areas for improvement and make necessary adjustments. One can accomplish this by utilizing surveys, feedback mechanisms, and data analysis. One example of a purpose-driven leader leveraging technology and measuring the impact of their work is Sal Khan, the founder of Khan Academy. Sal Khan, a former hedge fund analyst, was inspired by his desire to make a world-class education available to everyone, regardless of socioeconomic background. With this goal in mind, he created Khan Academy. This non-profit organization offers free online courses, lessons, and practice exercises for students across the globe. Khan leveraged technology to realize his purpose by creating and utilizing an online platform, harnessing the power of the internet and digital tools to reach a vast and diverse audience. He developed quickly accessible educational materials, including videos and interactive exercises, which catered to various learning styles, ensuring the content was engaging and effective. To measure the impact of his work, Khan and his team analyzed data from user engagement and performance metrics, such as the number of registered users, completed courses, and improvements in students' test scores. This data-driven approach allowed Khan Academy to continuously refine its offerings and better understand the efficacy of its educational content, ultimately driving the organization's growth and success.

As a result of Sal Khan's purpose-driven leadership, leveraging technology, and commitment to measuring impact, Khan Academy has transformed the educational landscape. Today, it serves over 100 million users worldwide, providing free, high-quality education and fostering lifelong learning for millions without access to such resources.

Effective communication is critical for aligning an organization's efforts with its purpose and vision. Therefore, purpose-driven leaders must develop communication strategies that are authentic, transparent, and inspiring. By leveraging storytelling techniques, technology, and measurement tools, leaders can communicate their purpose and vision in a way that resonates with stakeholders and inspires them to act. The examples below show that purpose-driven communication is essential for aligning an organization's efforts and can drive business success and positively impact society and the environment.

In 2018, the multinational corporation Walmart announced a new initiative called "Project Gigaton," aimed at reducing greenhouse gas emissions in its supply chain by one gigaton by 2030. The initiative involved working with suppliers to reduce their emissions through various measures, such as energy efficiency improvements, renewable energy procurement, and sustainable agriculture practices.

To effectively communicate this purpose-driven initiative to its suppliers, Walmart employed several strategies. First, it provided clear and concise communication about the goals and expectations of the initiative. It offered support and resources to help suppliers achieve their targets. Walmart also engaged in ongoing dialogue and collaboration with suppliers to identify and address implementation barriers and share best practices and success stories.

Another critical strategy Walmart employed was aligning its communication with its overall purpose and vision. Walmart has long been committed to sustainability and corporate social responsibility. Project Gigaton naturally extended from these values. By framing the initiative in terms of its broader purpose and vision, Walmart was able to inspire and motivate its suppliers and communicate the issue's importance and urgency to a broader audience.

The success of Project Gigaton is a testament to the power of purpose-driven communication. By effectively communicating its purpose and vision, Walmart could mobilize its suppliers and stakeholders to act towards a common goal. In addition, it resulted in significant environmental and social impact and benefits to Walmart's brand and reputation.

We find ourselves retracing the steps of legendary business leaders who have left an indelible mark on the world through their purpose-driven communication. Visionaries like Steve Jobs, who galvanized Apple with his compelling storytelling, or Richard Branson, whose charisma and genuine passion for innovation continue to inspire generations. One where the echoes of great leaders, such as Nelson Mandela and Abraham Lincoln, reverberate through time, reminding us of the power that purposeful communication can hold. As we ponder their lessons, we must recognize the immense potential within each of us and embrace the responsibility to share our vision with the world.

These iconic leaders have demonstrated that effective communication of purpose and vision can ignite a spark within teams and organizations, propelling them toward extraordinary success. As you absorb the wisdom from their experiences, remember that you can inspire and unite others with your unique vision.

The task ahead is not simple but a worthy endeavor, as the stakes are high and the rewards bountiful. In learning to communicate our purpose and vision, we empower ourselves and kindle a fire within others, sparking change that transcends individual aspirations and reverberates globally. Let the wisdom and strategies gathered in these pages embolden you to become the architects of a future defined by unity, passion, and an unwavering commitment to your purpose. May the strategies and insights shared within these pages fuel your journey as you forge a path of purposeful leadership that inspires those around you to pursue greatness.

III. INSPIRING YOUR TEAM

"Leadership is the art of sparking a fire in others. Inspire your team not just to dream more and do more, but to become more, for the true power of a team lies in the heart of its people."

IMAGINE STANDING AT the helm of a ship, surrounded by a team of dedicated and talented individuals, each ready and eager to embark on a voyage into uncharted waters. The winds of change swirl around you, threatening to capsize your vessel, and it is your responsibility to guide your crew safely through the storm. What does it take to inspire and motivate them to work in harmony, driven by a shared purpose, and willing to overcome any obstacle? What does it take to become a beacon of inspiration that lights the way for those who follow?

In the intricate fabric of leadership, the threads of inspiration are woven with the utmost care, binding together a team more significant than the sum of its parts. A single spark of inspiration can ignite a fire within each team member, propelling them to achieve their fullest potential and surpass their expectations. It is the power of purposeful leadership to harness your team's collective strength and wisdom and channel it toward a common goal.

The story of Ernest Shackleton, the famed Antarctic explorer who led the ill-fated Endurance expedition in 1914, is an extraordinary tale of resilience and leadership. When his ship became trapped and ultimately crushed by ice, he and his crew found themselves stranded in Earth's harshest and most unforgiving environment. Yet, despite these dire circumstances, Shackleton inspired his men to endure unimaginable hardships and ultimately brought them all safely home. He did this by instilling in them a shared purpose, never losing sight of their goal, and fostering a sense of camaraderie and mutual trust among the crew.

As a leader, how can you evoke this same unwavering dedication and commitment within your team? How can you ignite that fire within, driving them to achieve greatness even in adversity? These questions we will unearth in our journey through purposeful leadership, drawing upon the wisdom and experience of those who have come before us.

The indomitable spirit of Franklin D. Roosevelt guided America through the trials of the Great Depression and World War II. Through his steadfast commitment to democratic ideals and his unwavering belief in the strength of the American people, he inspired a nation to persevere and ultimately triumph over unimaginable hardship. Roosevelt's leadership transcended the boundaries of politics. It resonated with people on a deeply human level, demonstrating the power of inspiration in bringing about monumental change.

And who can forget the charisma and vision of Apple's Steve Jobs, a titan of industry who revolutionized how we live, work, and communicate? His ability to inspire his team to push the boundaries of what was possible in technology and design and his unyielding pursuit of perfection made Apple a symbol of innovation and an icon in the technology industry.

As we set sail on this voyage into the heart of inspiring leadership, we will examine the strategies and principles that have enabled these and other leaders to inspire their teams to achieve extraordinary success. We will discover how to create a shared purpose, communicate your vision effectively, and harness each team member's strengths and abilities to propel your organization forward.

Inspiring your team is one of a leader's most important tasks. A team that is encouraged is more engaged, motivated, and productive. But inspiring a team is not always easy. It requires a deep understanding of the individuals on the team, as well as a clear vision and purpose that everyone can rally around. We will study the strategies and techniques that purpose-driven leaders use to inspire their teams and the impact that inspiration can have on organizational success.

1. **Understanding Your Team:** The first step in inspiring your team is understanding them. It means understanding their strengths, weaknesses, interests, and values. Purpose-driven leaders take the time to get to know their team members as individuals and as part of the team. As a result, they create a culture of trust and respect where team members feel comfortable sharing their thoughts and ideas. One example of a purpose-driven leader who understands his team is Jeff Bezos, the founder and former CEO of Amazon. Bezos is known for his intense focus on customer satisfaction and willingness to experiment and take risks. But he also understands the importance of his team. In a letter to shareholders, he wrote, "Our success at Amazon is a function of how many experiments we do per year, per month, per week, per day... The success of Amazon, including its ability to create shareholder value, comes from our employees' ingenuity and hard work. "By understanding his team and empowering them to experiment and take risks, Bezos was able to inspire his

team to create new and innovative products and services and ultimately drive the success of Amazon.

2. **Creating a Shared Vision:** Once you understand your team, the next step is to create a shared vision that everyone can rally around. It means articulating the organization's clear purpose and direction and communicating it to inspire and motivate the team. One example of a purpose-driven leader who created a shared vision is Satya Nadella, the CEO of Microsoft. When he became CEO in 2014, Microsoft struggled to keep up with the rapidly changing technology landscape. Nadella recognized that the company needed a new direction and purpose.

   He articulated a new vision for Microsoft, centered around empowering people and organizations to achieve more through technology. He communicated this vision in a way that inspired and motivated the team and led the company through a successful turnaround.

3. **Empowering Your Team:** Empowering your team is another crucial strategy for inspiring them. It means giving them the autonomy and resources they need to achieve their goals and recognizing and rewarding their contributions.

   One example of a purpose-driven leader who empowers his team is Tony Hsieh, the former CEO of Zappos. Hsieh was known for his emphasis on company culture and customer service and his willingness to experiment and take risks. But he also understood the importance of empowering his team. So he created a culture of trust and empowerment where team members were encouraged to take risks and make decisions. He also recognized and rewarded their contributions through various incentives and rewards. It empowered his team to create a unique and successful company culture and drive the success of Zappos.

4. **Communicating Your Purpose:** Finally, communicating your purpose is critical for inspiring your team. It means articulating your purpose clearly, compelling, and relevant to your team members. One example of a purpose-driven leader who communicated his purpose effectively is Howard Schultz, the former CEO of Starbucks. Schultz was known for emphasizing company culture, social responsibility, and customer experience. He communicated his purpose in a way that inspired and motivated his team and led Starbucks through rapid growth and success. Schultz also communicated his purpose externally through various marketing and public relations.
5. **Celebrate achievements and milestones:** It is important to celebrate accomplishments and milestones to keep team members motivated and inspired. Celebrations can take many forms, from team outings to bonuses to public recognition. Leaders should take the time to acknowledge their team member's hard work and accomplishments and celebrate them meaningfully and personally.
6. **Provide opportunities for growth and development:** Providing opportunities for growth and development is crucial for keeping team members inspired and motivated. For example, leaders can offer training and development programs, mentorship, coaching, and stretch assignments that challenge team members to learn new skills and take on new responsibilities. As a result, leaders build a stronger team and create a culture of continuous learning and improvement by investing in their team members' growth and development.
7. **Foster a culture of innovation**: Encouraging creativity and innovation can inspire and motivate team members. Leaders can foster a culture of innovation by creating a safe space for experimentation and risk-taking, providing resources

and support for new ideas, and recognizing and rewarding creative thinking. By giving team members the freedom to innovate and explore new ideas, leaders can keep their team members engaged and motivated.

8. **Lead with empathy and compassion:** Leaders who lead with empathy and compassion can inspire and motivate their team members by creating a culture of trust, respect, and understanding. Empathetic leaders take the time to listen to their team members, understand their needs and concerns, and provide support and guidance. Leaders who lead with empathy and compassion create a sense of belonging and connection that inspires and motivates team members to do their best work.
9. **Encourage work-life balance**: Finally, leaders who encourage it can inspire and motivate their team members by showing that they value their well-being and recognize the importance of a healthy work-life balance. Leaders can encourage work-life balance by setting realistic expectations, providing flexible work arrangements, and promoting self-care and wellness. By prioritizing work-life balance, leaders can help their team members feel more fulfilled and motivated both in and outside of work.

A purpose-driven leader who inspires their team is Natarajan Chandrasekaran, the Chairman of Tata Sons. Under Chandrasekaran's leadership, Tata Sons has experienced significant growth and expansion across various industries. Chandrasekaran is known for his strategic vision and ability to drive organizational transformation. He has emphasized the importance of innovation, technology adoption, and sustainability in Tata Sons' operations. Chandrasekaran has been instrumental in fostering a culture of collaboration and teamwork within Tata Sons. He believes in empowering employees and encouraging them to think creatively to solve complex challenges. Chandrasekaran has motivated his team to embrace new ideas and drive innovation by promoting continuous learning and development.

His commitment to purpose-driven work characterizes Chandrasekaran's leadership style. He recognizes the significance of making a positive impact on society. He has integrated this ethos into Tata Sons' corporate strategy. Chandrasekaran actively encourages initiatives that contribute to social welfare, environmental sustainability, and community development.

Chandrasekaran's leadership approach aligns with the values of collaboration, innovation, and purpose-driven work, much like Satya Nadella. His strategic vision, focus on teamwork, and commitment to creating a positive societal impact make him an inspiring leader in his own right.

Inspiring your team is a critical component of purpose-driven leadership. By leading by example, fostering a supportive work environment, providing resources and support, and recognizing achievements, you can empower your team to achieve their full potential and drive purposeful work that positively impacts society.

We find ourselves standing at the edge of a vast, unexplored territory brimming with potential. The stories of great leaders like Shackleton, Gandhi, and Jobs have illuminated the path before us, revealing the power of purposeful leadership to ignite a spark within each team member, driving them toward greatness. The challenge now lies before you is to apply these lessons to your unique context, breathing life into your vision and inspiring those around you.

Embarking on this journey will not be easy. However, the rewards are bountiful; when your team is truly inspired, they become an unstoppable force capable of conquering the most daunting challenges. Remember, as a purposeful leader, you can weave the intricate tapestry of inspiration that unites your team and propels them to achieve the seemingly impossible. So, dare to embrace your role as the visionary guide and embark on the journey toward purposeful leadership, leaving an indelible mark on the world that will echo through the ages.

Leading by Example

"Leadership is less about the words we say, and more about the actions we take. Be the torchbearer; illuminate the path with your deeds, for your actions echo louder in the hearts of your team."

An ancient proverb states, "A leader is best when people barely know he exists." This timeless wisdom highlights the power of leading by example, where a leader's actions speak louder than words, and their impact reverberates throughout the organization. In these unspoken gestures, true leadership flourishes, cultivating an environment that inspires team members to follow suit and achieve greatness.

Sir Richard Branson, the charismatic founder of the Virgin Group, is known for his fearless approach to risk-taking and dedication to customer service, which has become the stuff of legend. Branson's willingness to roll up his sleeves and work alongside his team has earned him respect and fostered a company culture that encourages innovation, creativity, and accountability. In addition, his leadership has inspired employees across his diverse empire to embody the values and principles he champions.

Or reflect upon the quiet strength of Rosa Parks, whose refusal to give up her seat on a bus in segregated Alabama became a catalyst for the Civil Rights Movement. Parks' steadfast resolve and unwavering commitment to equality sent a powerful message to her fellow citizens, sparking a revolution that would forever change the course of history.

These stories remind us that leading by example is not merely a management technique but a profound manifestation of a leader's vision, values, and character. Through these tangible demonstrations of purposeful leadership, leaders ignite the spirit of inspiration, propelling teams to overcome adversity and reach the highest peaks of success.

Leading by example is an essential aspect of purpose-driven leadership. It involves setting a standard of behavior and demonstrating a commitment to the organization's purpose and values. Leaders who lead by example inspire and motivate their teams to do the same. We will understand the importance of leading by example and how purpose-driven leaders can use this strategy to inspire their teams.

Leading by example is an essential strategy for purpose-driven leaders. It involves demonstrating a commitment to the organization's purpose and values through your actions and behavior. Leaders inspire their teams to do the same when they lead by example. It created a culture of purpose and shared values that can drive the organization's success.

Leaders who lead by example demonstrate their commitment to the organization's purpose and values. In addition, it creates a sense of trust and respect among team members, as they see their leader paying lip service to the organization's values and living them. Finally, it can lead to increased engagement and motivation among team members.

Leaders who lead by example also set a standard of behavior for their teams. When leaders commit to the organization's values, they actively communicate and clarify expectations for team members. In addition, it fosters a culture of accountability, where leaders hold team members to the same high standards they uphold. Finally, leading by example can be incredibly inspiring. When team members see their leader demonstrating a deep commitment to the organization's purpose and values, they are inspired to do the same. As a result, it can create a shared purpose and a culture of excellence to drive the organization's success.

Leading by example is an essential strategy for purpose-driven leaders. It involves demonstrating a commitment to the organization's purpose and values through your actions and behavior. Leaders who lead by example inspire and motivate their teams to do the same, creating a culture of purpose and shared values that can be incredibly powerful in driving the organization's success. Many examples of purpose-driven leaders have used the strategy of leading by example to inspire their teams. By following in their footsteps, purpose-driven leaders can create a culture of excellence, innovation, and social responsibility to drive their organizations to new heights.

The Power of Authenticity and Vulnerability in Leadership

Once upon a time, a quiet revolution began to unfold in a world where leadership was often synonymous with authority and control. Yet, at its core were the principles of authenticity and vulnerability, shattering long-held beliefs and breathing new life into how leaders guided their teams. As the curtain of pretense lifted, purpose-driven leaders revealed their true selves, establishing a profound connection with their teams. This connection sparked a surge of trust, collaboration, and innovation.

Brené Brown is a renowned researcher and thought leader whose groundbreaking work on vulnerability transformed how countless leaders view their role. By embracing vulnerability and sharing her own experiences, Brown forged a deep, authentic connection with her audience, inspiring numerous individuals to embrace their imperfections and redefine the very essence of leadership.

When we look at the iconic figure of Oprah Winfrey, whose personal story of triumph over adversity resonates deeply with millions worldwide, we find inspiration in her journey and the impact she has made through her various endeavors. Her ability to openly share her struggles and emotions, whether in her television show or as a business leader, has fostered a level of trust and loyalty seldom seen. Oprah's authentic approach to leadership inspires her team and followers to strive for self-improvement and growth while staying true to their unique journey.

These compelling stories exemplify hope and inspiration, showcasing the transformative power of authenticity and vulnerability in leadership. They challenge us to cast aside the shackles of expectation and bravely embrace our truths, allowing the light of genuine connection and purposeful leadership to shine.

As leaders, we often feel pressure to maintain a specific image of strength and competence. Expectations are placed upon us to possess all the answers, make decisions quickly and decisively, and project an aura of invincibility. But what if we told you that the most influential leaders embrace vulnerability and authenticity?

There has been a growing recognition of the power of vulnerability and authenticity in leadership in recent years. When leaders are willing to show their humanity, acknowledge their weaknesses and imperfections, and connect with their teams on a deeper, more emotional level, they create an environment of trust, respect, and empathy. Leadership is a complex and challenging role that requires various skills, including inspiring and motivating others. Authenticity and vulnerability are one of the most powerful ways to do this. Authenticity involves being true to oneself, while vulnerability is the willingness to show one's weaknesses and limitations. These qualities can create a powerful connection between leaders and their teams, fostering trust, openness, and a sense of shared purpose. We will discover the power of authenticity and vulnerability in leadership and how these qualities can help leaders to build strong and effective teams.

Real-world examples abound of leaders who have embraced vulnerability and authenticity and reaped the rewards of doing so. For instance, Jacinda Ardern, the former Prime Minister of New Zealand, has been praised for her empathetic leadership style. Ardern has been willing to show her vulnerability by openly weeping with shooting victims' families or sharing her experiences with anxiety and motherhood. By doing so, she has created a sense of connection with her people and has been able to lead with both strength and compassion.

The Power of Authenticity:

Authenticity is a crucial component of effective leadership. Authentic leaders are true to themselves and their values, and they inspire trust and respect from their teams. Authenticity requires self-awareness, a willingness to be vulnerable, and a commitment to honesty and transparency. When leaders are authentic, they create an environment of trust and openness where team members feel comfortable sharing their ideas, opinions, and concerns. Authenticity can help leaders build stronger relationships with their teams, customers, partners, and other stakeholders.

Howard Schultz, the former CEO of Starbucks, is known for Authenticity. Schultz was known for his commitment to his values and belief in the company's power to create positive social and environmental impact. Schultz was also willing to take risks and make bold decisions, such as closing all Starbucks stores for a day of racial bias training in response to racial profiling at one of the company's stores. Schultz's authenticity and commitment to his values helped create a strong and loyal customer base and a culture of social responsibility within the company.

The Power of Vulnerability:

Traditional leadership often perceives vulnerability as a weakness. However, it can be a powerful tool for building trust and connections with others. The vulnerability involves showing one's flaws, limitations, and mistakes and asking for help when needed. When leaders are vulnerable, they create a culture of openness and acceptance, where team members feel comfortable sharing their vulnerabilities and working together to overcome challenges.

Bill Gates is an example of a vulnerable leader, the co-founder of Microsoft. Gates has been open about his struggles with anxiety and depression and his early failures in business. Gates has also been willing to take risks and make bold decisions, such as shifting the company's focus from software to cloud computing. Gates' vulnerability and willingness to take risks helped create a culture of innovation and creativity within Microsoft and a shared purpose among team members.

The Power of Authenticity and Vulnerability in Combination:

When leaders combine authenticity and vulnerability, they connect with their teams. Authenticity helps build trust and respect, while vulnerability creates a culture of openness and acceptance. Together, these qualities can foster a sense of shared purpose, where team members feel motivated and inspired to work towards a common goal.

Another leader who embodies authenticity and vulnerability is Sheryl Sandberg, the COO of Facebook. Sandberg has been open about her struggles with grief and loss following the sudden death of her husband. She has also been a vocal advocate for diversity and inclusion in the workplace. In addition, she has written extensively about the challenges women face in leadership. Sandberg's authenticity and vulnerability have helped to create a culture of openness and empathy within Facebook, as well as a strong sense of purpose and commitment to social responsibility.

It is vital to examine the science behind these concepts, look at real-world examples of leaders who have successfully embraced them and provide practical tips and strategies for cultivating authenticity and vulnerability in your leadership style and creating a culture of openness, trust, and empathy within your team. Here are some practical tips and strategies for incorporating these qualities into your leadership style:

- **Be transparent**: Share your goals, successes, and failures with your team. Being open about your experiences and challenges can help build trust and create a shared purpose.
- **Listen actively**: Pay attention to your team's feedback and concerns and demonstrate that you value their input by acting on their suggestions.
- **Be approachable**: Create an environment where your team feels comfortable approaching you with questions or concerns and they feel confident that you will listen to them and take their problems seriously.
- **Lead by example**: Model the behavior you want to see in your team. For example, if you want your team to be more open and vulnerable, start by being more open and vulnerable yourself.

- **Foster a culture of empathy**: Encourage your team to be empathetic and supportive of each other. Let us encourage individuals to be there for one another and provide support through challenges and difficult times.
- **Embrace failure**: Don't be afraid to fail or make mistakes. Instead, view failure as an opportunity to learn and grow and encourage your team to do the same.
- **Be yourself**: Don't try to be someone you're not. Instead, embrace your unique qualities and strengths, and use them to inspire and motivate your team.
- **Encourage feedback and collaboration:** Creating a culture of feedback and collaboration is critical for setting the tone in your organization. Encourage your team to share their ideas, perspectives, and feedback, and listen to what they say. Foster a collaborative environment where everyone feels empowered to contribute to the team's success. When you value your team's input and ideas, you create a culture of inclusivity and innovation.
- **Invest in your team's development:** Investing in your team's story is essential to setting the tone in your organization. Provide opportunities for learning and growth, such as training programs, mentorship, and coaching. Encourage your team to develop new skills, pursue their passions, and support them in their professional and personal goals. When you invest in your team's development, you demonstrate your commitment to their success and well-being.
- **Embrace diversity and inclusion:** Diversity and inclusion are essential for setting the tone in your organization. Embrace diversity in all forms, including race, gender, age, religion, and sexual orientation. Create a culture of inclusivity where everyone feels valued and respected. Encourage your team to share their unique perspectives and experiences and celebrate the diversity that makes your team strong.

By incorporating these tips and strategies into your leadership style, you can create a culture of openness, trust, and empathy within your team. As a result, it can help build stronger relationships, increase motivation and engagement, and drive better results.

Being authentic and vulnerable may seem counterintuitive, as there is a long-standing expectation that leaders should always have everything together and be in control. However, this expectation is changing, and research has shown that leaders willing to show vulnerability and authenticity can build stronger relationships with their teams and create a more positive and productive work environment.

By acknowledging their flaws and mistakes, leaders can show their teams that it is okay to be imperfect and make mistakes and that growth and learning are always possible. In addition, it can create a culture of psychological safety and trust within the team, where team members feel comfortable expressing their vulnerabilities and seeking help and support from each other.

Authenticity and vulnerability in leadership also involve being honest and transparent with your team about the challenges and uncertainties of the business. When leaders are open and transparent about the organization's challenges, it can help create a shared sense of purpose and commitment to finding solutions and overcoming obstacles.

Leaders who embrace authenticity and vulnerability can create a more positive, collaborative, and productive work environment where team members feel valued and supported. In addition, by being true to themselves

Let us ponder the indelible mark these qualities can leave in the hearts and minds of those who follow. By stripping away the veneer of invincibility and embracing our true selves, we unlock a reservoir of human potential, foster deep connections, and cultivate an environment where innovation and collaboration thrive. Like the fabled phoenix that rises from the ashes, leaders who dare to expose their vulnerabilities are reborn with newfound strength, inspiring their teams to follow suit and reach for the stars. The transformative power of authenticity and vulnerability in leadership is undeniable, offering a beacon of hope for those seeking to change the world one heartfelt, genuine connection at a time.

Remember that the path to purposeful leadership is one where authenticity and vulnerability pave the way. Embrace these qualities, and watch as your team is inspired to reach new heights, united by the bonds of trust and shared purpose.

Encouraging Creativity and Innovation

"Innovation is the magic born when creativity meets courage. Encourage it, foster it, for it's the force that not only breaks the shackles of status quo, but also propels us into the realms of extraordinary."

In a realm where purposeful leadership reigns supreme, creativity and innovation are the powerful forces that propel organizations to the summit of success, like the brushstrokes of a master painter or the symphony of an acclaimed composer, leaders who are skilled at unlocking their teams' latent potential cultivate these twin pillars of progress, enabling them to create a tapestry of ideas that forever changes the world.

Take, for instance, the inspiring tale of Elon Musk, a visionary leader whose unrelenting passion for innovation has spawned companies such as Tesla, SpaceX, and Neuralink. He is said to foster a culture of creativity, urging his teams to push boundaries and challenging conventional wisdom at every turn. This fearless pursuit of innovation has revolutionized industries and given birth to technologies that were once the stuff of science fiction.

In another corner of the world, the inimitable Sheryl Sandberg, COO of Facebook, has championed the cause of creativity by encouraging her teams to "move fast and break things." By nurturing a dynamic environment that embraces risk-taking and does not fear failure, Sandberg has played a pivotal role in guiding the social media giant to new heights, fundamentally altering how people connect and communicate globally.

These captivating stories stand as a testament to the remarkable power of creativity and innovation in shaping the destiny of organizations and, indeed, the world. Purposeful leaders must respond to the clarion call and actively foster environments where imaginative ideas can flourish and they fully realize the boundless possibilities of human potential.

Innovation has perennially been the pulsating heart of advancement, driving transformation across diverse industries and sectors. From technology and healthcare to the intricate landscapes of manufacturing and finance, organizations prioritizing creativity and innovation often flourish and conquer. Yet, the pertinent question remains: What does it take to nurture an innovation environment within a team or organization? What strategies and methodologies do influential leaders employ to invigorate their teams and fuel groundbreaking ideas?

Central to this endeavor is a fundamental shift in mindset - a transition from the status quo and an openness to embracing novel ideas, even if they appear hazardous or unorthodox. It necessitates a willingness to challenge presuppositions and reevaluate entrenched practices, to experiment and navigate uncharted territories, and to acknowledge failure as an indispensable stepping stone on the path to success.

We will explore the significance of advocating creativity and innovation in leadership, offering practical strategies and techniques for fostering a culture of innovation within your team or organization. Drawing inspiration from real-world examples spanning various industries, we will scrutinize inventive leaders' quintessential traits and behaviors, examining how they have harnessed creativity and innovation to catalyze growth and prosperity. Thus, whether you are a fledgling startup founder eager to disrupt your industry or a seasoned executive striving to stay at the forefront of the curve, the insights and methods presented will empower you to unleash the full potential of your team and generate revolutionary results.

Creativity and innovation are indispensable cornerstones of success in today's competitive business landscape. Innovation can help organizations maintain a competitive edge by launching novel products, services, and processes, elevating customer satisfaction, and augmenting revenue. In addition, by championing creativity and innovation, leaders can cultivate a perpetual improvement and expansion culture, leading to enhanced productivity and profitability.

Innovation can enable businesses to adapt to fluctuating market conditions and evolving customer needs. As a result, agile and adaptable organizations are more likely to thrive in today's rapidly transforming business milieu. By embracing creativity and innovation, leaders can position their organizations to be more responsive to market shifts and stay ahead of their rivals.

Barriers to Creativity and Innovation:

Imagine the seemingly insurmountable barriers that once constrained the ingenuity of leaders like Sir Richard Branson and Mark Zuckerberg, challenging their ability to innovate and create. In purposeful leadership, recognizing and dismantling these barriers is essential for unleashing the full potential of creativity and innovation, ultimately steering organizations toward the heights of success. Yet, despite the criticality of creativity and innovation, numerous organizations grapple with cultivating a culture of innovation. Unfortunately, there exist various barriers that can stymie innovation, including:

- Resistance to change: People frequently resist change, adhering to standard methodologies rather than venturing into untested territories.

- Fear of failure: The apprehension of failure can deter individuals from assuming risks and exploring novel ideas, crucial components of innovation.
- Resource constraints: Absent the appropriate resources such as time, capital, and tools, fostering innovation becomes an arduous task.
- Lack of diversity: A dearth of diversity can curtail the spectrum of ideas and viewpoints within a team, impeding innovation.
- Inadequate leadership support: Strong leadership support is indispensable in establishing a culture of innovation within an organization.

Strategies for Encouraging Creativity and Innovation:

Business history archives brim with luminary leaders like Jack Welsh and Sara Blakely, who transformed their once-fledgling enterprises into global powerhouses through their unrelenting pursuit of creativity and innovation. Under the canopy of such visionary leadership, teams find inspiration to break free from conventional thinking, igniting a flame of ingenuity that illuminates the path to groundbreaking solutions and uncharted success. Yet, despite these impediments, numerous strategies are available to leaders to stimulate creativity and innovation within their teams. These encompass:

- Encouraging experimentation: Inspire team members to test new ideas and approaches while extending support throughout their endeavors. Google's co-founders, Larry Page, and Sergey Brin, are known for fostering a culture of experimentation. For example, they implemented a policy called "20% time," encouraging employees to spend 20% of their work time pursuing innovative projects they are passionate about.

This approach has led to creation of products like Gmail and Google Maps.

- Fostering a culture of learning: Motivate team members to learn from their failures and triumphs and continuously refine and expand their knowledge. Billionaire entrepreneur Elon Musk exemplifies the importance of fostering a learning culture. He famously taught himself rocket science, leading to the successful establishment of SpaceX. Musk constantly learns from his successes and failures and promotes continuous learning throughout his companies, driving their remarkable growth.
- Supplying the right resources: Equip team members with the required time, finances, and innovation tools. IBM has consistently provided its employees with resources to foster innovation. Under the leadership of Ginni Rometty, the company prioritized research and development and invested heavily in cutting-edge technologies like artificial intelligence and quantum computing, positioning IBM as a technology leader.
- Embracing diversity: Champion diversity within the team by actively seeking many perspectives and ideas. Indra Nooyi, the former CEO of PepsiCo, recognized the value of diversity in driving innovation. Under her leadership, PepsiCo prioritized diversity and inclusion, assembling a diverse workforce with different perspectives and ideas. This approach enabled the company to create innovative products tailored to a global customer base.
- Leading by example: Demonstrate innovation and creativity and embody the behavior you wish to see in others. Sir Richard Branson, the founder of the Virgin Group, is a prime example of leading by example. He is a risk-taker known for his bold ventures and ideas. Branson's adventurous spirit has

helped shape the culture of his organization, inspiring employees to innovate and push boundaries.

- Creating a safe environment: Forge a secure atmosphere where team members feel at ease taking risks and experimenting with new concepts, unshackled by the fear of failure. Ed Catmull, the co-founder of Pixar Animation Studios, fostered an environment where employees felt comfortable taking risks and sharing ideas without fear of failure. As a result, the creation of Braintrust, a group of creatives who openly and candidly discuss projects, enabled Pixar to produce innovative films and maintain its reputation as an industry leader.
- Encouraging collaboration: Advocate for collaboration among team members and create opportunities for cross-functional teams to synergize. New Zealand's Prime Minister Jacinda Ardern has emphasized the importance of collaboration in addressing complex issues. By fostering a spirit of cooperation and unity within her government and among the public, Ardern has successfully navigated challenges like the COVID-19 pandemic and natural disasters, demonstrating the power of collaboration in driving effective solutions.

Creativity and innovation are essential for success in today's business world. Therefore, leaders must foster a culture of innovation within their teams by providing the right resources, embracing diversity, leading by example, and creating a safe environment where team members feel comfortable taking risks and trying new things. By doing so, leaders can position their organizations for success, driving growth, productivity, and profitability.

The Role of Creativity and Innovation in Team Success

Amid fierce competition and rapid change, creativity and innovation are the pillars of team success and the cornerstones of success in today's fast-paced world, propelling teams to greatness. For example, think of the groundbreaking impact of how Netflix, under the leadership of Reed Hastings, disrupted the entertainment industry by championing streaming technology and changing the way we consume content. Another prime example is Amazon, led by Jeff Bezos, which revolutionized e-commerce, transforming how we shop and access goods. These inspiring tales exemplify the remarkable power of nurturing creativity and innovation, showcasing that when leaders actively foster these attributes, teams can break new ground and redefine the possibilities within their domains.

Creativity and innovation are essential to team success in today's dynamic and ever-changing business landscape. With technology evolving at a breakneck pace, businesses that do not embrace innovation and creativity risk becoming obsolete. We will demonstrate the significance of creativity and innovation in team success and provide tips for fostering a culture of innovation within your team.

What is Creativity?

Creativity refers to thinking outside the box, coming up with new and innovative ideas, and approaching problems from a fresh perspective. It is a process of generating, developing, and transforming ideas into something new and valuable. Creative individuals are unafraid to take risks, challenge the status quo, and experiment with new approaches.

Why is Creativity Important in Team Success?

In today's fast-paced business world, the ability to be creative and innovative is essential for teams to stay competitive and meet the evolving needs of their customers. Creativity allows teams to identify new opportunities, develop novel solutions, and differentiate themselves from competitors. As a result, teams that embrace creativity and innovation are better equipped to adapt to changes in the market, stay ahead of the curve, and drive business growth.

Examples of Creativity in Action

Some of the world's most innovative and successful companies, such as Apple, Google, and Amazon, are known for their culture of creativity and innovation. Apple, for example, is renowned for its cutting-edge products, such as the iPhone and iPad, which have revolutionized how we communicate and access information. Likewise, Google's innovative search algorithms have transformed how we find information online. Amazon's disruptive business model has completely revolutionized the retail industry.

Tips for Fostering Creativity in Your Team

- **Create a Culture of Psychological Safety**: One of the most critical factors in fostering creativity is creating a culture of psychological safety, where team members feel comfortable sharing their ideas and opinions without fear of criticism or ridicule. To achieve this, leaders actively promote open communication, encourage feedback, and create an environment where mistakes are valuable opportunities for learning and growth.

- **Encourage Diversity of Thought:** Diversity of thought is critical for creativity and innovation. Encouraging team members from different backgrounds, experiences, and perspectives can lead to more diverse and creative solutions to problems.
- **Provide Resources for Creativity:** Resources such as time, funding, and training can help facilitate creativity and innovation. In addition, encourage team members to attend conferences, workshops, and other events to gain insights and learn new skills.
- **Celebrate Creativity**: Celebrating and rewarding creativity can help encourage it within your team. Recognize team members who develop innovative ideas or take risks to succeed.

What is Innovation?

Innovation refers to transforming creative ideas into tangible products, services, or techniques that add value to the business. It involves identifying new and unique ways of doing things that can lead to improved efficiency, increased revenue, and enhanced customer satisfaction.

Why is Innovation Important in Team Success?

Innovation is critical for team success, enabling teams to stay ahead of the competition by continually improving products, services, and processes. Innovation can help teams identify new opportunities, create new markets, and differentiate themselves from competitors. In addition, teams that embrace innovation are better equipped to adapt to changing customer needs, market trends, and technological advancements.

Examples of Innovation in Action

One of the best examples of innovation in action is Tesla, which has completely revolutionized the automotive industry with its electric vehicles. Tesla's innovative approach has led to the development of cutting-edge technology, such as self-driving capabilities and over-the-air updates, which have disrupted the traditional automotive market. Another example of innovation is Airbnb, which has transformed the travel industry by providing travelers with a unique and personalized experience.

Tips for Fostering Innovation in Your Team

- **Encourage Risk-taking:** Innovation requires taking risks and trying new things. Encourage team members to think outside the box and experiment with new ideas, even if they may not initially seem feasible or practical. Jeff Bezos, the founder and former CEO of Amazon, is a prime example of a leader who encourages risk-taking. He made bold and ambitious bets on the future of online retail, digital streaming, and cloud computing, which have paid off incredibly. Bezos encourages his team to think big, innovate, and take risks to achieve success.
- **Foster a Culture of Collaboration:** Collaboration and teamwork are essential for innovation. Encourage team members to collaborate and share their ideas and expertise to create something new and innovative. Indra Nooyi, the former CEO of PepsiCo, is known for her emphasis on collaboration and teamwork. She encourages her team members to collaborate, share their ideas and expertise, and leverage their diverse backgrounds and experiences. This approach has led to innovative products such as PepsiCo's Frito-Lay Baked chips and the Tropicana Probiotics line.

- **Embrace Failure:** Innovation often involves taking risks, and with risks comes the possibility of failure. Embrace failure as a learning opportunity and encourage team members to learn from their mistakes and try again. Reid Hoffman, the co-founder of LinkedIn, is a leader who embraces failure as a critical component of innovation. He believes failure is necessary to learn and grow and encourages his team to take risks and experiment with new ideas. Hoffman's experience of founding several startups that failed before co-founding LinkedIn demonstrates his belief in the value of failure as a learning opportunity.
- **Provide Resources for Innovation:** Resources such as time, funding, and access to technology can help facilitate innovation. Encourage team members to attend conferences, take courses, and experiment with new tools and technologies. Mark Zuckerberg, the CEO of Meta, is a leader who provides resources for innovation. Facebook encourages employees to attend hackathons, take courses, and experiment with new technologies. In addition, the company's "Bootcamp" program provides employees with the resources and mentorship needed to develop their innovative projects.
- **Celebrate Innovation:** Celebrating and recognizing innovation can help encourage it within your team. Recognize team members who come up with new and innovative ideas and highlight their impact on the business. Bill Gates, the co-founder of Microsoft, is a leader who truly celebrates innovation. Gates personally acknowledges and rewards team members who generate new and innovative ideas, often taking the initiative to send them handwritten notes or personal emails.

One example of Gates celebrating innovation comes from the early days of Microsoft. One of the company's employees,

> Charles Simonyi, proposed a new software program that would eventually become Microsoft Word. When Simonyi presented his idea to Gates, Gates immediately recognized the program's potential and gave Simonyi the resources and support he needed to develop it.
>
> Years later, when Microsoft Word became one of the most popular word-processing programs in the world, Gates made a point to recognize Simonyi's contribution and thank him for his innovative idea. Gates' recognition and celebration of Simonyi's idea not only helped motivate Simonyi and his team to continue pushing the boundaries of innovation but also demonstrated to the entire company the importance of celebrating and recognizing innovative ideas and their impact on the business.

Innovation and creativity are at the heart of every successful team, and it fuels that drive businesses to new heights of achievement and success. Look at the technological advancements of the last century - from the discovery of electricity to the invention of the internet. All these innovations have changed the way we live, work, and interact with each other.

Innovation is about creating something new and solving and improving problems. Take, for example, the COVID-19 pandemic. In the face of this global crisis, businesses had to innovate to survive. As a result, many companies pivoted their business models, embracing new technology and finding creative ways to reach customers. For example, remote work, virtual events, and online shopping are all innovative solutions that emerged during the pandemic.

Consider the story of SpaceX, founded by visionary entrepreneur Elon Musk. SpaceX has revolutionized space travel through innovation and creativity, paving the way for a new human exploration and discovery era. In addition, by building reusable rockets and spacecraft, SpaceX has dramatically reduced the cost of space travel, making it more accessible to the masses.

Creativity and innovation are not just for the tech giants of Silicon Valley. They are essential for every business, regardless of industry or size. By fostering a culture of psychological safety, diversity of thought, and risk-taking and providing resources and recognition for innovation and creativity, teams can unleash their full potential and achieve unprecedented success. As the famous quote goes, "The only way to do great work is to love what you do." Embracing creativity and innovation is the key to creating a fulfilling and successful career and building a better future.

As we reflect upon the remarkable stories of companies that have risen to the pinnacle of success through creativity and innovation, we must ask ourselves: What could our teams achieve if we unleashed their full creative potential? Can we, as leaders, inspire and support our teams to break through barriers and redefine what's possible in our industries? Embracing a leadership mindset that values, nurtures, and celebrates creativity and innovation is a powerful way to unlock the untapped potential of our teams. The message is clear: To foster a future of continued growth and unparalleled success, leaders must champion creativity and innovation within their organizations, paving the way for teams to create lasting impact in the ever-evolving world.

Strategies for Fostering a Creative and Innovative Environment

Creating a thriving environment for innovation requires leaders to recognize and implement effective strategies. Reflect upon Google's work culture, where creativity and innovation are deeply ingrained in the company's DNA, led by Sundar Pichai's vision. Adobe's Kickbox program, an initiative supported by Shantanu Narayen, empowers employees to explore new ideas and launch novel projects. Such real-world examples remind us that fostering a creative and innovative environment is not an abstract concept; instead, it is a deliberate and strategic approach that, when effectively executed, unleashes the boundless potential of teams and organizations.

Creativity and innovation are essential for success. Thinking outside the box, developing new ideas, and approaching problems from a fresh perspective sets successful teams apart. Companies that fail to embrace creativity and innovation risk falling behind their competitors and becoming irrelevant in their industries.

Just look at Kodak, a once-great company that failed to innovate and adapt to the digital age. Despite being the leader in photography for over a century, Kodak's failure to embrace digital technology led to its downfall. As a result 2012, the company filed for bankruptcy, a stark reminder of the consequences of failing to innovate.

On the other hand, companies like Google, Amazon, and Apple have embraced creativity and innovation, using it to drive their success and stay ahead of the competition. These companies have created work environments that foster creativity and innovation, encouraging their team members to take risks, experiment with new ideas, and develop innovative solutions.

The tips outlined in the previous section for fostering innovation focus more on the innovation process, including taking risks, embracing failure, and providing resources for innovation. In addition, these tips offer more practical, actionable steps for fostering innovation within a team.

We will deep down some of the most effective strategies for fostering a creative and innovative environment within your team. The strategies outlined are more comprehensive, covering innovation and creativity. They also delve deeper into the various aspects of creating a culture of innovation and creativity, such as promoting diversity, providing opportunities for learning and development, and fostering a culture of psychological safety.

Overall, the strategies and tips provide valuable insights and recommendations for fostering a culture of creativity and innovation within a team. The techniques offer a more holistic approach to creating an innovative work environment. In contrast, the tips provide practical steps for promoting innovation in the team's day-to-day operations. Both techniques are essential for creating a culture of innovation and creativity to drive team success in today's fast-paced business landscape.

Fostering a team culture of creativity and innovation is essential for success in today's rapidly evolving business landscape. However, creating such an environment is not always easy.

- **Encourage a Growth Mindset: -** The first step in fostering a creative and innovative environment is to encourage a growth mindset within your team. A growth mindset believes individuals can learn and develop their abilities through hard work, dedication, and persistence. This mindset is essential for fostering creativity and innovation. It encourages team members to take risks, learn from their mistakes, and continuously improve their skills. An excellent example of a leader fostering a growth mindset within their team is Microsoft CEO Satya Nadella. In his book, "Hit Refresh," he emphasizes the importance of a growth mindset in driving innovation and success within his team. Nadella believes that learning and growth are never-ending journeys, and he encourages his team to embrace new challenges, take risks, and learn from their failures. As a result, under his leadership, Microsoft has transformed into a more innovative and customer-centric organization with a focus on continuous learning and development.

- **Promote Collaboration and Diversity: -** Collaboration and diversity are critical for fostering creativity and innovation within a team. Encourage team members to collaborate, share their ideas and expertise, and leverage their backgrounds and experiences. By promoting collaboration and diversity, you can generate more diverse and innovative ideas, leading to better outcomes for your team. Sundar Pichai, CEO of Alphabet, is an excellent example of a leader who encourages collaboration and diversity. Pichai understands the importance of diversity in driving innovation and fostering a creative work environment. As a result, he has implemented various initiatives to promote diversity within the company, such as unconscious bias training and increasing the number of women and underrepresented minorities in leadership positions. Pichai also encourages collaboration among his team members, providing them with the resources and support they need to work together and develop innovative solutions.
- **Provide Opportunities for Learning and Development -** Providing opportunities for learning and development is essential for fostering creativity and innovation within your team. Encourage team members to attend conferences, take courses, and participate in training programs to help them develop new skills and gain insights. By providing these opportunities, you can help your team members stay updated with the latest trends and technologies and apply them to their work. One leader who places a significant emphasis on learning and development is Jeff Bezos, founder, and CEO

of Amazon. Bezos believes continuous learning is essential for driving innovation and growth within his team. He encourages his employees to attend conferences, take courses, and participate in training programs. In addition, he attends many industry events to stay up to date with the latest trends and technologies. Under Bezos's leadership, Amazon has become a leader in innovation, regularly introducing new products and services.

- **Foster a Culture of Psychological Safety -** Creating a culture of psychological safety is crucial for fostering creativity and innovation within your team. A culture of psychological safety is one where team members feel safe to express their ideas and opinions without fear of criticism or reprisal. This environment encourages risk-taking and experimentation, which are essential for innovation. One leader who has successfully fostered a culture of psychological safety is Ed Catmull, co-founder and president of Pixar Animation Studios. Catmull understands that creating an environment where team members feel comfortable sharing their ideas and opinions is essential for driving creativity and innovation. He encourages his team to speak up, ask questions, and take risks without fear of criticism or retribution. This culture of psychological safety has helped Pixar produce some of the most innovative and successful animated films in history.
- **Embrace Technology: -** Finally, embracing technology is essential for fostering creativity and innovation within your team. Today's technology offers many tools and resources to help your team members collaborate more effectively, develop new ideas, and streamline their work processes. By embracing technology, you can create a more efficient and innovative work environment to help your team succeed. A leader who has embraced technology to foster creativity and innovation is Tim Cook, CEO of Apple. Cook understands

> the importance of technology in driving innovation and providing new opportunities for his team. Under his leadership, Apple has embraced cutting-edge technology, such as artificial intelligence and augmented reality, to develop new products and services. Cook also encourages his team to experiment with new technology, providing them with the resources and support they need to develop innovative solutions.

Many successful companies have embraced these strategies to foster a culture of creativity and innovation within their teams. One example is Google, known for its innovative and creative work environment. Google encourages its employees to take risks and experiment with new ideas, providing them with resources such as time and funding to pursue their passions.

Another example is 3M, a global company known for its innovative culture. 3M encourages collaboration and diversity, allowing team members to collaborate across different departments and specialties to develop innovative solutions. The company also provides opportunities for learning and development, focusing on continuous improvement and skill-building.

Fostering a culture of creativity and innovation within your team is essential for success in today's dynamic and ever-changing business environment. By embracing a growth mindset, promoting collaboration and diversity, providing opportunities for learning and development, fostering a culture of psychological safety, and adopting technology, you can create a work environment that encourages risk-taking, experimentation, and innovation.

We cannot overstate the power of innovation and creativity. From the development of life-saving medical technology to the creation of sustainable energy solutions, innovation can transform the world as we know it. By fostering a culture of innovation and creativity within your team, you are setting your business up for success and contributing to the betterment of society.

Real-world examples of the impact of innovation and creativity abound. For example, innovative companies like Tesla have transformed the automobile industry, which has developed electric vehicles that are changing how we think about transportation. Similarly, innovations like CRISPR gene editing have revolutionized the healthcare industry, holding the potential to cure genetic diseases that were once deemed incurable.

But innovation and creativity are not just the purview of large corporations and industries. Every business, regardless of size or industry, can benefit from fostering a culture of innovation and creativity within its team. By encouraging risk-taking, promoting collaboration and diversity, providing opportunities for learning and development, fostering a culture of psychological safety, and embracing technology, businesses can unleash their full potential and achieve unprecedented success.

Fostering a culture of creativity and innovation within your team is not just about achieving business success but about creating a better future for us all. By developing new and innovative solutions to our challenges, we can create a more sustainable, equitable, and prosperous world for ourselves and future generations. As leaders, it is our responsibility to inspire and motivate our teams to think creatively, take risks, and embrace innovation, so that we can all contribute to making the world a better place.

As we examine the profound impact of fostering a creative and innovative environment on organizations, we must ask ourselves: Are we doing enough to cultivate and embrace the full spectrum of our team's creative potential? Reflect upon the success stories of trailblazing companies like Google, Apple, Amazon, Microsoft, and Adobe, and let us recognize that the strategies these leaders have employed are not just for the elite; they are within reach of all who are willing to invest time, effort, and trust in their teams. As leaders, it is our responsibility to foster an atmosphere where creativity and innovation flourish, enabling our teams to soar to new heights of success. The message resounds with unmistakable clarity: Embrace creativity and innovation wholeheartedly and witness these forces' transformative power on teams and organizations. The future awaits those bold enough to seize the opportunity, shaping a world where innovative ideas thrive, and success knows no bounds.

Providing Opportunities for Growth and Development

"Growth is the cornerstone of success, both for individuals and organizations. As leaders, we not only provide opportunities, but also kindle the desire to reach for the stars and evolve beyond the ordinary."

Have you ever wondered what distinguishes exceptional leaders from their counterparts? As we navigate the narratives of some of the world's most influential business and political leaders, a shared principle becomes evident: the unwavering dedication to offering opportunities for growth and development within their teams. What is the driving force behind this approach, and how do these leaders kindle an insatiable hunger for progress in their people?

Envision the metamorphosis of a caterpillar into a breathtaking butterfly, emerging renewed and empowered. This transformation illustrates the role of purpose-driven leaders in shaping their teams. Individuals like Nandan Nilekani, co-founder of Infosys, and Narendra Modi, the Prime Minister of India, epitomize this philosophy, painstakingly constructing an environment that encourages their team members to unleash their potential and soar to new heights of success.

Contemplate the relentless pursuit of excellence demonstrated by leaders such as Nilekani and Modi as they tirelessly commit to the growth and development of those under their guidance. How do they realize this remarkable endeavor? Through perpetual reflection, assessment, and creating a setting that promotes learning and personal progress.

These visionary leaders have reaped the rewards of a deeply engaged and motivated workforce by fostering an environment conducive to growth and development. Their commitment to nurturing the innate potential in their teams has not only propelled individual triumphs but catapulted entire organizations and nations to greater levels of accomplishment. Each inspiring story illuminates the profound impact of providing opportunities for growth and development on the world stage.

As we embark on this journey to uncover the essence of leadership wisdom, let us remain vigilant to the insights, strategies, and transformative power of providing opportunities for growth and development. Within this realm, we discover the blueprint for exceptional leadership and the future of our organizations and societies.

Imagine entering your office on a Monday morning, greeted by a group of driven, enthusiastic individuals poised to conquer the day's challenges. As you initiate your morning meetings, you observe that your team members are fully engaged, brimming with novel ideas, and eager to collaborate. Their self-assurance shines, as does their hunger to learn and progress. While this scenario may seem like an idyllic vision, it is entirely achievable when you, as a leader, create an environment that fosters growth and development within your team.

Prioritizing your team's growth and development is not only an investment in their future but also in the success of your organization. So the question remains: how do you cultivate a culture of growth and development within your team? How do you facilitate opportunities for your team members to expand their skill sets while promoting your organization's success? Next, we will delve into the most powerful strategies for providing growth and development opportunities for your team.

From training and education programs to mentorship and coaching, job shadowing and cross-training, performance feedback, and development plans, various approaches can help your team members hone their skills and capabilities. We will also examine real-world examples from organizations that have adeptly implemented these strategies to establish a culture of growth and development within their teams.

Ultimately, offering growth and development opportunities is not solely about helping your team members advance their careers. Instead, it is about forging a culture of success that propels the success of your organization. When team members feel valued, supported, and invested, they are more likely to be motivated, inspired, and committed to achieving their objectives. Consequently, as your team members flourish, so does your organization.

As a leader, one of your most crucial responsibilities is to create opportunities for growth and development for your team members. It not only contributes to the enhancement of their skills and abilities but also signifies your dedication to their success and well-being. Therefore, we will scrutinize some of the most efficient strategies for nurturing growth and development within your team.

- **Training and Education Programs -** One of the most common and effective ways to provide opportunities for growth and development is through training and education programs. These can include online courses, workshops, seminars, and more formal programs such as certifications or degrees. By providing these resources, you can help your team members develop new skills, stay updated with the latest industry trends, and position themselves for future career opportunities. Infosys Founder N.R. Narayana Murthy is a strong advocate of training and education programs as a means of providing growth and development opportunities for employees. He has implemented a program called "Infosys' Global Education Center," which provides employees access to online courses, in-person training, and certification programs. Murthy believes that investing in employee development benefits individual employees and helps Infosys stay competitive and innovative in a fast-changing industry.

- **Mentorship and Coaching** - Another powerful way to provide opportunities for growth and development is through mentorship and coaching. Pairing team members with more experienced mentors or coaches can provide them with valuable guidance and support, as well as opportunities to learn from the experiences of others. It can be particularly effective in helping team members develop leadership skills or navigate complex organizational challenges. For example, as CEO of IBM, Ginni Rometty implemented a mentorship program called "IBM P-TECH," which pairs high school students with IBM employees who serve as mentors. This program provides valuable guidance and support to students and helps IBM employees develop coaching and mentoring skills. Rometty also emphasizes the importance of coaching and mentorship for IBM employees at all levels, encouraging them to seek mentors to help them develop their skills and achieve their professional goals.
- **Job Shadowing and Cross-Training** - Job shadowing and cross-training are also effective ways to provide opportunities for growth and development within your team. Job shadowing allows team members to observe and learn from colleagues with different roles or responsibilities. At the same time, cross-training provides opportunities to develop new skills or gain experience in different areas of the organization. Both strategies can help team members broaden their knowledge and skills and better understand the organization. Amazon

CEO Jeff Bezos is known for emphasizing cross-training and job shadowing to provide employee growth and development opportunities. Amazon's "Career Choice" program provides employees with opportunities to gain new skills and certifications in healthcare, transportation, and information technology. Bezos believes that cross-training and job shadowing help employees develop new skills and foster a culture of continuous learning and innovation within the company.

- **Performance Feedback and Development Plans: -** Providing regular performance feedback and development plans is another critical aspect of providing opportunities for growth and development. By setting clear goals and objectives and providing regular feedback and support, you can help team members identify areas for improvement and develop action plans for achieving their professional goals. Former General Electric CEO Jack Welch was a strong proponent of performance feedback and development plans. He implemented a system called "Rank and Yank," which involved ranking employees regularly, rewarding top performers, and removing low performers. While controversial, this system emphasized the importance of setting clear performance goals and providing regular feedback to employees. Welch also encouraged employees to take ownership of their development by identifying areas for improvement and developing action plans to address them.

By implementing these strategies to provide growth and development opportunities, leaders like Nadella, Rometty, Bezos, and Welch have created learning, development, and innovation cultures within their organizations. Their success demonstrates the value of investing in employee growth and development to drive business success.

As a leader, providing opportunities for growth and development for your team members is critical for achieving long-term success and driving innovation within your organization. Investing in your team's development empowers them to achieve their full potential and create a continuous learning and improvement culture.

Some of the most successful companies in the world have prioritized growth and development for their employees. Amazon, for example, has a program called "Career Choice," which provides funding for employees to pursue training and education programs outside of work. This program helps Amazon employees develop new skills and advance their careers. In addition, it positions them for future success within the company.

Google has a reputation for being one of the most innovative and successful companies in the world, in part because of its commitment to employee development. The company offers a range of training and education programs and mentorship and coaching opportunities to help its team members develop their skills and capabilities. By doing so, Google attracts and retains top talent and fosters a culture of innovation and growth.

Another example comes from Salesforce, a global software company known for its innovative approach to employee development. For example, Salesforce offers job shadowing, cross-training opportunities, and regular performance feedback and development plans. The company also provides its employees with opportunities to pursue their passions through a program called "Volunteer Time Off," which allows them to volunteer for causes they care about.

Ravi Kumar S., Former President of Infosys, championed the idea of continuous learning and development. He has spearheaded the establishment of multiple "Digital Hubs" in the US. Apart from delivering digital services, these hubs are also centers for training new and existing employees in advanced technologies like machine learning, artificial intelligence, user experience, and advanced digital design, to name a few. This focus on training reflects his belief in nurturing talent within the organization and fostering a culture of continuous learning.

However, providing opportunities for growth and development is essential for individual and organizational success. By investing in your team's development, you can create a culture of continuous learning and improvement that can help your organization stay ahead of the competition and adapt to changing market conditions.

Providing opportunities for growth and development is no longer just a "nice-to-have"; it is a necessity for success. As a leader, you are responsible for investing in your team's development and creating a continuous learning and improvement culture that will drive success for your team and your organization. So, take the time to develop a comprehensive growth and development strategy, and watch as your team and organization thrive.

The Importance of Professional Development in Motivating Teams

Think of the hum of a finely tuned engine, purring with power and efficiency, propelling a vehicle to greater speeds and distances. Now imagine your team is that engine, each member a vital component, working in perfect harmony, driving your organization to unparalleled heights of success. But, of course, the secret ingredient that fuels this engine is professional development. But why is professional development the lifeblood of motivated teams, and how can leaders harness its transformative potential?

As a leader, you must ask yourself: How can I ignite the passion for growth within my team? How can I inspire them to exceed their limitations, scale new heights, and achieve extraordinary results? This section will unravel the intricate tapestry of professional development, weaving together real-life examples of trailblazing leaders, practical techniques, and groundbreaking insights.

As a leader, you have a critical role in creating an engaging, inspiring, and motivating work environment for your team members. But with so many factors to consider, from managing competing priorities to navigating complex organizational structures, it can be challenging to know where to begin.

At the heart of effective leadership is a deep understanding of the importance of purpose. The purpose is the foundation upon which everything else is built - from the mission and vision of the organization to the day-to-day activities of individual team members.

When you lead purposefully, you create a sense of meaning and direction that inspires and motivates your team members to achieve their full potential. Purpose provides a framework for decision-making, a compass for navigating challenges and obstacles, and a source of energy and resilience in adversity.

Let's look at Patagonia, the outdoor clothing and gear company known for its environmental and social responsibility commitment. From its founding in 1973, Patagonia has been driven by a deep sense of purpose - to build the best products while doing the least harm to the planet.

Every aspect of the company embodies this purpose, from the materials and processes utilized to create its products to its active advocacy and activism on environmental protection and social justice issues. By leading purposefully, Patagonia has built a loyal customer base and a passionate team of employees who are deeply committed to the company's mission and values.

Dr. Paul Farmer and Partners in Health, a non-profit organization, exemplify the power of purpose through their work in providing healthcare services to some of the poorest and most vulnerable communities worldwide.

Dr. Farmer has dedicated his life to providing high-quality healthcare to those who need it most, regardless of their ability to pay. His commitment to this purpose has inspired a global movement of healthcare workers and advocates who share his vision of health equity and social justice.

Through his leadership, Dr. Farmer has demonstrated the transformative power of purpose in driving positive change and inspiring others to act.

These examples illustrate the importance of purpose in leadership and the impact that purpose-driven leadership can have on organizations and individuals. You can create a meaningful work environment by leading purposefully, engaging and inspiring your team members, and driving improved performance, increased job satisfaction, and better business outcomes.

As a leader, one of your primary responsibilities is to inspire and motivate your team members to achieve their full potential. One of the most effective ways to do this is by providing opportunities for professional development. Professional development refers to acquiring new skills, knowledge, and experience to help individuals enhance their job performance and achieve their career goals.

We will examine the importance of professional development in motivating teams and discuss some of the most effective strategies for providing these opportunities within your organization.

- **Enhancing Job Satisfaction**: - One of the primary ways professional development can motivate teams is by improving job satisfaction. Employees who feel they are growing and developing are more likely to be engaged and committed to their work. By providing opportunities for professional development, you can help your team members feel more satisfied and fulfilled in their jobs and increase their motivation and productivity. Satya Nadella, the CEO of Microsoft, has been a strong advocate for professional development to enhance job satisfaction and motivate employees. Under his leadership, Microsoft has launched several initiatives to provide employees with opportunities for growth and development, allowing employees to assess and develop their skills, and its "Hackathon" event encourages employees to collaborate and innovate on new projects.
- **Building Confidence and Competence: -** Professional development can also help build confidence and competence within your team. You can help your team members develop new skills and expertise by providing training, education, and mentorship opportunities. It can improve their job performance and give them the confidence to take on new challenges and responsibilities. Sheryl Sandberg, the COO of Facebook, has long been an advocate for building confidence and competence through professional development. She has written extensively on the topic, including in her book "Lean In," where she emphasizes the importance of taking on new challenges and seeking opportunities for growth and development. At Facebook, Sandberg has championed a culture

of continuous learning and improvement, encouraging employees to take risks and learn from their experiences.

- **Fostering a Culture of Learning** - Professional development can also help foster a learning culture within your organization. You can inspire your team members to do the same by demonstrating your commitment to ongoing learning and growth. It can create a culture of continuous improvement, where team members are encouraged to seek out new knowledge and skills and to share their experiences and insights with others. For example, Sundar Pichai, the CEO of Alphabet, has been a strong proponent of fostering a learning culture within his organization. Under his leadership, Google has launched several initiatives to encourage employees to seek out new knowledge and skills, such as its "Google Learning Center," which offers a range of training and education programs. Pichai has also emphasized the importance of collaboration and learning from others, encouraging employees to share their experiences and insights.
- **Attracting and Retaining Top Talent** - Professional development can be a powerful tool for attracting and retaining top talent. In today's competitive job market, employees often seek opportunities to grow and develop. By providing these opportunities, you can attract top talent to your organization and retain your existing team members by demonstrating your commitment to their growth and development. For example, Marilyn Hewson, the former CEO of Lockheed Martin, recognized the importance of professional development to attract and retain top talent. Under her leadership, Lockheed Martin launched several initiatives to provide employees with opportunities for growth and development, such as its "Leadership Development Program," which helps employees develop the skills and capabilities needed for future leadership roles. Hewson's commitment to employee

> development helped make Lockheed Martin a top employer for engineering and technology professionals.

Companies that prioritize professional development for their teams are more likely to succeed. Apple, for instance, has implemented the "Today at Apple" program, which offers free classes and workshops on various subjects, such as photography, videography, coding, and app development. This initiative helps employees acquire new skills and expertise and positions them for future success within the company.

Global consulting firm Deloitte places a strong emphasis on employee development. They offer a variety of training and educational programs, as well as mentorship and coaching opportunities, to enhance the skills and capabilities of their team members. In addition, Deloitte's "Greenhouse" program allows employees to explore their passions and interests through innovative projects outside their regular responsibilities.

Professional development is crucial to motivating and inspiring teams to reach their full potential. Professional development can propel your organization toward success by improving job satisfaction, boosting confidence and competence, fostering a learning culture, and attracting and retaining top talent. Therefore, take the initiative to design a comprehensive professional development strategy and watch your team members excel and achieve their career objectives.

Purpose-driven leadership extends beyond a feel-good concept; it is essential to success in today's dynamic business environment. By leading with purpose and prioritizing the well-being and growth of your team members, you can cultivate an engaging, inspiring, and meaningful work environment, leading to enhanced performance, increased job satisfaction, and superior business outcomes.

Moreover, purpose-driven leadership aims to make a positive impact on the world. By establishing and communicating a clear mission and vision for your organization and leading with integrity, authenticity, and passion, you can encourage your team members to utilize their skills and talents to make a difference in the lives of others.

Today's world faces numerous challenges, including climate change, social inequality, political polarization, and economic instability. However, these challenges present opportunities for leaders willing to embrace purpose-driven leadership and exert their influence to create positive change. Greta Thunberg, the Swedish environmental activist, exemplifies the transformative power of purpose-driven leadership, inspiring millions to address climate change and urging governments and businesses to take more substantial measures.

Purpose-driven leadership is not exclusive to activists and social entrepreneurs; anyone aspiring to create a positive impact within their sphere of influence can adopt it. Whether leading a team of employees, running a small business, or merely seeking to make a difference in your community, purpose-driven leadership can help you attain your goals and significantly contribute to the world.

As we confront the challenges of the 21st century, purpose-driven leadership will become increasingly crucial. The world needs leaders committed to creating positive change, driven by a profound sense of purpose, and willing to leverage their influence to make a difference. To become a leader, define your purpose and values, communicate them clearly to your team members, and lead with integrity, authenticity, and passion. Purpose-driven leadership is about achieving success, positively impacting the world, and leaving a legacy of change and progress.

Think of yourself standing atop a mountain, gazing at the horizon, seeing the limitless potential of your team stretch out before you. At this moment, you realize the true power of professional development and its ability to transform individuals and entire organizations.

The evidence is undeniable – the most successful leaders prioritize the growth and development of their team members, fostering an environment that breeds innovation, collaboration, and adaptability. When employees feel valued, challenged, and supported, they flourish, and their newfound confidence and enthusiasm ripple throughout the organization, creating an unstoppable momentum.

As a leader, the responsibility of steering your team towards greater heights rests on your shoulders. Take a moment to reflect on the stories and lessons shared. Consider the extraordinary achievements of leaders who have embraced professional development as a vital ingredient for success. The question that now remains is this: Are you ready to embark on this transformative journey and unlock the full potential of your team?

The path to purposeful leadership lies in your hands. By investing in professional development, you have the power to inspire, engage, and elevate your team, driving your organization to new heights of success. So, take that first bold step and unleash your team's true potential, igniting the spark of greatness within them and leading them toward a future filled with accomplishment and triumph.

Techniques for Creating a Culture of Learning and Growth

Envision entering an organization where curiosity, passion, and an unquenchable thirst for knowledge permeate every corner, where employees are empowered to challenge the status quo, break boundaries, and navigate unexplored paths. A place where enthusiasm and creativity reign supreme and growth is not just an empty promise but a fundamental part of the organizational fabric. How do leaders cultivate such a fertile environment characterized by a culture of learning and growth? And what role do they play in its creation?

Consider the transformational leadership of Hubert Joly, who, during his tenure as CEO of Best Buy, turned the company around by fostering a culture of learning and growth. Joly believed in empowering employees, providing opportunities for continuous improvement, and leading by example. He championed initiatives like "Renew Blue," focusing on employee training, collaboration, and innovation. As a result, Best Buy not only survived the so-called "retail apocalypse" but emerged as a thriving, competitive force in the industry.

When we reflect upon the visionary leadership of Jim Citrin, who leads Spencer Stuart's CEO Practice, a leading executive search firm specializing in finding top-notch CEOs. Citrin has consistently advocated for the importance of a learning mindset within organizations, emphasizing continuous development, adaptability, and embracing failure as an essential component of growth. By cultivating a culture of learning and growth within Spencer Stuart, Citrin has helped the firm become a recognized authority in identifying and developing exceptional leaders.

Building a culture of learning and growth goes beyond developing the following innovative product or service; it's about creating an environment where individuals feel empowered, valued, and inspired to stretch their capabilities and contribute to collective success. So the pressing question is, how can leaders transform their organizations into fertile grounds for learning, growth, and continuous improvement? This section will delve into the techniques, strategies, and mindset shifts that leaders can adopt to establish a flourishing culture of learning and growth within their teams and organizations.

Have you ever contemplated what distinguishes exceptional leaders from mediocre ones? What defining factor sets thriving companies apart from those barely staying afloat? The answer resides in purpose.

Purpose serves as the catalyst that propels individuals and organizations towards excellence. It acts as the guiding beacon for decision-making, infusing a sense of direction and meaning while encouraging action even in the face of adversity.

But how can leaders effectively leverage purpose to inspire and motivate their teams? This article will unveil techniques for purpose-driven leadership and cultivating a culture of learning and growth that triggers enhanced performance, heightened job satisfaction, and superior business outcomes.

To comprehend the transformative power of purpose-driven leadership, let us examine NASA's Apollo 11 mission. When President John F. Kennedy set the ambitious objective of landing a man on the moon by the end of the 1960s, he ignited a profound sense of purpose and possibility, inspiring the nation to accomplish what seemed impossible.

Thanks to a colossal endeavor involving thousands of individuals nationwide, NASA accomplished this goal in 1969, marking one of humanity's most outstanding achievements. However, it wasn't solely the technological innovation that made the mission possible; the unyielding sense of purpose and commitment to a shared objective propelled the team forward.

The Apollo 11 mission is a powerful testament to the significance of purpose in leadership and the impact that purpose-driven leadership can have on individuals and society. By leading purposefully, you can inspire and motivate your team members to unleash their full potential and create a positive ripple effect.

Establishing a culture of learning and growth is crucial for inspiring and motivating team members to reach their full potential. In addition, when team members sense investment in their growth and success from their employer, it increases the likelihood of their engagement and motivation at work. In turn, this leads to increased productivity and improved business outcomes.

In the subsequent sections, we will look at techniques for fostering a culture of learning and growth that boosts performance and job satisfaction. We will investigate how to offer ongoing training and development opportunities, nurture curiosity and a continuous improvement mindset, and supply regular feedback and support. Collectively, these elements lay the groundwork for purpose-driven leadership and offer a blueprint for inspiring and motivating team members to realize their full potential. Together, these elements form the foundation of purpose-driven leadership and provide a roadmap for inspiring and motivating your team members to achieve their full potential.

- **Provide Opportunities for Ongoing Training and Development** - One of the most effective ways to create a culture of learning and growth is to provide opportunities for ongoing training and development. It can take many forms, from on-the-job training and mentoring to attending industry conferences and taking courses or workshops. The key is finding the best approach for each team member and aligning with their goals and interests. For example, some team members may prefer self-paced online courses, while others may prefer in-person workshops or conferences. Real-world examples of practical training and development programs abound. For instance, Google's "20% time" policy allows employees to spend 20% of their work time pursuing projects that interest them, which has led to the development of some of the company's most innovative products. At the same time, Google also provides extensive training and development opportunities for its employees, including on-site courses and workshops and tuition reimbursement programs.

- **Foster a Mindset of Curiosity and Continuous Improvement** - Another critical technique for creating a learning and growth culture is fostering a curiosity and continuous improvement mindset. It means encouraging team members to ask questions, challenge assumptions, and seek new knowledge and skills. One effective way to do this is to create opportunities for team members to share their knowledge and expertise. For example, holding "brown bag" lunches or "learning circles" where team members can share their experiences and insights can help to foster a sense of community and encourage ongoing learning and growth. Companies like Microsoft provide real-world examples of this technique, empowering employees to share their knowledge and expertise through online forums and internal blogs. It not only helps to foster a culture of continuous learning but also helps to build a sense of community and collaboration within the organization.
- **Provide Regular Feedback and Support** - Finally, regular feedback and support are essential for creating a culture of learning and growth. It means providing constructive feedback on performance and offering support and guidance to help team members develop their skills and achieve their goals. One effective way to provide feedback and support is to hold regular one-on-one meetings with team members. These

meetings can allow team members to discuss their progress, set goals, and receive feedback and guidance from their manager. Companies like Deloitte serve as real-world examples of effective feedback and support programs, as they have implemented a "check-in" system that promotes regular feedback and coaching between managers and team members. It has led to improved communication, increased engagement, and better performance among team members.

Creating a culture of learning and growth is essential for inspiring and motivating your team members to achieve their full potential. By providing opportunities for ongoing training and development, fostering a mindset of curiosity and continuous improvement, and providing regular feedback and support, you can create a work environment that is engaging, inspiring, and meaningful, driving improved performance, increased job satisfaction, and better business outcomes.

By leading with purpose and prioritizing the well-being and growth of your team members, you can create an engaging, inspiring, and meaningful work environment. In addition, you can drive improved performance, increased job satisfaction, and better business outcomes by providing opportunities for ongoing training and development, fostering a mindset of curiosity and continuous improvement, and providing regular feedback and support.

But purpose-driven leadership is not just about success in the workplace - it is also about making a positive impact on society. Leading with purpose and integrity can inspire others to act and make a difference in their spheres of influence.

Malala Yousafzai, a Pakistani activist, has become a global symbol of the fight for girls' education. Malala's leadership and commitment to her cause have inspired millions worldwide to act and advocate for the rights of women and girls.

Malala's example demonstrates the power of purpose-driven leadership and a single individual's impact on the world. By leading with purpose and a commitment to a cause, you can make a difference in the lives of others and create a legacy of positive change.

But purpose-driven leadership is not just for activists and social entrepreneurs - it is for anyone who wants to make a difference in their sphere of influence. Whether you are leading a team of employees, running a small business, or simply seeking to make a positive impact in your community, purpose-driven leadership can help you to achieve your goals and make a meaningful contribution to the world.

So, if you want to be a leader who makes a difference, start by defining your purpose and values, communicating them clearly to your team members, and leading with integrity, authenticity, and passion. Remember that purpose-driven leadership is about achieving success, positively impacting the world, and leaving a legacy of change and progress.

In a world facing many challenges, purpose-driven leadership will become increasingly important. The world needs leaders committed to creating positive change, driven by a deep sense of purpose, and willing to use their influence to make a difference.

So, the question is: what is your purpose, and how can you use it to inspire and motivate others to achieve greatness and positively impact the world?

IV. MOTIVATING YOUR TEAM

"Motivation is the heartbeat of a thriving team. Stoke it not with mere words, but by fostering a culture of recognition, respect, and relentless pursuit of a shared purpose."

CONSIDER THE DECEPTIVE tranquility preceding a storm, the air pregnant with unspoken potential, luring you into a false sense of serenity. Within it, however, lies the latent power for a tempest. It is akin to your team - still yet pulsating with untapped prowess, dormant yet capable of feats beyond imagination. The question that looms, both imminent and pressing, is how you, as a leader, can stir this tranquil sea into a tidal wave of productivity, engagement, and innovation.

Let's draw a parallel with the world of orchestras. Visualize an esteemed conductor, such as Leonard Bernstein. Picture him poised on the stage, baton aloft, a myriad of musicians awaiting his cue. In silence, they linger, their latent abilities awakened. Then, with a single, assured stroke, Bernstein commands a symphony, metamorphosing dormant potential into a harmonious ballet of action, each musician executing their part with fervor and precision. His craft lies in this transformation: From silence to the symphony, from potential to performance.

Such is the art of motivation—the leader's baton nudges potential into kinetic energy. The spark lights the fuse, the switch that sets the engine in motion, and the ripple swells into a wave. As we embark on this journey, we shall delve into the heart of this art, unraveling the techniques, methods, and strategies that extraordinary leaders like Bernstein use to rouse their teams into action. We will scrutinize the 'why,' the 'what,' and the 'how' of their maneuvers, to illuminate the path for you to orchestrate your team with finesse.

Your role as a leader is not to master every instrument but to ignite the passion in every musician. So, are you prepared to raise your baton?

What elevates the exceptional from the commonplace in the world of leadership? What fuels some organizations' surge to success while others stumble and falter? The answer lies encapsulated in a single, powerful term: Purpose.

The purpose is the beacon that shepherds individuals and organizations towards extraordinary achievements. It underpins decision-making, confers a sense of direction and value, and incites action even in the face of daunting adversity.

But the conundrum remains: How can leaders employ this potent instrument of purpose to kindle inspiration and motivation within their teams? In this discourse, we will plumb the depths of purpose-driven leadership, cultivating a culture steeped in learning, growth, and enhanced performance. Finally, we endeavor to comprehend how this can bolster job satisfaction and yield superior business results.

Let's envision a world where a profound purpose and unwavering dedication to a cause propel everyone forward. We envision a world where motivation arises from material gain and a fervent aspiration to make a positive difference. Sounds utopian? Yet, it's not as far-fetched as it may appear.

History is a testament to numerous leaders and organizations, fueled by purpose, who have accomplished astounding feats and etched their names indelibly on the world stage. Reflect on Mahatma Gandhi, the paragon of non-violence and civil disobedience, who led India to independence. Gandhi's leadership and allegiance to his cause didn't merely inspire millions globally; it changed the face of a nation and reshaped the world's view of peaceful resistance.

The odyssey of Steve Jobs, a visionary entrepreneur who redefined technology and communication with Apple. Jobs' relentless pursuit of innovation, design perfection, and ability to foresee consumers' needs inspired his team. It catalyzed a technological revolution that continues to shape our world.

These instances underscore the transformative potential of purpose-driven leadership and the extensive impact such organizations can imprint on the world. By leading with purpose, you can fan the embers of potential within your team members, helping them to realize their fullest potential and contribute positively to the world.

As we traverse this exploration, we will reveal strategies for constructing a culture that fosters learning, growth, and peak performance. We will dissect the cornerstones of purpose-driven leadership, offering a blueprint for inspiring and motivating your team members to scale the heights of their potential.

Purpose-driven leadership is a beacon of hope in a world often driven by profit and short-term gains. It shows us that it is possible to create thriving organizations that achieve excellent financial results and significantly impact their employees, communities, and the world.

So, as we embark on this journey, let's remember that, as leaders, our task is not just to manage people or oversee projects. Instead, our mission is to ignite the spark of purpose in others, to fan the flames of their potential, and to guide them as they transform that potential into action.

As we lift our baton, like Bernstein, we are not simply conducting an orchestra of individuals. Instead, we are creating a symphony of purpose, a harmony of effort, and a melody of achievement. We are not just leading a team; we are leading a movement, a crusade of purpose that has the potential to change not just our organizations but the world. So, are you ready to conduct your symphony? Are you prepared to lead with purpose?

Setting Clear Goals and Expectations

"Clarity in goals is the roadmap to success. It's the beacon that guides, aligns, and unifies your team's efforts, transforming scattered strides into a purposeful march towards achievement."

When you set yourself sailing on a journey across the vast, unexplored expanses of the ocean, the sea mirrors the sky, brilliant and blue, and the breeze is gentle, yet you're adrift. Without a compass, a map, or a clear destination, how far could you venture before the sea's whims take control?

This maritime adventure is a potent metaphor for the tumultuous journey of leading a team without explicit goals and expectations. Like mariners sailing the open sea, your team depends on the beacon of well-set plans to plot their course. Recall the monumental accomplishments of the team behind the Mars Rover landing or the architects who crafted the magnificent Burj Khalifa. Their triumph hinged on possessing specific, explicit objectives and expectations, transforming audacious dreams into awe-inspiring realities. As we delve into "Setting Clear Goals and Expectations," we aim to equip you, as a leader, to be the lighthouse guiding your team towards their Mars landing or architectural wonder.

But what does it indeed mean to lead with purpose? Is it simply about delegating duties and managing projects, or is there something more intrinsic involved? The answer is both more straightforward and complex than we might anticipate. Purpose-driven leadership's crux is the capacity to inspire and motivate your team members to actualize their potential and make a positive dent in the universe.

Reflect on a time when you were part of a team that excelled extraordinarily. What was the secret sauce that made the team tick? Was it just the individual prowess of team members, or was there something more? In reality, high-performing teams are greater than the sum of their parts. They comprise individuals bonded by a shared purpose and an unwavering dedication to achieving a common goal. This shared objective is the adhesive that binds the team, and fuels improved performance.

So, how can leaders utilize the power of purpose to inspire and motivate their teams? It starts with establishing clear goals and expectations that resonate with your organization's purpose and strategy. Doing so gives your team members a sound understanding of what they are working towards and why it counts. This clarity of purpose forms the cornerstone of purpose-driven leadership. In addition, it lays the roadmap for motivating your team members to realize their potential.

We will understand the critical role of clear goals and expectations in enhancing team performance. We will scrutinize techniques for setting realistic and inspiring goals that motivate your team members to reach their potential and make a positive impact. Along the journey, we will delve into the science of motivation and probe the role of feedback, recognition, and accountability in driving performance enhancement.

So, let's decode the techniques for setting clear goals and expectations. Starting with your organization's purpose and strategy, utilizing the SMART framework, engaging your team members, breaking goals into digestible steps, and providing continual feedback and support, you can set precise, achievable, and aligned with your organization's purpose and strategy. Doing so can ignite your team members to reach their potential and leave a legacy in the world.

The Importance of Goal Setting in Driving Team Performance

When we look at the grandeur of the Great Wall of China, a spectacle so immense that it's visible from space, or the intricate engineering that conceived the International Space Station, a testament to human collaboration and innovation. Neither of these wonders emerged from ambiguity but from clear objectives and meticulous planning.

In the sphere of leadership, goal setting is a mirror of this very principle. It's an alchemy that transmutes the abstract into the concrete, the vision into reality. It is the architectural blueprint for a team's journey, defining undertakings 'what,' 'why,' and 'how.' As we traverse the terrain of "The Importance of Goal Setting in Driving Team Performance," we will probe into the mechanics of how setting precise, attainable goals underpins the success of high-performing teams, converting formidable challenges into resounding victories. Just as the Great Wall and the Space Station were erected brick by brick, bolt by bolt, your team's triumph will be built, goal by goal.

What ingredients make up the recipe for a high-performing team? Is it simply about recruiting top-notch individuals and equipping them with the right tools and resources, or is a more profound, fundamental element involved?

The response, intriguingly, is both more straightforward and more intricate than it might seem. The lifeblood of any high-performing team is a sense of purpose, a lucid comprehension of the team's goals and the significance of these goals.

But how can leaders channel this sense of purpose to kindle inspiration and motivation in their teams? In this exploration, we will excavate the techniques that engender purposeful leadership and cultivate a culture of learning and growth, driving enhanced performance, heightened job satisfaction, and superior business outcomes.

Reflect on an instance when you were part of a team that soared. What was the magic ingredient that powered this team's effectiveness? Was it team members' skills, or was there a more potent force at work?

The reality is that high-performing teams transcend the sum of their parts. They comprise individuals united by a sense of purpose and a commitment to realizing a shared objective. This shared purpose acts as the adhesive bonding the team and the fuel powering improved performance.

Consider the narrative of the Apollo 11 mission, which transported astronauts Neil Armstrong and Buzz Aldrin to the moon in 1969. This landmark achievement resulted from an enormous collective effort involving thousands of engineers, scientists, and support staff striving towards a shared goal. The mutual purpose of landing a man on the moon furnished the motivation and focus required to accomplish this insurmountable feat.

Similarly, by leading with purpose, you can ignite the potential within your team members, inspiring them to impact the world positively. We will excavate the techniques for nurturing a culture that promotes learning and growth, enhancing performance and job satisfaction. We will scrutinize how to offer continuous training and development opportunities, foster a mindset of curiosity and perpetual improvement, and provide regular feedback and support. These elements collectively constitute the bedrock of purpose-driven leadership, offering a roadmap to inspire and motivate your team members to reach their potential.

Understanding the importance of goal setting in driving team performance is essential. Goal setting is a critical component of purpose-driven leadership, providing the clarity, focus, motivation, and collaboration needed to achieve shared objectives. Goal setting is a crucial component of driving team performance. When team members have clear, measurable goals, they are more motivated, focused, and committed to achieving their objectives.

- **Provides Clarity and Focus -** One of the primary benefits of goal setting is that it allows for clarity and focus for team members. When team members know `what they need to achieve, they can better prioritize their time and resources and stay on track toward their objectives. For example, consider the story of the U.S. women's soccer team. When the team set a goal to win the World Cup in 2019, they could focus their efforts and prioritize their training and preparation to achieve their objective. This clear goal gave the team a sense of purpose and direction and helped drive improved performance on the field. Likewise, former U.S. President John F. Kennedy's plan to land a man on the moon by the decade's end gave NASA clarity and focus. Again, this clear goal provided a sense of purpose and direction and helped improve performance and technological advancement.
- **Drives Motivation and Commitment -** Another critical benefit of goal setting is that it drives motivation and commitment among team members. When team members have a clear, compelling goal to work toward, they are more motivated and committed to achieving their objectives. For example, consider the story of the pharmaceutical company Pfizer. When the company set a goal to develop a new cholesterol-lowering drug, Lipitor, they were able to mobilize its resources and drive innovation and collaboration across the organization. This clear goal provided a sense of purpose and

urgency for the company. It helped to drive improved performance and business outcomes. Likewise, Tesla CEO Elon Musk's plan to accelerate the transition to sustainable energy has driven innovation and collaboration. This clear goal provided a sense of purpose and urgency for the company. It helped to drive improved performance and environmental impact.

- **Facilitates Communication and Collaboration** - Goal setting also enables communication and collaboration among team members. When team members work toward a common objective, they are more likely to share information and ideas and collaborate to achieve their goals. For example, consider the story of the software company Adobe. When the company set a goal to transform its business model from selling software to providing cloud-based services, they were able to foster collaboration and innovation across the organization. This clear goal provided a sense of purpose and direction for the company. It helped to drive improved performance and customer satisfaction. Likewise, Facebook CEO Mark Zuckerberg's goal is to connect people and build a community that has fostered collaboration and innovation across the organization. This clear goal provided a sense of purpose and direction for the company. It helped to drive improved performance and social impact.
- **Enables Continuous Improvement** - Finally, goal-setting allows team members to improve continuously. When team members work toward clear, measurable objectives, they can track their progress and identify areas for improvement. For example, consider the story of the sports apparel company Under Armour. When the company set a goal to improve its supply chain efficiency, it identified opportunities for improvement. As a result, it implemented new processes and technologies to achieve its objectives. This clear goal enabled

> the company to drive continuous improvement and achieve better business outcomes. Likewise, Amazon Founder Jeff Bezos' plan to provide customers with the best possible shopping experience has driven innovation and continuous improvement across the company's operations. This clear goal operated the company to improve performance, customer satisfaction, and business outcomes.

Goal setting is a critical component of driving team performance. By providing clarity and focus, driving motivation and commitment, facilitating communication and collaboration, and enabling continuous improvement, effective goal setting can help inspire and motivate team members to achieve their full potential and positively impact the world.

Leading with purpose is not just a nice-to-have but a must-have for any leader who wants to build a high-performing team and achieve extraordinary results. Purpose-driven leadership can help inspire and motivate team members to achieve their full potential and positively impact the world by providing a clear sense of direction and motivation.

We have explored the various techniques for leading with purpose, including creating a learning and growth culture, fostering a curiosity and continuous improvement mindset, and setting clear and compelling goals. When applied thoughtfully and intentionally, these techniques can help create a purpose-driven culture that drives improved performance, job satisfaction, and business outcomes.

But leading with purpose is not just about achieving better results but also about making a difference in the world. Purpose-driven leaders find their drive not in mere financial gain or personal success but in a deep desire to impact the world and leave a lasting legacy positively.

Consider the story of Bill Gates, the co-founder of Microsoft and one of the world's most successful entrepreneurs. After achieving unprecedented success in the tech industry, Gates has dedicated his life to philanthropy and has pledged to give away most of his wealth to address global challenges such as poverty, disease, and climate change.

These examples demonstrate that purpose-driven leadership is not just about achieving business success but also about using that success as a platform for positively impacting the world.

So, as you think about your leadership journey, ask yourself: What is my purpose? What motivates me to do the work that I do? And how can I harness the power of purpose to inspire and motivate my team members to achieve their full potential and positively impact the world?

The answers to these questions may not be easy to find, but they are worth pursuing. By leading with purpose, you can unlock the full potential of your team and achieve extraordinary results that make a difference in the world.

Techniques for Establishing Clear and Achievable Goals

Reflect upon the momentous achievement of Sir Edmund Hillary and Tenzing Norgay, the first climbers confirmed to have reached the summit of Mount Everest. Their journey, fraught with danger and uncertainty, was grounded in a singular, crystal-clear goal: to conquer the world's highest peak. It was a challenging yet achievable objective, guiding their every step and decision on their arduous climb.

Much like mountaineering, leadership also involves a journey towards a peak, albeit metaphorical. It calls for establishing clear and achievable goals that can guide a team's efforts, much like a guiding star in the vast expanse of the night sky. As we journey into the subject of "Techniques for Establishing Clear and Achievable Goals," we will unveil how leaders can craft these guiding stars, these goals, to direct their teams toward success. Drawing upon lessons from luminaries across fields, from innovative entrepreneurs like Jensen Huang, CEO of Nvidia, to visionary scientists like Marie Curie, we will explore how goal setting is not just about reaching the peak but about motivating the climb.

Leadership is more than just managing tasks and projects. It's about inspiring and motivating your team members to achieve their full potential and positively impact the world. One of the essential tools in a leader's arsenal is the ability to establish clear and achievable goals that align with their organization's purpose and strategy.

Consider the story of Jensen Huang, CEO of Nvidia. When he co-founded Nvidia, he envisioned a world where graphics computing would revolutionize how we interact with technology. This clear and ambitious goal drove his team to develop the Graphics Processing Unit (GPU), which has since transformed gaming, film production, and scientific research. Huang's ability to set clear, ambitious goals has propelled Nvidia to become a global leader in AI and graphics processing and transformed the technology landscape.

In future exploration, we will explore the techniques for setting clear and achievable goals. In addition, we will learn how leaders at all levels can inspire and motivate their team members to achieve their full potential, making a lasting impact on the world.

So, let's identify the techniques for establishing clear and achievable goals. By starting with your organization's purpose and strategy, using the SMART framework, involving your team members, breaking goals into manageable steps, and providing ongoing feedback and support, you can set goals that are well-defined, achievable, and aligned with your organization's purpose and strategy.

- **Start with Your Organization's Purpose and Strategy.** The first step in establishing clear and achievable goals is to start with your organization's purpose and strategy. First, align your goals with your organization's mission, vision, and values. Then, design them to assist in accomplishing your strategic objectives. For example, suppose your organization's purpose is to improve access to healthcare in underserved communities. In that case, your goals might include increasing the number of patients served, improving patient outcomes, and expanding your reach to new communities. For example, Jeff Immelt, the former CEO of General Electric, directed his efforts towards establishing clear goals for the company's digital transformation, aligning it with GE's strategic vision of becoming a digital industrial company. It allowed the company to set clear objectives and priorities for its digital initiatives. As a result, it resulted in improved performance and increased revenue.
- **Use the SMART Framework -** The SMART framework helps set clear and achievable goals. SMART stands for Specific, Measurable, Achievable, Relevant, and Time-bound. Following these principles ensures that your goals are well-defined and aligned with your organization's purpose and strategy. For example, a SMART goal for a sales team might be to increase revenue by 10% within the next six months by acquiring five new customers per month. For example, Mary Barra, CEO of General Motors, used the SMART

framework to set clear goals for the company's sustainability efforts. By establishing specific, measurable targets for reducing the company's environmental impact, Barra was able to align the company's sustainability goals with its overall strategic objectives.

- **Involve Your Team Members** - Another critical technique for establishing clear and achievable goals is to involve your team members in the process. By actively soliciting their input and feedback, you can ensure the relevance and feasibility of your goals and foster a sense of investment among your team members in achieving them. For example, suppose you are setting goals for a project team. In that case, you might involve team members in a brainstorming session to identify the project's most essential objectives and critical aspects. For example, Mark Parker, the former CEO of Nike, was known for involving his team members in setting clear goals for the company's innovative product lines and sustainable initiatives. Parker established clear objectives aligned with the company's overall strategic vision by soliciting input from employees across the organization.
- **Break Goals into Manageable Steps** - Breaking goals into manageable steps can help ensure they are achievable and that team members progress toward their objectives. Setting milestones and tracking progress can ensure that team members stay on track and achieve their goals. For example, suppose your goal is to launch a new product within the next six months. In that case, you might break the project into manageable steps, such as conducting market research, developing product specifications, creating a prototype, and conducting user testing. For example, Alan Mulally, a former CEO of Ford, broke the company's goal of achieving profitability into a series of manageable steps. It allowed the

company to focus on achieving small wins and building momentum toward its goal of financial stability.

- **Provide Ongoing Feedback and Support** - Finally, ongoing feedback and support are critical to achieving your goals. By providing regular feedback, you can ensure that team members are staying on track and making progress toward their objectives. You can help team members overcome obstacles and achieve their goals by providing support and resources. For example, you might hold regular progress meetings to review team members' progress toward their goals, provide coaching and support to help them overcome obstacles, and recognize and reward team members for achieving their objectives. Ursula Burns, the former CEO of Xerox, provided ongoing feedback and support to her team members to achieve the company's goal of becoming a digital services provider. By investing in employee training and development, Burns built a culture of innovation and collaboration that helped the company achieve its goals.

Practical goal setting is critical to driving team performance. By starting with your organization's purpose and strategy, using the SMART framework, involving your team members, breaking goals into manageable steps, and providing ongoing feedback and support, you can establish clear, measurable goals that are achievable and aligned with your organization's purpose and strategy. By doing so, you can inspire and motivate your team members to achieve their full potential and positively impact the world.

Establishing clear and achievable goals is a critical component of effective leadership. Setting goals aligned with your organization's purpose and strategy can inspire and motivate your team members to achieve great things and positively impact the world. But goal setting is not just about achieving short-term objectives. It's about creating a continuous improvement and growth culture where team members are empowered to pursue their passions and make meaningful contributions to the world.

Consider the story of Amazon CEO Jeff Bezos. From the beginning, Bezos set a clear and ambitious goal for his company: to provide customers with the best shopping experience. But Bezos didn't stop there. He recognized that he needed to establish a culture of innovation and experimentation to achieve this goal, empowering team members to take risks and pursue their passions. This culture has driven continuous improvement and growth at Amazon. It has enabled the company to make a lasting impact on the world.

So, as you think about establishing clear and achievable goals for your team, remember that it's not just about achieving short-term objectives. It's about creating a continuous improvement and growth culture, empowering team members to pursue their passions and positively impact the world.

By setting clear goals that are aligned with your organization's purpose and strategy, using the SMART framework, involving your team members, breaking goals into manageable steps, and providing ongoing feedback and support, you can create a culture of continuous improvement and growth that inspires and motivates your team members to achieve their full potential and make a positive impact on the world.

Remember, as a leader; it's not just about achieving results. It's about creating a legacy that inspires and motivates others to achieve great things and positively impact the world. So go forth and lead with purpose and inspire your team members to reach their full potential and make a lasting impact on the planet.

Providing Recognition and Rewards

"Recognition fuels the spirit of achievement. Reward not just the results, but the effort, resilience, and the courage to dare, for these are the seeds from which great victories grow."

Reflect on the thrill of success, the euphoria accompanying a well-deserved accolade or the satisfaction of recognition for a well-done job. Think of how the awards received by Nobel laureates fuel further innovation or how an Oscar winner's acceptance speech often kick-starts a flood of new creative endeavors. These moments exemplify the power of recognition and rewards, not just in affirming personal achievement but in motivating continued excellence and fostering a sense of shared success.

For simplicity, imagine you have been working tirelessly on a project for weeks, pouring your heart and soul into every aspect. You have been burning the midnight oil, working long hours, and putting in extra effort to ensure everything is perfect. Then, finally, the project is complete, and you present it to your team leader with pride and anticipation.

And what do you get in return? Nothing. No recognition. No appreciation. Just a quick nod and a "thanks" before your leader moves on to the next item on their to-do list.

How does that make you feel? Unimportant? Unappreciated? Demotivated?

Now, let's flip the script. Imagine instead that your team leader takes the time to acknowledge your hard work, expressing gratitude for your efforts and highlighting how your contributions have made a difference. They give you a tangible reward, such as a bonus or a gift card, as a token of their appreciation.

How does that make you feel now? Valued? Respected? Motivated?

The difference between these two scenarios is the power of recognition and rewards in motivating teams. When leaders take the time to acknowledge and appreciate their team members' hard work, it can profoundly impact morale, job satisfaction, and performance.

Providing recognition and rewards is a critical component of leading with purpose and motivating your team members to achieve their full potential. At its core, recognition, and rewards are about acknowledging your team member's hard work and contributions and showing them their efforts are valued and appreciated.

But how do recognition and rewards impact team performance? And what are the best ways to recognize and reward team members to maximize their impact?

Consider the story of John, a sales manager at a software company. John noticed that his team was feeling burned out and disengaged, and he knew that he needed to do something to boost morale and motivation. So he decided to implement a recognition program where team members could nominate each other for outstanding contributions and achievements. The program included formal recognition, such as awards and bonuses, and informal recognition, such as public shoutouts and thank-you notes.

The results were astounding. Team members felt more appreciated and motivated, and their performance and productivity increased dramatically. In addition, they were more engaged in their work, and turnover rates decreased.

This story illustrates the power of recognition and rewards in motivating teams. But what are the best practices for recognizing and rewarding team members effectively? How can you ensure your recognition program is meaningful, effective, and sustainable?

Identifying the power of recognition and rewards in motivating teams and the creative and effective ways to recognize and reward team members is essential. We will examine the psychological principles behind recognition and rewards, the different types of recognition and rewards, and the strategies for implementing an effective recognition program.

Recognition and rewards are rooted in the basic human need for validation and validation. By recognizing and rewarding team members for their contributions and achievements, you are fulfilling this need and providing a powerful motivation for improved performance and job satisfaction. The key lies in ensuring that you tailor your recognition program to the needs and preferences of your team members while aligning it with your organization's purpose and values.

There are many types of recognition and rewards, including formal awards, bonuses, promotions, and public recognition, as well as informal recognition, such as thank-you notes, public shoutouts, and small gestures of appreciation. The key is to find the right mix of recognition and rewards that works for your team and your organization.

Effective recognition programs exhibit several key elements, including establishing clear and consistent criteria for recognition, regularly communicating and providing feedback, creating opportunities for team members to recognize one another, and emphasizing the values and purpose of the organization. By following these best practices, you can create a recognition program that is meaningful, effective, and sustainable. That drives improved performance, increased job satisfaction, and better business outcomes.

Whether you are a seasoned leader or a new manager, it will provide you with the tools and techniques needed to inspire and motivate your team members through the power of recognition and rewards. So, let's dive in and explore the art of recognizing and rewarding your team members!

In the following subsections, we will identify the power of recognition and rewards in motivating teams and the creative and effective ways to recognize and reward team members. Then, we will examine the different types of recognition and rewards, their psychological principles, and the strategies for implementing an effective recognition program. By this end, you will clearly understand how to use recognition and rewards to inspire and motivate your team members to achieve their full potential and positively impact the world.

The Power of Recognition and Rewards in Motivating Teams

Every team leader knows the importance of motivation in achieving outstanding results. But how can you effectively motivate your team members to perform at their best? One of the most powerful tools at your disposal is recognition and rewards. Recognizing and rewarding your team members for their hard work and achievements can inspire them to go above and beyond and achieve even greater success.

As a leader, imagine you walk into your office on a Monday morning, still groggy from the weekend. Sitting at your desk, you notice a note on your computer screen. It's a thank-you note from your boss, acknowledging the hard work you put in last week to complete a project. Suddenly, you feel a surge of energy and motivation coursing through your veins. You feel appreciated, valued, and inspired to tackle the week ahead.

This scenario illustrates the power of recognition and rewards in motivating teams. When people feel appreciated and recognized for their contributions, they are likelier to feel engaged, motivated, and committed to their work. As a result, they are more likely to go above and beyond to meet goals and exceed expectations. On the other hand, when people feel undervalued and ignored, they are more likely to become disengaged, demotivated, and apathetic toward their work.

As a leader, it's your responsibility to create a culture of recognition and rewards that motivates and inspires your team members to achieve their full potential. But how do you go about doing that? What are the best practices for recognizing and rewarding your team members? How do you ensure that your efforts are effective and meaningful?

We will understand the power of recognition and rewards in motivating teams and the techniques for creating a culture of recognition and rewards that drive improved performance, increased job satisfaction, and better business outcomes. We will examine how to provide recognition and rewards aligned with your organization's purpose and values, foster a culture of collaboration and teamwork, and encourage ongoing growth and development. Together, these elements form the foundation of purpose-driven leadership and provide a roadmap for inspiring and motivating your team members to achieve their full potential.

There are many benefits to recognizing and rewarding your team members.

- **Improved performance**: Leaders who recognize and reward their team members for their hard work and achievements often see improved performance from their team. According to a study by Gallup, organizations that recognize their employees have a 14% higher employee engagement rate, leading to increased productivity and profitability. For example, Cisco Systems, a technology company, implemented a program called "Catch Someone Doing Something Right" that encourages employees to recognize and reward their colleagues for their achievements. This program has resulted in increased employee morale and productivity, as well as improved the organization's overall performance.

- **Increased motivation**: Recognition and rewards can be powerful motivators for employees. When employees feel their contributions are valued and appreciated, they are more likely to be motivated to continue performing at a high level. For example, Google's effective employee recognition programs have earned them recognition. The company uses a peer-to-peer recognition system called "gThanks" that allows employees to recognize and reward their colleagues for their contributions. This program has improved employee engagement and motivation and promoted a positive organizational culture.
- **Higher job satisfaction**: Employees who feel appreciated and recognized for their contributions are more likely to be satisfied. It can increase retention rates, morale, and a positive work environment. For example, the Ritz-Carlton Hotel Company has a renowned employee recognition program called "The Ritz-Carlton Gold Standards." This program rewards employees for delivering exceptional customer service and encourages them to go above and beyond their job requirements. The program has resulted in increased employee retention and loyalty, as well as improved customer satisfaction and brand reputation.
- **Better teamwork**: Recognition and rewards can also help foster teamwork and collaboration among team members. When employees feel their contributions are valued, they

are more likely to work together effectively and support one another. For example, the software company, Atlassian, has a unique employee recognition program called "Kudos," which allows employees to give virtual high-fives to their colleagues for their contributions. This program has improved team collaboration and communication, promoting a positive work environment and culture.

- **Improved customer service**: In industries where customer service is critical, recognition and rewards can help incentivize employees to provide exceptional service. For example, the Ritz-Carlton hotels have implemented a "Wow Stories" program that recognizes employees who go above and beyond to create memorable guest experiences. This program actively fosters a culture of exceptional customer service throughout the hotel chain and receives credit for its impact.
- **Increased innovation**: Leaders who recognize and reward their team members for innovative ideas and solutions can encourage a culture of creativity and innovation within their organization. 3M, a diversified technology company, has a long-standing employee recognition program called "The Genesis Grant" that rewards employees for their innovative ideas and contributions. This program has increased the company's innovation and creativity and fostered a continuous improvement culture.
- **Improved employer brand**: Recognition and rewards can also help improve an organization's reputation. When employees feel valued and appreciated, they are more likely to speak positively about their employer and recommend the organization to others as a great workplace. It can help to attract top talent and improve the employer's brand.

Some industry examples are Salesforce, a leading cloud-based software company with a program called "Ohana," which means family in Hawaiian. The program recognizes and rewards employees who embody the company's trust, growth, innovation, and equality values. In addition, this program receives credit for helping create a strong company culture and fostering high employee engagement.

The grocery chain Whole Foods has a program called "Spotlight," which recognizes and rewards team members who provide exceptional customer service. This program has helped to create a culture of customer service excellence within the company.

The social media company LinkedIn has a program called "InCredible Awards," which recognizes and rewards employees who have significantly impacted the company's culture, strategy, or results. This program has helped to foster a culture of innovation and collaboration within the organization.

As we have seen, purpose-driven leadership is not a one-size-fits-all approach. It requires a deep understanding of your organization's purpose, culture, and values, as well as the needs and aspirations of your team members. It requires empathy, patience, and the willingness to learn from mistakes and embrace new ideas and perspectives.

But most importantly, leading with purpose requires the courage to take a stand and make a difference, even in the face of uncertainty and adversity. As the late civil rights leader and activist, Dr. Martin Luther King Jr. once said, "The ultimate measure of a man is not where he stands in moments of comfort and convenience, but where he stands at times of challenge and controversy."

The same is true for leaders. During times of challenge and controversy, leaders have the most incredible opportunity to demonstrate their commitment to their organization's purpose and values and inspire their teams to do the same.

So, as you embark on your journey as a purpose-driven leader, remember the power of purpose, the importance of learning and growth, the value of setting clear and achievable goals, and the impact of recognition and rewards. Finally, and most importantly, remember that leadership is not about personal glory or achievements but about empowering others to achieve their full potential and positively impact the world.

Ultimately, the accurate measure of your success as a leader will not be the profits you generate or the accolades you receive but the impact you have on the lives of your team members, your organization, and the world around you. So, lead with purpose, and make a difference.

Creative and Effective Ways to Recognize and Reward Team Members

Imagine being part of a team where your hard work and achievements are consistently recognized and appreciated. A team where everyone feels valued and motivated to perform at their best. As a leader, you should aspire to build this type of team. And the good news is that it is possible through creative and effective recognition and rewards.

Recognition and rewards can come in many forms, from a simple thank-you note to an elaborate celebration. And when done right, they can be a powerful tool for motivating and inspiring your team members. We saw in an earlier chapter that The benefits of recognizing and rewarding your team members are clear: increased engagement, improved job satisfaction, higher levels of productivity, and reduced turnover.

To understand the impact of recognition and rewards, consider the story of the software company Atlassian. The company introduced a program called "FedEx Days," granting employees 24 hours to work on a project they chose to deliver a tangible outcome. After 24 hours, teams presented their projects, and winners were chosen based on creativity, innovation, and impact. The program was a huge success, leading to improved morale, increased innovation, and even new product ideas.

But providing effective recognition and rewards requires more than just handing out prizes or throwing a party. It requires a deep understanding of your team members, their motivations, and what drives them to excel. It also requires creativity and innovation to ensure that recognition and rewards are meaningful and impactful.

Not all recognition and rewards hold equal value. Recognition and rewards must be personalized, timely, and meaningful to each team member to be effective. They should also align with your organization's values and goals. You can tailor these strategies to suit your organization's unique needs and culture. By implementing these strategies, you can foster a culture of appreciation and motivation that propels improved performance and business outcomes.

- **Personalized Gifts and Experiences**: Personalized gifts and experiences are a great way to show your team members that you appreciate their hard work and dedication. Whether it's a custom-made piece of jewelry, a spa day, or tickets to a sporting event, personalized gifts and experiences show that you have taken the time to understand your team members' interests and preferences. This type of recognition and reward is especially effective for milestone achievements, such as hitting a sales goal or completing a significant project.

- **Public Recognition and Praise:** Public recognition and praise can be a powerful motivator for team members. Whether in a company-wide meeting, an email to the entire team, or a shoutout on social media, public recognition and praise can help build a culture of appreciation and positivity in your organization. It also demonstrates your investment in the success of your team members. It highlights the organization's appreciation for their hard work. Patagonia's CEO, Rose Marcario, initiated an award ceremony to recognize and reward the company's most innovative employees. This ceremony entails a grand party where winners receive awards in the presence of their peers. This recognition helps foster a culture of innovation at Patagonia, and the event helps to build camaraderie among employees.
- **Flexible Work Arrangements:** Flexible work arrangements, such as telecommuting or flexible schedules, can be a valuable reward for team members who have demonstrated exceptional performance or achieved significant milestones. This type of recognition and reward indicates your trust in your team member's ability to manage their schedules. In addition, it reflects your investment in their work-life balance. In the post-Covid-19 era, the workplace dynamic has undergone significant changes, and many companies provide flexibility to their employees.
- **Professional Development Opportunities:** Providing professional development opportunities, such as attending industry conferences or participating in leadership training programs, can effectively recognize and reward team members committed to their personal and professional growth. This type of recognition and reward shows that you are invested in your team members' long-term success and value their contributions to the organization. In addition, Microsoft allows employees to participate in the company's mentoring program.

This program pairs employees with mentors who help them develop skills and achieve their career goals. By investing in employee development, Microsoft creates a more engaged and motivated workforce.

- **Provide opportunities for volunteer work:** Providing opportunities for employees to engage in volunteer work can be a powerful way to recognize and reward them. For example, IBM allows employees to volunteer for up to 8 hours of paid time off each year. This program will enable employees to positively impact their communities while fostering a culture of giving back at IBM.
- **Offer unique experiences**: Offering employees unique experiences, such as attending an industry conference or traveling to a new city, can be a memorable and effective reward. For example, Zappos offers its employees the opportunity to participate in an annual event called "Zapponian Carnival," which includes games, food, and entertainment. This event fosters a sense of community among employees and helps them feel appreciated and valued by the company.

Leaders can create a more engaged, motivated, and productive workforce by using creative and effective ways to recognize and reward team members. These strategies help foster a culture of appreciation and recognition, positively impacting employee retention and job satisfaction.

As leaders, we have the power to shape the culture of our organizations and inspire our teams to achieve great things. By understanding the importance of recognizing and rewarding team members and implementing creative and effective strategies, we can create a workplace that fosters a sense of purpose, engagement, and commitment.

The examples and techniques we've explored demonstrate the power of recognition and rewards in motivating teams. From personalized and meaningful gestures to public recognition and shared experiences, there are countless ways to show our team members their contributions are valued and appreciated.

But the benefits of recognition and rewards go far beyond just motivating individual team members. When we create a workplace culture that prioritizes recognition and rewards, we foster a sense of community and collaboration that can drive improved performance, increased job satisfaction, and better business outcomes.

So let us embrace the power of recognition and rewards in our leadership approach. Let us celebrate our team member's hard work and achievements and create a workplace that inspires and motivates everyone to do their best work. And remember that showing gratitude and appreciation can profoundly impact the lives and careers of those around us.

As leaders, we have the power to make a difference. Let us use it to build purpose-driven teams that positively impact the world.

Fostering a Positive Work Environment

"A positive work environment is more than just a place, it's a culture. Cultivate it with respect, nurture it with trust, and watch as it blossoms into a powerhouse of productivity and creativity."

Imagine working in an environment where you're constantly stressed, overworked, and underappreciated. You step into your workplace, and the air is thick with tension. Your coworkers huddle in small groups, whispering to each other, and the atmosphere is gloomy and stifling. You try to ignore it and focus on your work but can't help feeling drained and unmotivated.

Now, contrast this with a workplace that exudes positivity and vibrancy. People are smiling, laughing, and collaborating effortlessly. You feel energized, inspired, and eager to tackle challenges. So what is the difference between these two scenarios? Now, think about how that affects your performance and overall well-being. It's no secret that a positive work environment can make all the difference in how you approach your job and how well you perform. But how do you create a positive work environment? How do you foster a culture where employees feel valued, supported, and motivated?

As a leader, it's your responsibility to create and maintain a positive work environment that inspires and motivates your team members. But how can you do that? As we advance, we will explore the techniques for fostering a positive work environment, including promoting open communication, encouraging collaboration, fostering a sense of community, and cultivating a culture of positivity.

Think of the most productive and successful organizations you know. What sets them apart from the rest? Is it their cutting-edge technology or their superior products? While these factors certainly play a role, the most successful organizations share a common thread: a positive work environment. When team members feel valued, supported, and inspired, they are more likely to be engaged, productive, and committed to achieving shared goals.

On the other hand, a toxic work environment can be detrimental to both individual and organizational performance. For example, when team members feel stressed, anxious, or undervalued, they are more likely to experience burnout, turnover, and decreased productivity. In extreme cases, a hostile work environment can lead to legal or ethical issues that damage the organization's reputation and bottom line.

The truth is that a positive work environment is more than just a nice-to-have; it's essential to the success of any organization. Employees who feel valued, supported, and motivated are more engaged, productive, and less likely to leave the company. But creating a positive work environment isn't just about providing free snacks or ping-pong tables; it's about building a culture that fosters engagement, collaboration, and trust.

Consider the story of Zappos, the online shoe and clothing retailer known for its customer service and employee-centric culture. Zappos CEO Tony Hsieh believed creating a positive work environment was critical to the company's success. So he focused on building a culture that valued employee happiness and engagement, offering perks like free lunches, on-site wellness programs, and a company culture book. The result? Zappos became a billion-dollar company with a loyal customer base and a reputation for exceptional customer service.

But creating a positive work environment isn't just for big companies like Zappos. Any organization can benefit from a positive workplace culture. We'll now identify the techniques for creating a positive work environment, including the importance of employee engagement, the role of leadership in fostering a positive culture, and the benefits of building trust, transparency, and collaboration. We'll also provide practical tips and real-world examples to help you transform your workplace into a thriving community that inspires and motivates your team to achieve their best.

Creating a positive work environment starts with employee engagement. When employees feel valued and supported, they're more likely to be engaged in their work and committed to the organization's goals. But how do you foster engagement? One way is to provide opportunities for employees to give feedback and share their ideas. Employees who feel their opinions are heard and valued are more likely to be engaged and committed to the organization's goals.

Another way to foster engagement is to provide opportunities for growth and development. When employees have a clear path to advancement and opportunities for learning and development, they're more likely to be engaged and committed to the organization's goals. Again, consider the example of LinkedIn, the professional networking platform. LinkedIn offers its employees a "Career Path Framework," which provides a clear path for advancement and opportunities for learning and development. As a result, LinkedIn has a highly engaged workforce and a reputation as a great workplace.

As a leader, you have the power to shape the culture and environment of your workplace. By fostering a positive work environment, you can inspire and motivate your team members to achieve their full potential and positively impact the world. We will examine the importance of a positive work environment in driving team performance and a few strategies or techniques for creating a positive work environment that drives improved performance, increased job satisfaction, and better business outcomes.

The Importance of a Positive Work Environment in Driving Team Performance

When we think of high-performing teams, we often consider team members' talents and skills. However, there's much more to a successful team than just having the right people on board. One critical factor often overlooked is the importance of a positive work environment. Creating a workplace culture that fosters positivity and well-being can significantly impact team performance, job satisfaction, and overall business outcomes. We will further understand the importance of a positive work environment in driving team performance and provide strategies for creating a workplace culture that supports employee well-being and success.

A positive work environment is one where employees feel valued, supported, and engaged. It's where people enjoy coming to work, feel motivated to do their best, and have a sense of pride and ownership in their work. A positive work environment can profoundly impact team performance, driving increased productivity, creativity, and collaboration among team members. On the other hand, a hostile work environment, characterized by low morale, high turnover, and a lack of trust and respect among team members, can be detrimental to team performance, leading to decreased productivity, increased absenteeism, and low job satisfaction.

Numerous studies have demonstrated the link between a positive work environment and team performance. For example, a study by the Harvard Business Review found that companies with a positive work culture outperformed their competitors in revenue growth, net income growth, and stock price. Similarly, a study by the Society for Human Resource Management found that organizations with high employee engagement had 22% higher profitability than those with low employee engagement.

But what makes a work environment positive? At its core, a positive work environment supports employee well-being and success. It's a place where employees feel safe, valued, and supported in their personal and professional growth. It's a place where people feel a sense of purpose and meaning in their work and are empowered to make a difference.

Creating a positive work environment requires a multifaceted approach that addresses employees' physical, emotional, and social well-being. It involves creating a workplace culture that fosters positivity, well-being, and a sense of community among team members.

It is essential to examine the characteristics that define such an environment to understand the importance of a positive work environment. These include:

- Respect and Trust: In a positive work environment, team members respect and trust each other. They acknowledge the value of each person's contributions and treat everyone with dignity and professionalism.
- Clear Communication: Team members communicate their ideas and opinions openly and transparently. They receive constructive and respectful feedback through clear communication channels.
- Collaboration and Support: The work environment promotes collaboration and support among team members. Leaders provide necessary resources and support for

employees to succeed, while colleagues assist each other in achieving common goals.

- Positive Attitude and Mindset: A positive work environment fosters an optimistic and constructive attitude. Team members focus on solutions rather than problems and cultivate a growth mindset.

The benefits of a positive work environment are numerous and far-reaching. Here are a few of the most significant:

- Improved Performance: A positive work environment drives improved team performance. When employees feel valued, respected, and supported, they are more motivated to perform at their best.
- Increased Job Satisfaction: A positive work environment also increases job satisfaction. When team members feel comfortable expressing their ideas and opinions and their colleagues and leaders support them, they are more likely to feel satisfied with their work.
- Lower Turnover: A positive work environment reduces turnover rates. Employees are more likely to stay with an organization when they feel valued and supported, reducing the costs and disruption associated with high turnover rates.
- Better Customer Service: A positive work environment leads to better customer service. When team members are motivated, engaged, and supported, they are more likely to provide exceptional service, increasing customer satisfaction and loyalty.

So how can leaders create a positive work environment? It starts with understanding the needs and preferences of your team members. It can include everything from physical workspace and amenities to company culture and values. In addition, understanding what motivates and inspires your team members can create a workplace that fosters collaboration, creativity, and innovation.

One example of a company that prioritizes a positive work environment is Google. The tech giant is known for its quirky office spaces, free gourmet food, and emphasis on work-life balance. But beyond the perks, Google also fosters a culture of openness and collaboration, encouraging employees to share ideas and work together to solve problems. By creating a positive work environment, Google has been able to attract and retain some of the brightest minds in the tech industry, driving innovation and growth.

But creating a positive work environment is not just the job of top leadership. It requires buy-in and support from team members at all levels of the organization. By involving team members in creating a positive work environment, you can foster a sense of ownership and commitment, driving improved collaboration and productivity.

In addition to improving collaboration and productivity, a positive work environment can significantly impact employee engagement and job satisfaction. According to a study by the Society for Human Resource Management, employees who are satisfied with their work environment are more likely to be engaged and motivated, leading to improved performance and job satisfaction.

Creating a positive work environment is critical to driving team performance and achieving organizational goals. By prioritizing a positive work environment, leaders can inspire and motivate their team members to reach their full potential and positively impact the world. It requires an understanding of the needs and preferences of team members, involvement and support from all levels of the organization, and a commitment to fostering a culture of collaboration, creativity, and innovation. By prioritizing a positive work environment, you can drive improved business outcomes and make a lasting impact on the world.

Remember, the power to create a positive work environment lies in our hands as leaders. Let us use that power wisely and positively impact the world.

Strategies for Building a Positive and Supportive Culture

In today's fast-paced business world, leaders need to be more than just managers – they need to be visionaries who inspire and motivate their teams to achieve their full potential. In addition, a positive and supportive culture at the heart of any successful team fosters trust, collaboration, and a shared sense of purpose. But how can leaders create such a culture?

We need to understand the strategies for building a positive and supportive culture. We will dive deep into establishing clear values and norms, creating opportunities for communication and feedback, fostering a sense of belonging and inclusion, and prioritizing employee well-being. Together, these strategies form the foundation of purpose-driven leadership and provide a roadmap for building a team culture that inspires and motivates team members to achieve their full potential.

- **Establishing Clear Values and Norms** - The first step in building a positive and supportive culture is establishing clear values and norms. Values are the guiding principles that underpin everything a team does. At the same time, leaders expect team members to exhibit norms encompassing their behaviors and attitudes. By defining these values and norms, leaders can create a shared sense of purpose and direction for their teams and provide a framework for decision-making and problem-solving. One leader who exemplified this strategy is Indra Nooyi, former CEO of PepsiCo. Nooyi understood the importance of establishing clear values and norms in building a positive and supportive culture. Under her leadership, PepsiCo created a set of guiding principles known as "Performance with Purpose," which defined the company's commitment to sustainability, health, and wellness. In addition, the company integrated these principles into its operations, encompassing areas such as product development and employee training and development.

- **Creating Opportunities for Communication and Feedback** - Effective communication is essential for building a positive and supportive culture. Leaders must create opportunities for open and honest communication and provide regular feedback to team members. It can help build trust, encourage collaboration, and ensure team members feel heard and valued. One leader who understood the importance of communication and feedback was Bill Campbell, former CEO and mentor to some of Silicon Valley's most successful leaders, including Steve Jobs and Jeff Bezos. Campbell believed regular communication and feedback were critical to building a positive and supportive culture. He emphasized the importance of creating a safe space for team members to share their ideas and concerns and providing constructive feedback to help them improve their performance.
- **Fostering a Sense of Belonging and Inclusion** - In a positive and supportive culture, leaders actively create a sense of belonging and foster an inclusivity environment where all team members feel valued and included. As a result, the company celebrates diversity and demonstrates respect for unique perspectives and contributions. Mellody Hobson, co-CEO of

Ariel Investments and a prominent advocate for diversity and inclusion exemplifies this strategy. Hobson actively fosters a culture of inclusivity where team members experience a sense of belonging and where their perspectives and contributions are valued. Under her leadership, Ariel Investments has implemented various initiatives to advance diversity and inclusion, such as unconscious bias training, mentorship programs, and affinity groups.

- **Prioritizing Employee Well-being -** Leaders must prioritize employee well-being to build a positive and supportive culture. It means creating an environment where team members feel professionally and personally supported and their physical and mental health is prioritized. One leader who prioritized employee well-being is Arianna Huffington, founder of The Huffington Post and CEO of Thrive Global. Huffington recognized that employee well-being was essential to building a positive and supportive culture and that burnout and stress were significant obstacles to success. Under her leadership, Thrive Global has implemented a range of initiatives.
- **Fostering a Growth Mindset**: Individuals with a growth mindset believe in developing skills and abilities through hard work, dedication, and perseverance. Leaders who foster a growth mindset among their team members can create an environment that promotes learning and development, which can help team members feel motivated and engaged. For example, leaders can foster a growth mindset by encouraging team members to embrace challenges, learn from mistakes, and seek feedback. They can also provide ongoing training and development opportunities through workshops, mentorship programs, or access to online learning platforms. For example, the CEO of Microsoft, Satya Nadella, implemented a growth mindset culture by encouraging team members to embrace challenges and learn from

failures. He also provided opportunities for ongoing training and development, such as through the Microsoft Academy, which offers courses on various topics related to technology and business.

- **Leading by Example**: Perhaps the most essential strategy for building a positive and supportive workplace culture is leading by example. When leaders model the behaviors and values they want to see in their team members, they can create a culture that promotes trust, respect, and integrity. Leaders can lead by example by demonstrating a commitment to their organization's purpose and values, treating team members with respect and empathy, and showing a willingness to learn and grow. They can also be transparent and authentic in their communication, admitting mistakes and seeking feedback from team members—the former CEO of Starbucks. Schultz was known for his hands-on leadership style and commitment to building a culture of excellence in his organization. He modeled the behavior he wanted to see in his team members by working alongside them, taking the time to get to know them personally, and always striving for excellence in everything he did. This approach helped to build a culture of collaboration, innovation, and customer service at Starbucks. As a result, it allowed the company to become one of the world's most successful and admired brands. Leading by example is not just about the big things in any case. It's also about the small actions and behaviors that leaders model daily. For example, suppose a leader wants to create a culture of respect in the workplace. In that case, they must model respectful behavior in their interactions with team members, colleagues, and customers. It means being attentive, empathetic, and responsive to the needs of others and treating everyone with dignity and respect.

Building a positive and supportive culture within your team is essential to creating a high-performing and motivated group of individuals. By focusing on the abovementioned strategies, such as leading by example, encouraging open communication, and prioritizing work-life balance, you can create a workplace where team members feel valued, respected, and supported in their personal and professional growth.

A positive work culture can have a ripple effect, not only improving team performance and job satisfaction but also contributing to the overall success of your organization. By investing in your team and creating a culture of purpose, recognition, and support, you can inspire and motivate your team members to achieve their full potential and make a lasting impact on the world.

Remember, leadership is not just about managing tasks and projects; it's about inspiring and empowering your team members to be the best versions of themselves. First, as a leader, you create a work environment that fosters positivity, creativity, and growth. Then, by implementing the strategies outlined, you can build a culture that supports your team members and drives improved performance, increased job satisfaction, and better business outcomes.

Leading with purpose requires a commitment to continuous improvement and a willingness to invest in the people you lead. So, act today and build a positive and supportive culture within your team. Your team members, the organization, and the world will thank you.

V. OVERCOMING CHALLENGES

"Challenges are not roadblocks, but stepping stones to greatness. Embrace them, for every adversity carries within it the seeds of growth and the forge for true leadership."

AS THE SUN sets on a bustling metropolis, a lone figure walks through the city streets. But this is not just any figure - this is a leader. And this leader has a purpose.

Leading with purpose is the foundation of effective leadership. A leader without purpose is like a ship without a rudder - directionless and vulnerable to being tossed about by the currents of circumstance. Conversely, a leader who embraces purpose becomes a formidable force.

Purpose gives a leader a north star - a guiding light that illuminates the path ahead. It provides clarity, focus, and motivation. But leading with purpose is not easy. Along the way, leaders will encounter challenges and obstacles that threaten to derail them from their course. These moments reveal the true measure of a leader.

Consider the story of Martin Luther King Jr., a man who embodied the power of purpose. Dr. King was a leader driven by a deep sense of purpose - the belief that all people are created equal and that racial discrimination had no place in American society. Despite facing immense opposition, including physical violence and incarceration, Dr. King pursued justice. He inspired and motivated others to join him in his cause and ultimately achieved a monumental victory in the passage of the Civil Rights Act 1964.

Or consider the story of Steve Jobs, a leader who revolutionized the technology industry through his unwavering sense of purpose. Jobs was a visionary who saw the potential of personal computing long before it became mainstream. Yet, driven by a belief that technology could change the world, he persisted in his vision, refusing to compromise even when it meant challenging conventional wisdom. Through his leadership, Jobs built Apple into one of the world's most valuable companies, transforming how we live, work, and communicate.

These stories illustrate the power of purpose in leadership. But leading with purpose is not just for the history books or the business world - it is a skill anyone can cultivate. Whether leading a team at work, volunteering in your community, or striving to improve, having a clear purpose can make all the difference.

We will explore some of the common challenges that leaders face and provide strategies for overcoming them. In addition, we will examine the importance of communication, motivation, and resourcefulness and provide real-world examples of leaders who have successfully navigated these challenges. Through these stories and strategies, we hope to inspire and motivate you to lead purposefully and achieve your personal and professional goals.

Dealing with Setbacks and Failures

"Setbacks are but lessons in disguise, failures are mere stepping stones to success. Embrace them with a resilient spirit, for they are the crucible in which the mettle of true leadership is tested."

A leader prepares for the tasks ahead with a deep sense of purpose. Leading with purpose is not just a job but a way of life for this individual. They understand that effective leadership is more than achieving success; it is about inspiring and motivating others to strive for their best, despite setbacks and failures.

Leading with purpose requires a steadfast commitment to one's values and objectives, the courage to take risks, the perseverance to overcome obstacles, and the humility to learn from mistakes. However, the rewards of effective leadership are immeasurable - from seeing a team achieve its goals to feeling a sense of fulfillment from making a positive difference in the lives of others and knowing one's work has a positive impact on the world.

Winston Churchill, a stalwart leader during the Second World War, is an example of a leader who embodies the power of purpose. Leading Britain in its darkest hours, Churchill remained committed to his goal of victory over the forces of tyranny, despite facing immense challenges and setbacks. Churchill's unwavering commitment to his cause made him an icon of resilience and determination, and his leadership profoundly impacted history.

Masayoshi Son, SoftBank's founder, and CEO, reflects similar traits in the business realm. Despite severe losses during the dot-com crash, Son remained committed to his vision of a digital future. As a result, he persevered, rebuilt his company, and is today recognized as a visionary leader whose investments have significantly shaped the technology landscape.

This segment delves into the challenges and opportunities of leading purposefully, providing strategies for inspiring and motivating teams to achieve their goals. We examine the importance of resilience, resourcefulness, and adaptability, giving real-world examples of leaders who have successfully navigated these challenges. Through these stories and strategies, we aim to motivate and inspire you to lead with purpose and to make a positive impact in your life and the lives of others.

The Role of Failure in the Journey of Purposeful Leadership

You're standing at the edge of a cliff, gazing out at the vast expanse of the world before you. You're a leader with a team of people looking to you for guidance and inspiration. You're filled with purpose and passion, ready to take on any challenge that comes your way. But as you step forward, you stumble and fall, tumbling down the rocky face of the cliff.

At that moment, everything seemed lost. Shame, regret, and doubt fill you, but something miraculous happens. You realize you've learned something valuable as you pick yourself up and dust yourself off. You've learned that failure is not the end. It's a part of the journey, a stepping stone to purposeful leadership.

Failure is something that all leaders experience at some point in their journey. It's natural to want to succeed in everything we do. However, the truth is that failure is an inevitable part of the process. It's often through our failures that we learn the most valuable lessons and develop the skills we need to become effective and purposeful leaders.

Throughout history, some of the most successful leaders have experienced failure on their journey. For example, the co-founder of Apple Inc., Steve Jobs, was ousted from the company he founded in 1985 in a highly publicized power struggle. This setback became a turning point in Jobs' leadership journey, as he found NeXT and Pixar, ultimately leading to his triumphant return to Apple, where he revolutionized the tech industry with the iPod, iPhone, and iPad. Jobs attributed his subsequent success to the lessons he learned during his failure, stating, "I'm convinced that the only thing that kept me going was that I loved what I did. You've got to find what you love" (Jobs, 2005).

One of the most influential media moguls and philanthropists, Oprah Winfrey, experienced numerous setbacks on her journey to success, including getting fired from her first television job as a news anchor. However, Winfrey's ability to learn from her failures and persevere despite adversity led her to create a media empire, revolutionizing the talk show format and inspiring millions worldwide.

Or consider J.K. Rowling, author of the Harry Potter series. Numerous publishers rejected her before finally finding success. But through her perseverance and determination, she became one of the best-selling authors ever.

Failure of Nokia, the once-dominant mobile phone manufacturer. Nokia failed to adapt to the rise of smartphones and ultimately lost its market share to companies like Apple and Samsung. However, Nokia's failure was not the end. The company has since reinvented itself and is now a leader in the telecommunications industry.

So, how can leaders use failure as a tool for growth? The first step is to embrace failure and recognize its importance in the journey toward purposeful leadership. Next, leaders should encourage their teams to embrace failure and use it as an opportunity for learning and growth.

Another critical aspect is to act and apply the lessons learned from failure. Finally, it requires a willingness to change and adapt. Leaders who can adapt and pivot in the face of failure are better equipped to navigate leadership challenges.

These stories illustrate the power of failure in the journey of purposeful leadership. It's not something to be feared or avoided but rather embraced as an opportunity for growth and development. As a leader, wanting to succeed in everything you do is natural. But the truth is that failure is an inevitable part of the journey. It's often through our failures that we learn the most valuable lessons and develop the skills we need to become effective and purposeful leaders. We'll explore the role of failure in leadership and how to use it to inspire and motivate your team. We'll examine how failure can be a learning opportunity, a source of resilience, and a catalyst for innovation. We'll dive deep into this critical aspect of purposeful leadership through real-world examples and industry-specific language.

- **Failure as a Learning Opportunity**: One of the most significant benefits of loss is that it provides a learning opportunity. When we fail, we must examine what went wrong, why it happened, and what we can do differently next time. This process of reflection and analysis is crucial for personal growth and development and equally important for building strong and effective teams. For example, let's say you're a CEO of a startup company, and your team has been working on a new product for months. You've invested much time, money, and resources into this project. However, when you launch it, it fails to generate the expected revenue. While seeing this as a setback is tempting, it is essential to use it as a learning opportunity. Sit down with your team and analyze what went wrong. Was it a product design flaw, a marketing issue, or something else entirely? By identifying the root cause of the failure, you can develop a plan to fix it and prevent similar problems from occurring in the future.

Satya Nadella, the CEO of Microsoft when he took over the company in 2014, inherited a stagnant corporate culture that was resistant to change. Under his leadership, Nadella encouraged his team to embrace failure and use it as a learning opportunity. In addition, he implemented a "growth mindset" throughout the organization, emphasizing the importance of experimentation, feedback, and continuous learning. As a result, Microsoft has become more innovative and agile, with new products and services like Azure and Teams driving the company's growth.

- **Failure as a Source of Resilience** - Another essential aspect of failure is that it builds resilience. In leadership, resilience is the ability to bounce back from setbacks, remain focused on goals, and adapt to change. When we experience failure, it can be demotivating and discouraging. However, it's important to remember that it's not the end of the road. We build resilience by learning from our mistakes and developing plans to move forward. As a result, we possess better equipped to handle future challenges. For example, let's say you're a project manager, and one of your team members misses a crucial deadline, causing a significant setback. While it's tempting to blame the team member or dwell on the setback, it's essential to use it as an opportunity to build resilience. Sit down with your team and discuss what happened and how you can work together to prevent it from happening again. By focusing on solutions and developing a plan to move forward, you build resilience and create a more cohesive and effective team: Sara Blakely, the founder and CEO of Spanx. Failure and setbacks, including multiple rejections from potential investors and manufacturers, marked Blakely's journey to success. However, she remained focused on her goal and refused to give up. By embracing failure as a source of resilience, Blakely developed a unique and innovative product that disrupted the fashion industry. Today, Spanx is a global brand with over $1 billion in annual revenue.

- **Failure as a Catalyst for Innovation** - Failure can also catalyze innovation. When we experience failure, it forces us to think outside the box and explore new solutions to problems. It's often through our failures that we discover new ideas, approaches, and technologies that can revolutionize our industries and lead to significant breakthroughs. For example, you're a research and development manager whose team has been working on a new drug for years. After countless trials and experiments, the medicine fails to meet the expected results. While it's natural to feel disappointed, it's essential to use this as an opportunity to explore new avenues for innovation. By analyzing the data and experimenting with new approaches, you might discover a breakthrough that leads to a new drug more effective than anything currently on the market: Elon Musk, the founder and CEO of SpaceX. Numerous failures and setbacks, including several failed launches and rocket explosions, marked Musk's journey to develop a reusable rocket. However, Musk used each failure as an opportunity to learn and innovate. He implemented a "fast failure" approach, emphasizing the importance of learning quickly from mistakes and moving forward. As a result, SpaceX successfully launched and landed a reusable rocket in 2015, paving the way for a new era of space exploration.

Failure is an inevitable part of the journey of purposeful leadership. While it can be challenging and demotivating, viewing it as an opportunity for learning, resilience, and innovation is essential. By embracing failure and using it as a tool for personal and team development, you can inspire and motivate your team to reach new heights of success. Remember, the most successful leaders are willing to take risks and learn from them.

The first step in leveraging the power of failure in purposeful leadership is changing how we perceive setbacks. Rather than viewing failure as a defeat, leaders must learn to embrace it as a valuable learning opportunity, an essential component of growth, and a stepping stone to success.

- **The Growth Mindset**: One of the critical attributes of purposeful leaders involves adopting a growth mindset, wherein they actively believe in developing intelligence, talent, and abilities through consistent effort, learning, and adaptation (Dweck, 2006). This mindset enables leaders to view failure as a necessary part of the learning process, thus fostering resilience and adaptability in the face of adversity.
- **Psychological Safety**: Creating a culture of psychological safety within the organization is essential for encouraging risk-taking, innovation, and learning from failure. As Harvard Business School professor Amy Edmondson described, psychological safety is "a climate in which people are comfortable expressing and being themselves" (Edmondson, 1999). By cultivating a psychologically safe environment, purposeful leaders empower their teams to share ideas, experiment, and learn from setbacks without fearing negative consequences.

Failure is a powerful learning tool, allowing leaders to glean valuable insights, identify gaps in knowledge or skills, and refine their strategies for future success. Learning from failure involves a combination of cognitive, emotional, and behavioral components, which work in tandem to facilitate personal and professional growth.

- **Cognitive Processing:** Upon encountering a failure, purposeful leaders thoroughly analyze the situation, evaluating the factors contributing to the setback and identifying areas for improvement. This process, known as cognitive processing, enables leaders to extract valuable lessons from their experiences and refine their strategies moving forward (Ellis & David, 2003).
- **Emotional Intelligence:** Purposeful leaders also exhibit high levels of emotional intelligence, which allows them to effectively manage their own emotions and those of their team members in the aftermath of failure (Goleman, 1995). By acknowledging and validating the feelings associated with setbacks, leaders can create a supportive environment for reflection, learning, and growth.
- **Behavioral Adaptation:** Finally, purposeful leaders use the insights gained from cognitive processing and emotional intelligence to inform their future actions and decisions. By adjusting their behaviors and strategies based on the lessons learned from failure, leaders can continuously evolve and adapt to the dynamic and ever-changing landscape of the business world.

Failure is not something to be feared or avoided in purposeful leadership. Instead, purposeful leaders should actively embrace it as a necessary and valuable component of growth and development. Through our failures, we learn the most important lessons, develop resilience, and discover new and innovative solutions to problems.

As a leader, it's essential to create a learning culture where failure is not stigmatized but celebrated as a valuable opportunity for growth. Encourage your team to take risks, experiment with new approaches, and learn from their mistakes. Creating an environment where failure is accepted and celebrated will foster a culture of innovation and creativity that will lead to significant breakthroughs and accomplishments.

Remember, the journey of purposeful leadership is not about achieving perfection or avoiding failure. It's about learning from our mistakes, growing as individuals and a team, and positively impacting the world. So, embrace failure as a necessary and valuable component of this journey. Use it to inspire and motivate yourself and your team toward tremendous success and fulfillment.

In the end, by embracing setbacks as valuable learning opportunities, cultivating a growth mindset, and employing strategies to harness the power of failure, leaders can drive innovation, resilience, and long-term success within their organizations. In the words of Winston Churchill, "Success is not final, failure is not fatal: It is the courage to continue those counts. "The most successful leaders are not those who have never failed, but those who have failed and used those experiences to become better, stronger, and more effective. So, take risks, embrace failure, and never stop learning and growing as a purposeful leader. With this mindset, you can achieve incredible things and make a lasting impact on the world.

Strategies for Overcoming Setbacks and Bouncing Back Stronger

The landscape for business and leadership is changing continuously; purposeful leaders face a myriad of challenges, unforeseen obstacles, and setbacks that can test even the most steadfast and resilient individuals. Yet, amidst these turbulent waters, the most successful leaders are those who not only navigate these storms but also use them as catalysts for growth, learning, and transformation. They rise like the mythical phoenix from the ashes of failure, emerging stronger and more determined than ever before. In this powerful and thought-provoking introduction to "Strategies for Overcoming Setbacks and Bouncing Back Stronger," we will explore the indomitable spirit of purposeful leaders who have turned setbacks into stepping stones for success.

In 1997, a young entrepreneur found himself ousted from his co-founded company. Faced with the bitter reality of failure, he might have retreated into obscurity or given up on his dreams. But instead, he chose to learn from his setback, adapt, and bounce back stronger. This entrepreneur was Steve Jobs, who went on to create groundbreaking products like the iPhone and the iPad, revolutionizing how we live and work. This inspiring example demonstrates the power of resilience, adaptability, and continuous learning in overcoming setbacks and achieving greatness.

Or consider the adaptability and tenacity of Howard Schultz, who steered Starbucks through the treacherous waters of the 2008 financial crisis and re-emerged stronger, more focused, and poised for even greater success. These are just a few of the countless examples of purposeful leaders who have faced failure and emerged triumphant, setting the stage for a new chapter in their journey.

As we delve into the captivating stories of these and other extraordinary leaders, we will uncover their powerful strategies to overcome setbacks, bounce back more robustly, and, ultimately, shape the course of history. We will discover how the combination of resilience, adaptability, and continuous learning can forge an unbreakable spirit capable of weathering the storms of adversity and emerging more robust than ever before.

In this comprehensive examination of the strategies for overcoming setbacks and bouncing back more vital, we will unveil the secrets behind the transformative journeys of these purposeful leaders. We will investigate the science behind resilience and adaptability, provide practical guidance on cultivating these essential qualities, and illustrate how the lessons learned from setbacks can become the foundation for future success.

As we embark on this remarkable exploration, we invite you to join us on a journey of discovery, growth, and inspiration. Together, we will learn to embrace setbacks as opportunities for learning, foster a spirit of resilience and adaptability, and ultimately unlock the true potential of purposeful leadership.

So, prepare yourself for an enthralling, thought-provoking, and transformative journey into the heart of what it truly means to overcome setbacks and bounce back stronger. As we turn the pages of history and unravel the captivating stories of these purposeful leaders, we hope to inspire, empower, and equip you with the strategies and insights necessary to turn your setbacks into stepping stones for success.

Purposeful leaders recognize the inevitability of setbacks and their essential role in driving personal and organizational growth. Therefore, it's necessary to explore a comprehensive analysis of the strategies for overcoming setbacks and bouncing back more robustly, focusing on resilience, adaptability, and continuous learning. We will delve into the science behind these concepts, provide real-world examples to illustrate their significance in leadership, and offer practical guidance on implementing these strategies in your leadership journey.

- **Building Resilience: The Foundation for Overcoming Setbacks** - Resilience, or the ability to recover quickly from adversity, is a crucial attribute of purposeful leaders who successfully navigate setbacks and emerge stronger. Resilience is not an inherent trait but a skill that can be developed and strengthened through intentional practice and reflection.

- **Develop a Growth Mindset**: As discussed in the previous section, adopting a growth mindset enables leaders to view setbacks as opportunities for learning and growth rather than permanent obstacles. By reframing challenges as opportunities for development, leaders can foster a resilient mindset that promotes adaptability and perseverance in the face of adversity (Dweck, 2006).
- **Cultivate Emotional Intelligence**: Emotional intelligence plays a critical role in building resilience, as it allows leaders to effectively manage their own emotions and those of their team members during times of crisis (Goleman, 1995). Developing empathy, self-awareness, and emotional regulation enables leaders to create a supportive environment that fosters resilience and recovery after setbacks.
- **Focus on Personal Values and Purpose**: Purposeful leaders clearly understand their values and overarching purpose, which guides them during adversity. Leaders can maintain perspective and prioritize long-term goals over short-term setbacks by staying grounded in their values and purpose.

- **Adaptability: Embracing Change and Thriving in Uncertainty** - Adaptability, or the ability to adjust to changing circumstances, is an essential skill for purposeful leaders seeking to overcome setbacks and bounce back stronger. By embracing change and fostering a culture of continuous improvement, leaders can navigate uncertainty and capitalize on new growth opportunities.
  - **Encourage Experimentation**: Fostering a culture of experimentation and innovation is crucial for promoting adaptability within organizations. By empowering team

members to take calculated risks and learn from their failures, purposeful leaders can drive continuous improvement and encourage the development of new skills, ideas, and solutions.

- **Promote Cross-Functional Collaboration**: Encouraging collaboration across departments and teams can help break down silos and facilitate the exchange of knowledge, skills, and perspectives. This cross-pollination of ideas can drive innovation, promote adaptability, and enable organizations to respond more effectively to changing market conditions.
- **Invest in Continuous Learning**: Purposeful leaders recognize the importance of lifelong learning for themselves and their teams. By investing in ongoing professional development, leaders can ensure that their organizations remain agile, adaptable, and equipped to navigate the challenges of an ever-changing business landscape.

- **Learning from Setbacks: Transforming Failure into Growth Opportunities** - As highlighted in the earlier conversations, learning from setbacks is a critical component of purposeful leadership. By extracting valuable insights from failures and using them to inform future decisions, leaders can continuously evolve and adapt in the face of adversity.
  - **Conduct Post-Mortem Analyses**: Leaders must thoroughly analyze the situation to identify the root causes of failure and learn from the experience after a setback. This process, known as a post-mortem analysis, enables leaders to extract valuable lessons and refine their strategies moving forward.
  - **Implement Feedback Loops**: Establishing organizational feedback loops can facilitate continuous learning and improvement. By creating channels for open communication and regular feedback, leaders can encourage team

members to share their insights, successes, and failures. This process can help identify areas for improvement, promote accountability, and drive collective learning in the aftermath of setbacks.

- **Foster a Culture of Reflection**: Encouraging regular reflection and introspection at the individual and organizational levels can help leaders and teams internalize the lessons learned from setbacks and apply them to future challenges. By promoting a culture of reflection, purposeful leaders can cultivate an environment of continuous learning and growth.

As we draw this comprehensive exploration of "Strategies for Overcoming Setbacks and Bouncing Back Stronger" to a close, let us pause for a moment to reflect on the power of the human spirit to rise above adversity, to learn, grow, and ultimately triumph in the face of seemingly insurmountable challenges. The stories of purposeful leaders who have navigated the stormy seas of setbacks and emerged victorious serve as a testament to the indomitable will within each of us, waiting to be harnessed and unleashed.

Picture, for a moment, a phoenix rising from the ashes, its wings outstretched as it soars towards the heavens, leaving behind the remnants of its previous incarnation, a symbol of renewal and rebirth. Such is the essence of resilience, adaptability, and the ability to learn from setbacks. These qualities define purposeful leaders as they navigate the ever-changing landscape of life and business.

But what does it indeed mean to bounce back stronger? It is not merely about recovering from setbacks and returning to the status quo. Instead, it is about using the crucible of adversity as a catalyst for transformation, a forge in which the raw materials of our experiences are shaped, tempered, and refined into the powerful instruments of purposeful leadership.

As we ponder the lessons gleaned from these pages, let us not shy away from the challenges that life inevitably presents, but instead, let us embrace them wholeheartedly, for it is through the alchemy of failure that we forge our greatest strengths. Let us not forget that setbacks, however painful they may be, are the crucibles in which our mettle is tested, our resilience fortified, and our wisdom deepened. In facing adversity, let us hold fast to our values, purpose, and vision, for they guide us through the darkest nights.

And so, as we embark on our journeys of purposeful leadership, let us embrace the knowledge that setbacks are not to be feared but rather welcomed as the invaluable teachers they are. Our true potential is revealed in moments of struggle. Through the fires of adversity, we forge the tools to build a brighter future for ourselves, our teams, and our organizations.

As you turn the final pages of this segment, consider the seeds of thought planted within your mind, the ideas that have taken root and begun to grow. Nurture, cultivate, and allow them to blossom into a thriving garden of resilience, adaptability, and continuous learning. Then, share the fruits of your labor with your team, your organization, and your world, and watch as the ripples of your impact spread far and wide, touching countless lives and leaving an indelible mark on the annals of history.

In embracing life's challenges and harnessing the transformative power of setbacks, purposeful leadership finds its true essence. It is through rising again that leaders genuinely shine. With this spirit in mind, we leave you with a final message—a timeless call to action that echoes through the ages.

Embrace the struggle, learn from your setbacks, and rise, like the phoenix, to conquer the skies. In doing so, you will become a more resilient, adaptable, and purposeful leader and ignite the inspiration that fuels the fires of greatness within yourself and those you lead.

Managing Conflict and Difficult Situations

"Conflict is an opportunity for growth, a crucible for forging stronger bonds. Navigate it with wisdom and compassion, turning challenges into catalysts for progress and harmony."

Think of a raging storm at sea. Thunder roars, lightning illuminates the dark skies, and colossal waves crash upon a ship's deck as it battles against the relentless forces of nature. Yet, the captain stands at the helm, resolute and unyielding, steering the vessel and its crew through the tempest, guided by a single unwavering vision: to reach the safety of calmer waters. This dear reader, is the essence of leadership in the face of conflict and difficult situations. As purposeful leaders, we are often called upon to navigate the stormy seas of discord and strife, charting a course through the turbulent waters of human emotions and clashing perspectives.

What separates the captains who triumph over adversity from those who succumb to the merciless grasp of the storm? How do the great leaders of our time –Mahatma Gandhi, Martin Luther King Jr., and Abraham Lincoln – manage to steer their ships through the most treacherous of waters, emerging more potent and more resolute than ever before? Can we, too, learn the art of navigating conflict and difficult situations, transforming these challenges into opportunities for growth and learning?

As we embark on this journey of discovery, we will explore the hidden depths of conflict and difficult situations, unraveling the complex tapestry of human emotions, desires, and motivations that give rise to these tumultuous storms. We will delve into the minds of the great leaders who have come before us, learning from their trials and tribulations, successes and failures, and the wisdom they have gleaned from their experiences. This exploration will uncover the strategies, techniques, and mindsets that enable purposeful leaders to triumph over adversity, transform conflict into collaboration, and steer their ships through even the most perilous of seas.

Consider, for a moment, the inspiring image of Martin Luther King Jr. standing on the steps of the Lincoln Memorial, delivering his legendary "I Have a Dream" speech. How did he rise above the pervasive racism and discrimination of his time to ignite a movement for civil rights and equality? What lessons can we learn from his remarkable journey, and how can we apply these insights to our lives and leadership?"

Or ponder the legendary story of Abraham Lincoln, who, in the throes of a nation torn apart by civil war, brought together a team of rivals, uniting them under a shared vision of a perfect union. What enabled Lincoln to navigate the treacherous waters of political intrigue, conflicting agendas, and deep-seated animosities, ultimately steering his nation towards a brighter future?

As we delve into the world of conflict and difficult situations, we will uncover the answers to these questions and, more, unearth the secrets of purposeful leadership in the face of adversity. We will illuminate the path before us, providing a guiding light for those who seek to navigate the stormy seas of human emotions and emerge stronger, wiser, and more resilient than ever before.

As we set sail on this voyage of discovery, prepare to cast off the shackles of fear and uncertainty, embrace the challenges, and chart a course toward a new horizon of growth, understanding, and purposeful leadership, for it is through the crucible of conflict and difficult situations that we forge the mettle of our character, the resilience of our spirit, and the wisdom of our hearts.

Purposeful leaders recognize that conflict and difficult situations are inevitable in leading diverse teams and managing complex organizational challenges. Navigating these situations fosters a productive, collaborative, and inclusive work environment. This section will delve into the various aspects of managing conflict and difficult situations, comprehensively analyzing the strategies, techniques, and mindsets that empower leaders to handle these challenges confidently and poise.

Before delving into the strategies for managing conflict, it is essential to understand the underlying nature and drivers of conflict. Conflict can arise from various sources, including differences in values, beliefs, priorities, expectations, and communication styles. By gaining a deeper understanding of the root causes of conflict, purposeful leaders can more effectively address the underlying issues and facilitate constructive resolution.

- **Intrapersonal Conflict:** This type of conflict arises within an individual, often resulting from internal struggles related to values, beliefs, or personal goals. Intrapersonal conflict can manifest in various ways, such as procrastination, indecision, or self-doubt. It can impact an individual's ability to contribute effectively to the team.
- **Interpersonal Conflict:** Interpersonal conflict occurs between two or more individuals and can result from differences in communication styles, expectations, or personal values. This type of conflict can lead to misunderstandings, tension, and friction within the team if not addressed effectively.
- **Intragroup Conflict:** Intragroup conflict arises within a team or group and can result from competition, differing goals, or misaligned priorities. This type of conflict can hinder collaboration and productivity, leading to a toxic work environment if left unresolved.

- **Intergroup Conflict:** Intergroup conflict occurs between two or more groups or teams within an organization, often stemming from competition for resources, conflicting goals, or organizational politics. This type of conflict can lead to inefficiencies, power struggles, and a breakdown in communication across the organization.

Effective conflict management requires a multifaceted approach that combines communication, negotiation, and problem-solving skills. Here, we outline the critical strategies for managing conflict and difficult situations purposefully and constructively.

- **Develop Active Listening Skills:** Active listening is the foundation for effective communication and conflict resolution. By listening attentively to others, asking clarifying questions, and summarizing their key points, purposeful leaders can demonstrate empathy, build rapport, and facilitate a deeper understanding of the underlying issues.
- **Foster Open Communication:** Encouraging open and transparent communication within the team can help to surface underlying tensions, promote understanding, and facilitate constructive dialogue around contentious issues. By creating an environment where team members feel comfortable expressing their thoughts and concerns, purposeful leaders can proactively address potential sources of conflict and promote a collaborative work environment.
- **Employ Conflict Resolution Techniques:** Various conflict resolution techniques can address and resolve conflict effectively, such as negotiation, mediation, and collaborative problem-solving. Purposeful leaders should be familiar with these techniques and adapt their approach based on the specific situation and individual needs.

- **Address Difficult Situations Proactively:** By addressing difficult situations proactively, purposeful leaders can prevent conflicts from escalating and becoming more challenging to resolve. It may involve initiating difficult conversations, providing constructive feedback, or implementing interventions to address performance or behavior issues.

Throughout history, numerous leaders have demonstrated the ability to navigate conflict and difficult situations gracefully and wisely. Here, we examine a few notable examples that illustrate the importance of effective conflict management in a purposeful context. Leadership:

Abraham Lincoln: As the 16th President of the United States, Lincoln faced numerous conflicts and difficult situations during his tenure, particularly during the Civil War. His ability to engage in open dialogue, listen to differing perspectives, and bring together a diverse team of advisors – known as his "Team of Rivals" – allowed him to navigate these challenges and ultimately preserve the Union.

Indra Nooyi: As the former CEO of PepsiCo, Nooyi faced numerous challenges and conflicts during her tenure, such as balancing the demands of shareholders with the company's long-term goals and navigating the complexities of a global organization. Her ability to communicate effectively, build consensus, and make difficult decisions under pressure was instrumental in her success as a leader.

Managing conflict and difficult situations is essential for purposeful leaders, enabling them to foster a collaborative, inclusive, and productive work environment. Leaders can effectively navigate the complexities of team dynamics and organizational challenges by developing a deep understanding of the nature of conflict, honing their communication and conflict resolution skills, and proactively addressing challenging situations.

As you reflect on the outlined strategies and techniques, consider how to incorporate these principles into your leadership approach. Doing so will enhance your ability to manage conflict and difficult situations and empower your team to overcome obstacles, grow, and thrive in adversity.

Remember, the mark of a genuinely purposeful leader is not merely the absence of conflict but the ability to harness the energy of differing perspectives and channel it toward the collective pursuit of a shared vision. In the words of the ancient Chinese philosopher Lao Tzu, "The best leaders are those the people hardly know exist. The next best is a leader who is loved and praised. The next is feared. The worst is one who is despised. If you fail to trust people, they will become untrustworthy. The best leaders value their words and use them sparingly. When they have accomplished their task, the people say, 'Amazing! We did it all by ourselves!'"

In the final moments of our exploration of "Managing Conflict and Difficult Situations," let us pause to consider the profound impact that effective conflict management can have on the fabric of our teams, organizations, and society. As we stand on the precipice of a new era characterized by rapid change, unprecedented challenges, and unparalleled growth opportunities, navigating conflict and difficult situations with grace, wisdom, and skill becomes more crucial.

If a world in which leaders from all walks of life – whether in business, government, or civil society – are equipped with the tools, knowledge, and mindset necessary to navigate the complex web of human interactions that shape our collective reality. In this world, conflict is not a force that drives us apart but a catalyst for growth, innovation, and progress.

Picture the countless conversations, negotiations, and problem-solving sessions every day in boardrooms, government offices, and community centers around the globe. Now imagine the transformative potential of these interactions if each participant were to approach them with a deep understanding of the nature of conflict, a commitment to open communication, and a genuine desire to find common ground.

Purposeful leaders can create a world where they harness conflict as a force for positive change and celebrate our differences as the raw materials for creativity, collaboration, and growth. Together, we can build this world one conversation, negotiation, and challenging situation at a time.

As we conclude this introduction, let us carry with us not only the strategies, techniques, and insights gleaned from these pages but also a renewed sense of purpose and conviction in the power of effective conflict management to transform our teams, organizations, and world.

In the words of the renowned American poet and philosopher Ralph Waldo Emerson, "Every wall is a door." So let us embrace the walls we encounter in conflict and difficult situations, recognizing that within each lies the growth potential for learning and the discovery of new pathways to success.

And so, as you embark on your journey of purposeful leadership, let us challenge ourselves to see conflict not as an obstacle to avoid but as an opportunity to seize. Let us take this opportunity to forge stronger connections, deepen our understanding, and unleash the full potential of our teams and organizations.

Embrace the challenge, harness the power of conflict, and transform your world. In doing so, you will become a more effective, purposeful leader and ignite a spark of inspiration that will ripple across the fabric of our collective reality, touching countless lives and leaving an indelible mark on human history.

Techniques for Navigating Conflict and Building Consensus

In the vast and intricate tapestry of human history, conflict and cooperation have woven into an elaborate dance, a constant interplay of opposing forces shaping the very fabric of our collective destiny. As we journey together into the uncharted realms of the future, the delicate balance between these forces becomes more crucial than ever before. Within this complex landscape of ever-evolving challenges and opportunities, the art of purposeful leadership takes on a newfound significance – for it is through the proficiency in navigating conflict and building consensus that leaders can ignite the transformative power of collaboration, unleashing the full potential of their teams and organizations.

For a moment, picture the bustling corridors of a modern-day business organization, a microcosm of our global society. Within these walls, individuals from diverse backgrounds, cultures, and belief systems come together, their unique perspectives and experiences converging to create a tapestry of ideas, opinions, and aspirations. Here, in the crucible of human interaction, the potential for conflict and consensus is born – for it is through the artful navigation of these opposing forces that leaders can harness the power of diversity, forging a path toward innovation, growth, and success.

Now, let us journey back to 1978, as the world watched with bated breath the unfolding of a historic event – the Camp David Accords.

Here, on the windswept mountaintop of Camp David, U.S. President Jimmy Carter skillfully navigated the treacherous waters of conflict and mistrust, bringing together two bitter adversaries – Egyptian President Anwar Sadat and Israeli Prime Minister Menachem Begin – in a groundbreaking peace agreement that would reshape the course of history. Through Carter's knowledge of conflict navigation and consensus-building techniques, he could bridge the chasm between these two nations, forging a lasting peace that would stand as a testament to the power of purposeful leadership.

Let the lessons of history and the wisdom of purposeful leaders who have come before us guide us as we explore the techniques for navigating conflict and building consensus. In the following pages, we will delve into conflict navigation and consensus-building, drawing from real-world examples and industry-specific insights to provide a comprehensive, in-depth analysis of this critical leadership skill. Together, we will discover the art of transforming conflict into a catalyst for growth, uniting diverse perspectives to pursue a shared vision, and harnessing the power of consensus to drive the engine of progress ever forward.

So, let us begin our journey into conflict navigation and consensus-building, armed with the knowledge that, as purposeful leaders, we hold within our grasp the power to shape not only the destiny of our teams and organizations but also the very course of human history. As we forge ahead, let us remember the words of American civil rights leader Martin Luther King Jr., who once said, "The ultimate measure of a man is not where he stands in moments of comfort and convenience, but where he stands at times of challenge and controversy." Purposeful leadership reveals its true power in these moments of challenge and controversy. By navigating conflict and building consensus, we unlock the full potential of our teams, organizations, and ourselves.

Navigating conflict and building consensus is paramount in the journey of purposeful leadership. As leaders strive to create cohesive, high-performing teams, they must have the skills and techniques to address disagreements, facilitate constructive dialogue, and foster collaborative decision-making. We will delve into the various methods for navigating conflict and building consensus. We will draw from real-world examples and industry-specific insights to provide a comprehensive, in-depth analysis of this critical leadership skill.

Effectively navigating conflict involves identifying the underlying sources of tension, facilitating open communication, and employing conflict resolution techniques to address the issues. The following are vital techniques that purposeful leaders can use to navigate conflict:

- **Active Listening**: Active listening is crucial for comprehending the perspectives, concerns, and emotions of those involved in a conflict. By actively listening, leaders can build rapport, establish trust, and create an environment conducive to open communication and collaborative problem-solving. Vaclav Havel was a leader who exemplified the power of active listening. As the leader of the Velvet Revolution and later as President of Czechoslovakia and the Czech Republic, he faced numerous conflicts and disagreements within his movement and with the communist regime. Havel's conflict resolution approach centered on listening intently to all parties involved, fostering an atmosphere of empathy and understanding. By actively listening, he could comprehend the needs and concerns of all stakeholders and develop solutions that addressed these issues, ultimately paving the way for a peaceful transition to democracy.
- **Emotional Intelligence**: Emotional intelligence is the ability to recognize, understand, and manage one's own emotions

and the emotions of others. By cultivating emotional intelligence, leaders can more effectively navigate conflict by empathizing with others, working on their feelings, and fostering a supportive and respectful environment. For example, Nelson Mandela demonstrated exceptional emotional intelligence during his tenure as South Africa's first Black president. After spending 27 years in prison, Mandela faced the monumental task of reconciling a deeply divided nation. He understood the importance of managing his own emotions, as well as empathizing with the feelings of others, to foster a sense of unity and progress. As a result, Mandela's emotional intelligence allowed him to navigate the complex dynamics of post-apartheid South Africa and play a pivotal role in facilitating the peaceful transition to democracy.

- **Establishing Ground Rules**: Setting ground rules for conflict resolution, such as taking turns speaking, avoiding personal attacks, and focusing on solutions rather than blame, can help create a structured and respectful environment for addressing disagreements and resolving conflict. As CEO of General Electric, Jack Welch was known for managing conflict effectively by establishing clear ground rules. He implemented a performance-based culture that held employees accountable for their actions and results. By setting expectations and guidelines for communication, Welch encouraged honest, solution-oriented discussions that minimized personal attacks and focused on resolving issues. Under his leadership, General Electric became one of the most successful companies in the world.
- **Utilizing Conflict Resolution Techniques**: Various conflict resolution techniques, such as negotiation, mediation, and collaborative problem-solving, can address and resolve conflict effectively. Purposeful leaders should be familiar with these techniques and adapt their approach based on the

specific situation and individual needs. For example, as a mediator during the Northern Ireland peace process, former U.S. Senator George Mitchell employed various conflict resolution techniques to help bring about the Good Friday Agreement in 1998. Mitchell's approach included fostering open communication, building stakeholder trust, and using his diplomatic skills to navigate the complex and deeply rooted conflicts between opposing factions. His ability to effectively employ conflict resolution techniques was critical in achieving lasting peace in Northern Ireland.

Building consensus involves bringing together diverse perspectives, fostering collaborative decision-making, and promoting a shared sense of ownership and commitment to the outcome. The following are vital techniques that purposeful leaders can employ to build consensus:

- **Encouraging Diverse Perspectives:** By inviting diverse perspectives and fostering an environment where team members feel comfortable expressing their thoughts and opinions, leaders can promote a richer, more nuanced understanding of the issues at hand and facilitate more informed decision-making. For example, as a mediator during the Northern Ireland peace process, former U.S. Senator George Mitchell employed various conflict resolution techniques to help bring about the Good Friday Agreement in 1998. Mitchell's approach included fostering open communication, building stakeholder trust, and using his diplomatic skills to navigate the complex and deeply rooted conflicts between opposing factions. His ability to effectively employ conflict resolution techniques was critical in achieving lasting peace in Northern Ireland.
- **Facilitating Open Dialogue**: Encouraging open dialogue and providing opportunities for team members to ask questions,

share ideas, and seek clarification can help to surface underlying concerns, address misconceptions, and promote a shared understanding of the issues at hand. As Prime Minister of the United Kingdom, Winston Churchill exemplified the power of facilitating open dialogue. During World War II, Churchill held daily meetings with his cabinet and military advisors, encouraging the free exchange of ideas, questions, and concerns. By promoting open dialogue, Churchill ensured that all perspectives were considered, ultimately leading to more effective decision-making and a stronger war effort.

- **Identifying Shared Values and Goals**: By specifying the shared values and goals that underpin the team's mission, leaders can help to build a sense of unity and purpose, providing a foundation for collaborative decision-making and consensus-building. For example, during her tenure as CEO of PepsiCo, Indra Nooyi emphasized the importance of identifying shared values and goals to build consensus. As a result, Nooyi implemented the "Performance with Purpose" initiative, which aimed to balance the company's financial goals with its social and environmental responsibilities. By aligning the organization around shared values and objectives, Nooyi fostered a sense of unity and purpose that contributed to the company's long-term success.
- **Engaging in Collaborative Problem-Solving**: Collaborative problem-solving involves working together as a team to develop solutions that address the needs and concerns of all stakeholders. By engaging in collaborative problem-solving, leaders can foster a sense of ownership and commitment to the outcome, promoting consensus and buy-in from the team. As CEO of Apple, Tim Cook has exemplified the power of collaborative problem-solving in building peace. Cook has fostered a culture of collaboration at Apple, encouraging

> employees to work together to develop innovative solutions to complex problems. By promoting teamwork and cooperation, Cook has helped to ensure that Apple remains at the forefront of technological innovation and maintains its position. In addition, by engaging in collaborative problem-solving, Cook has contributed to Apple's continued success and fostered a sense of ownership and commitment among employees, promoting a solid consensus around the company's vision and goals.

The following real-world examples illustrate the power of effectively navigating conflict and building consensus in the context of purposeful leadership:

The Montreal Protocol: In 1987, representatives from 46 countries came together to negotiate the Montreal Protocol, an international treaty aimed at phasing out the production of ozone-depleting substances. Navigating the diverse interests and concerns of the participating nations required exceptional conflict management and consensus-building skills. However, experts and stakeholders have hailed it as one of the most successful examples of international cooperation on environmental issues, recognizing the negotiators' active efforts in fostering open dialogue, identifying shared goals, and engaging in collaborative problem-solving, leading to successful treaty adoption.

The Merger of Daimler-Benz and Chrysler: In 1998, German automaker Daimler-Benz and American car manufacturer Chrysler presented significant challenges, including cultural differences, divergent management styles, and conflicting strategic visions. The successful integration of the two companies required exceptional conflict management and consensus-building skills on the part of the leadership team. By fostering open communication, addressing underlying tensions, and promoting a shared vision for the future, the leaders of the newly formed DaimlerChrysler were able to navigate these challenges and ultimately create a more competitive and innovative global organization.

In the realm of purposeful leadership, the ability to navigate conflict and build consensus is essential for fostering cohesive, high-performing teams and driving organizational success. By mastering the techniques outlined, leaders can effectively address disagreements, facilitate constructive dialogue, and promote collaborative decision-making, ultimately enabling their teams to overcome obstacles, adapt to change, and achieve their shared goals.

As we conclude this exploration of conflict navigation and consensus-building techniques, let us remember the transformative potential of purposeful leadership when we wield these skills. By embracing the challenges and opportunities that arise from diverse perspectives and complex situations, purposeful leaders can forge stronger connections, unlock the full potential of their teams, and contribute to a more collaborative, innovative, and harmonious world.

In the words of Mahatma Gandhi, "Unity to be real must stand the severest strain without breaking." Therefore, as purposeful leaders, let us cultivate this unbreakable unity within our teams and organizations, harnessing the power of conflict and consensus to propel us toward a brighter, more prosperous future.

As we conclude this exploration of techniques for navigating conflict and building consensus, let us pause to envision the powerful, transformative impact that effective conflict management and consensus-building can have on our teams, organizations and the broader world in which we live.

Consider the potential that lies dormant within each disagreement, each clash of perspectives, and each seemingly insurmountable challenge we encounter on our journey of purposeful leadership. Within these moments of conflict and discord lie the seeds of growth, innovation, and progress, waiting to be cultivated and nurtured by those who possess the skills, the mindset, and the courage to embrace them.

Envision the countless opportunities that active consensus-building can unlock for collaboration, shared understanding, and unity. In a world that often seems increasingly divided, the ability to bring people together, find common ground, and to co-create solutions that benefit all stakeholders is a skill of immeasurable value. This talent can shape history's course and redefine human achievement's limits.

As purposeful leaders, we can harness these techniques and transform the landscape of conflict and disagreement into fertile ground for growth, connection, and progress. By mastering the art of conflict navigation and consensus-building, we can become architects of a new reality where our differences are not barriers to overcome but rather bridges to new possibilities and untapped potential.

In this spirit, let us embrace the challenge and the opportunity that lies before us. Let us wield the tools and techniques of conflict navigation and consensus-building with skill, wisdom, and unwavering commitment to our shared purpose. In doing so, we will not only become more effective, purposeful leaders, but we will also inspire those around us to rise above the limitations of division and discord to reach new heights of collaboration and collective achievement.

As we stand at the precipice of a new era, an era defined by rapid change, unprecedented challenges, and boundless growth opportunities, let us remember the words of the great poet and philosopher Rumi, who once wrote, "Out beyond ideas of wrongdoing and right doing, there is a field. I'll meet you there."

In this field, where we transform conflict into collaboration and forge consensus from the fires of disagreement, let us, as purposeful leaders, unite to build a brighter, more harmonious, and more prosperous future for all.

Strategies for Resolving Conflict and Finding Common Ground

In the bustling corridors of a large multinational corporation, the CFO and the COO stand face-to-face, their voices escalating and their words sharp as knives. The tension in the room is palpable as employees in the vicinity hold their breath, unsure of the outcome. It is the climax of a conflict brewing for weeks, which began with differing opinions on the company's strategic direction. Though this disagreement started as a mere difference in perspective, it has evolved into a personal battle, threatening the harmony and productivity of the entire organization.

As dramatic as it may seem, this scene represents the reality that unfolds within countless organizations and teams worldwide. Conflict is an inescapable aspect of human interaction, manifesting in various forms in the workplace. From the spirited debates between engineers and designers over the features of a new product to the subtle undercurrents of tension that ripple through a team as members vie for scarce resources or recognition, conflict is an omnipresent force that has the potential to disrupt even the most high-functioning and cohesive groups.

However, not the presence of conflict poses the greatest danger but rather our inability to navigate and resolve these disagreements effectively. Unresolved conflict can have dire consequences, eroding trust, damaging relationships, and stiffening the flow of innovative ideas that fuel an organization's success. On the other hand, when harnessed and managed effectively, conflict can become a powerful catalyst for growth, propelling a team to greater heights of creativity, collaboration, and achievement.

In 2008, a high-stakes conflict unfolded within the leadership team at Starbucks, a globally renowned coffeehouse chain. The company struggled with declining sales, and its identity was at stake. The founder, Howard Schultz, returned as CEO and faced the difficult task of revitalizing the company amidst internal disagreements on the best course of action. The conflict centered around whether Starbucks should focus on aggressive expansion, return to its core values, and concentrate on the in-store experience.

Schultz's leadership played a crucial role in navigating this conflict. He demonstrated the importance of understanding the underlying issues, fostering open communication, and embracing the power of compromise. By closing underperforming stores, slowing expansion, and refocusing on the customer experience, Schultz was able to steer Starbucks toward a successful future.

In the spirit of fostering such transformative outcomes, we explore strategies for resolving conflict and finding common ground. In the following chapters, we will delve into the intricacies of the human psyche, the subtle dance of interpersonal dynamics, and the practical techniques that can help leaders navigate the often-treacherous terrain of conflict resolution. By equipping leaders with this knowledge, they will be better prepared to face the challenges that inevitably arise in the complex and ever-evolving landscape of the modern workplace.

As we embark on this journey, we invite you to reflect on your own experiences with conflict – the triumphs, the failures, and the lessons learned. Please take a moment to consider the conflicts that have shaped your leadership journey and their impact on your team and organization. Through these real-world examples, we can truly understand the power and potential of effective conflict resolution and, in doing so, unlock the secrets to leading with purpose, inspiring our teams, and driving our organizations toward unparalleled success.

In the complex world of purposeful leadership, conflicts are an inevitable part of the journey. To create a harmonious and productive work environment, leaders must develop strategies for resolving conflicts and finding common ground. We will delve into various techniques to help leaders effectively address conflicts and facilitate collaborative problem-solving, drawing from real-world examples and industry-specific insights to provide a comprehensive, in-depth analysis of this critical aspect of leadership.

Before we delve into conflict resolution strategies, it is crucial to grasp the nature of conflict. We can classify conflicts into three main types: substantive, procedural, and relational. Substantive conflicts arise from disagreements over the content of decisions. In contrast, procedural conflicts stem from differences in the decision-making process. Relational conflicts, on the other hand, involve personal or emotional issues between individuals. By identifying the type of conflict, leaders can more effectively tailor their approach to resolving the issue.

Purposeful leaders must be well-versed in various conflict resolution strategies to address disagreements and find common ground among team members. The following are critical strategies for resolving conflicts:

- **Identify and Address the Root Causes**: Leaders must first identify the underlying issues driving the disagreements to resolve conflicts effectively. By addressing the root causes of conflict, leaders can foster a more productive and harmonious work environment. Ajay Banga, Mastercard's former CEO, is a great example. When he stepped into the role, he identified a lack of inclusion and diversity limiting the company's potential. He determined that the root cause of this issue was an organizational culture that wasn't sufficiently embracing diverse perspectives. As a result, he championed a more inclusive culture that values diverse perspectives. As a result, under his leadership, Mastercard saw a significant increase in employee satisfaction and company performance.
- **Foster Open Communication**: Open communication is essential for resolving conflicts and finding common ground. Leaders should create an environment where team members feel comfortable expressing their thoughts, feelings, and concerns without fear of judgment or retaliation. For example, Indra Nooyi, the former CEO of PepsiCo, encouraged open communication by creating a diverse and inclusive workplace where employees felt comfortable sharing their ideas and concerns. She also made various channels for feedback, such as town hall meetings and online platforms, to facilitate communication. This approach helped her to resolve conflicts effectively and build a culture of collaboration and innovation.
- **Promote Collaboration**: Encouraging collaborative and cooperative problem-solving can help team members work together to discover solutions that address the needs and concerns of all stakeholders, leading to more effective and

enduring conflict resolution. As the first African American President of the United States, Barack Obama faced numerous conflicts between political and social groups. He consistently advocated for bi-partisan cooperation and dialogue in response to these issues. This approach encouraged collaboration and cooperation to find resolutions that addressed the needs and concerns of all stakeholders. His leadership style, emphasizing open dialogue and negotiation, played a significant role in resolving disputes peacefully and promoting unity and understanding across diverse groups.

- **Utilize Mediation Techniques**: In some cases, conflicts may require the involvement of a neutral third party to facilitate resolution. Mediation techniques, such as active listening, empathy, and impartiality, can help leaders guide the parties involved toward a mutually beneficial solution. For example, Kofi Annan, the former Secretary-General of the United Nations, used his diplomatic skills to mediate conflicts in different parts of the world, including the Balkans, Iraq, and Syria. He employed active listening, empathy, and impartiality to facilitate a resolution between conflicting parties. As a result, his efforts led to peaceful negotiations. Moreover, they helped to resolve some of the most contentious conflicts in recent history.

Finding common ground is a critical aspect of conflict resolution, as it helps to promote a sense of unity and shared purpose among team members. The following are essential strategies for finding common ground:

- **Identify Shared Values and Goals**: By identifying the shared values and goals that underpin the team's mission, leaders can help to build a sense of unity and purpose, providing a foundation for collaborative decision-making and consensus-building. For example, Bob Chapman, the CEO of Barry-Wehmiller, implemented a "truly human leadership" approach that emphasized the company's values of trust, communication, and collaboration. By focusing on these shared values, he built a teamwork culture and fostered a sense of purpose among his employees.

- **Focus on Interests, Not Positions**: Leaders should encourage team members to focus on their interests and needs rather than their positions or demands when navigating conflicts. This approach can help uncover common ground areas and facilitate more productive discussions. For example, Bob Chapman, the CEO of Barry-Wehmiller, implemented a "truly human leadership" approach that emphasized the company's values of trust, communication, and collaboration. By focusing on these shared values, he built a teamwork culture and fostered a sense of purpose among his employees.
- **Seek Win-Win Solutions**: Leaders should strive to develop solutions that address the needs and concerns of all stakeholders, ultimately leading to win-win outcomes that promote harmony and collaboration among team members. For example, Jacinda Ardern, the former Prime Minister of New Zealand, implemented policies that addressed the needs and concerns of all stakeholders, such as introducing a zero-carbon bill that aimed to reduce carbon emissions while supporting businesses and workers in affected industries. Her approach helped to promote collaboration and unity among different groups and led to positive outcomes for all stakeholders.
- **Promote a Culture of Compromise**: By fostering a culture of compromise, leaders can encourage team members to be more flexible and open to finding common ground, ultimately leading to more effective conflict resolution. Angela Merkel, the former Chancellor of Germany. She encouraged

collaboration and compromise among political parties to solve complex issues such as immigration and climate change. Her approach helped to build consensus.

The following real-world examples illustrate the power of effectively resolving conflict and finding common ground in the context of purposeful leadership:

In the aftermath of apartheid in South Africa, the government established the Truth and Reconciliation Commission (TRC) to address the human rights abuses that had occurred during this period. Led by Archbishop Desmond Tutu, the TRC sought to promote healing and reconciliation by encouraging open communication, fostering empathy, and acknowledging the shared values and goals of a unified South Africa. Through the process of truth-telling, the TRC facilitated a sense of common ground, ultimately contributing to the country's peaceful transition to democracy.

The Good Friday Agreement: In 1998, the Good Friday Agreement marked the culmination of the Northern Ireland peace process, ending decades of conflict. Key stakeholders, including political leaders from Northern Ireland, the Republic of Ireland, and the United Kingdom, worked together under the guidance of mediator George Mitchell to identify shared goals, focus on interests rather than positions, and seek win-win solutions. The resulting agreement has been instrumental in fostering peace and stability in the region.

In the journey of purposeful leadership, effectively resolving conflict and finding common ground are essential skills for fostering a harmonious and productive work environment. By employing strategies such as addressing root causes, fostering open communication, encouraging collaboration, and promoting a culture of compromise, leaders can navigate conflicts with skill and finesse, ultimately facilitating more effective decision-making and promoting a sense of shared purpose among team members.

As real-world examples illustrate, effectively resolving conflict and finding common ground can have profound and lasting impacts within organizations and globally. Moreover, by developing and honing these essential leadership skills, purposeful leaders can inspire and motivate their teams, fostering an environment of unity, collaboration, and progress.

As we draw this comprehensive exploration of strategies for resolving conflict and finding common ground to a close, let us reflect on the power and potential that lies within the hands of a skilled leader. The ability to transform discord into harmony, reshape challenges into opportunities, and foster an environment of growth and collaboration is a testament to the true essence of effective leadership.

Imagine the bustling atmosphere of a diverse and talented team, each member bringing their unique skills and experiences to the table. The air is charged with the energy of creativity and passion as they work together towards a shared vision. Yet, as with any group of individuals, differences, and disagreements are bound to arise. It is in these moments of discord that a leader's skills are truly put to the test.

As you embark on your journey as a leader, consider the impact you can have on your team by mastering the art of conflict resolution. Envision the ripples of positive change that can spread throughout your organization as you effectively navigate the challenges and complexities that come with leading a group of diverse individuals.

As you stand at the helm of your team, guiding them through the stormy seas of conflict, remember that the most powerful and lasting change occurs not by suppressing disagreements but by embracing them as opportunities for growth. Doing so will cultivate an environment where each team member can thrive and create a beacon of inspiration and resilience that will reverberate throughout your organization.

So, as we conclude this in-depth exploration of strategies for resolving conflict and finding common ground, allow the lessons you've learned to become a part of your leadership toolbox. Embrace the challenge of transforming the inevitable disputes that arise within your team into catalysts for growth, creativity, and innovation. In doing so, you will become a more effective leader and leave a lasting impact on your team and your organization.

Let this ending serve as an invitation to contemplate the profound role you play in shaping the culture and success of your team. Reflect on the strategies and techniques shared within these pages and consider how you can apply them to create an environment where conflict is managed and harnessed for the betterment of all.

Remember that, as a leader; your influence extends far beyond the confines of your team. The way you manage conflict and foster collaboration has the potential to impact not only the individuals within your organization but also the broader community and society at large. In these moments of resolution and unity, we collectively build a stronger, more compassionate, and more innovative world.

So, dear reader, as you embark on your journey toward mastering the art of conflict resolution, may you find inspiration, wisdom, and courage within these pages. May the lessons you've learned serve as a beacon of light, guiding you through the challenges that lie ahead. And most importantly, may you never forget the power and potential that resides within your hands – the power to create a world where conflict becomes a catalyst for growth, understanding, and unity.

With this final thought, we leave you to contemplate the possibilities that await you as you embark on this journey of transformation and growth. As you venture into the world, armed with the knowledge and tools necessary to navigate the complexities of conflict and find common ground, remember that the power to create meaningful change resides within you. So embrace the challenge, seize the opportunity, and become the leader your team and the world desperately need.

And, as you forge ahead into the uncharted waters of leadership, may the wisdom and insight gleaned from these pages serve as your guiding light, illuminating the path towards a more harmonious, innovative, and inspiring future for all.

Staying on Course: The Ongoing Journey of Purposeful Leadership

"Leadership is a voyage, a pursuit of purpose that remains unwavering amidst changing tides. Keep your compass steady, for the journey to success is not a sprint, but a marathon of relentless determination and resilience."

Leadership is not a destination; it is a journey. It is a journey that requires continuous growth, reflection, and adaptation. Purposeful leaders understand that leading with purpose is not a one-time event but rather an ongoing process that requires them to stay on course, continuously developing their leadership skills to inspire and motivate their team to achieve their full potential.

But what does it mean to stay on course as a purposeful leader? First, it means understanding leadership is a lifelong growth, reflection, and adaptation journey. It means continuously learning, leading with a vision, and building solid relationships with your team members and other stakeholders.

Staying on course requires purposeful leaders to be self-aware, empathetic, and resilient. It needs them to navigate complex challenges, inspire and motivate their team, and stay focused on their goals, even in adversity.

Purposeful leaders understand that they cannot achieve their goals alone. They need to build a team of talented individuals who share their vision and are committed to achieving it. They must create a culture of trust, collaboration, and innovation where team members feel empowered to take risks and bring their ideas to the table.

One example of a purposeful leader who stayed on the course is Tim Cook, the CEO of Apple. Cook inherited the role from Steve Jobs and faced the challenge of maintaining Apple's innovation and success. As a result, he led Apple to achieve the milestone of becoming the first US company to reach a valuation of $2 trillion. He achieved this by creating new products and services while prioritizing sustainability and diversity. In addition, Cook's leadership style emphasizes empathy, communication, and collaboration, which has helped him build strong relationships with his team and stakeholders.

Another example is Jacinda Ardern, the Prime Minister of New Zealand. Ardern is known for her compassionate leadership style and response to the 2019 Christchurch Mosque shootings. She demonstrated empathy and unity, bringing her country together in the face of tragedy. Ardern's leadership style is rooted in a vision of kindness and compassion, and she has prioritized issues such as climate change, child welfare, and mental health during her time in office.

To stay on course as a purposeful leader, you must be willing to take risks, embrace failure, and learn from your mistakes. In addition, you must adapt to changing circumstances and find new ways to overcome obstacles. Finally, it would help if you were committed to continuous learning and development, seeking feedback from your team and other stakeholders, and always looking for new knowledge and skills to improve your leadership.

Staying on course as a purposeful leader is not easy. However, inspiring and motivating your team to achieve great things is essential. It requires a deep commitment to your purpose, a willingness to learn and adapt, and a relentless focus on your goals—a few critical elements of staying on course as a purposeful leader.

- **Continuous Learning** - One of the most critical aspects of staying on course as a purposeful leader is continuous learning. Purposeful leaders understand that leadership is a lifelong journey that requires ongoing learning and development. As a result, they are curious and open-minded and constantly seek new ways to improve their leadership skills. One way to ensure continuous learning is to seek feedback from your team and other stakeholders. Actively seeking feedback can help you identify hidden spots, areas for improvement, and growth opportunities.
- Additionally, purposeful leaders always seek new knowledge and skills by reading books, attending conferences, and taking courses. For example, Jeff Bezos, the founder, and CEO of Amazon, has always emphasized the importance of continuous learning. He is known to read extensively and encourages his team to do the same. Bezos also attends conferences and meets with industry experts to gain new insights and knowledge.
- **Leading with Vision** - Another critical element of staying on course as a purposeful leader is leading with a vision. Purposeful leaders understand that a clear and compelling vision is essential to inspire and motivate their team to achieve great things. They are adept at articulating their vision in a way that resonates with their team and helps them understand how their work contributes to the bigger picture. Purposeful leaders, to lead with a vision, must be able to communicate clearly and effectively. They should be able to distill complex ideas into simple and compelling messages that resonate with their team. Purposeful leaders also understand that leading with a vision requires them to be authentic and genuine. They must be enthusiastic about their vision and be willing to take risks to achieve it. For example, Elon Musk, the CEO of Tesla and SpaceX, is known for his

bold vision and ability to inspire his team to achieve great things. His vision of creating a sustainable future and colonizing Mars has inspired his team to work towards a shared goal. Musk's ability to communicate his vision clearly and authentically has been a critical driver of his success.

- **Building Strong Relationships** - Another essential element of staying on course as a purposeful leader is building solid relationships. Purposeful leaders understand that leadership is about building trust, fostering collaboration, and creating a sense of community within their team. Therefore, they prioritize building strong relationships with their team members, peers, and other stakeholders. To build strong relationships, purposeful leaders must be good listeners and empathetic. They should take the time to understand the needs and concerns of their team members and show genuine interest in their well-being. Purposeful leaders should also be transparent and honest, sharing successes and failures with their team. For example, Mary Barra, the CEO of General Motors, has prioritized building solid relationships with her team members and other stakeholders. She is known for her empathy and listening ability, which has helped her build a culture of trust and collaboration within General Motors. Barra's focus on building strong relationships has been a critical driver of General Motors' success in recent years.

Staying on course as a purposeful leader requires continuous learning, leading with a vision, and building solid relationships. Purposeful leaders understand that leadership is an ongoing journey of growth and development. Therefore, they constantly seek new knowledge and skills, articulate a clear and compelling vision, and build strong relationships with their team members and other stakeholders.

Staying on course as a purposeful leader is not easy. However, inspiring and motivating your team to achieve great things is essential. Through the stories of purposeful leaders like Tim Cook and Jacinda Ardern, we can learn what it takes to stay on course as a purposeful leader and how we can apply these lessons to our leadership journeys. So, let's begin this journey together and discover what it means to stay on course as a purposeful leader. Through their stories, we will learn what it takes to stay on course as a purposeful leader and how we can apply these lessons to our leadership journeys.

The Importance of Resilience and Perseverance in Purpose-Driven Leadership

Resilience and perseverance are vital components of effective leadership, particularly purpose-driven leadership. As leaders strive to inspire and motivate their teams toward a common goal, they must possess an unwavering commitment to their mission and the capacity to bounce back from setbacks.

In the grand tapestry of human history, purpose-driven leadership weaves its thread throughout, leaving a lasting and transformative impact on societies across the globe. These leaders' indomitable spirit, unwavering determination, and ability to overcome adversity have profoundly shaped the world. As we explore the importance of resilience and perseverance in purpose-driven leadership, We invite you to step into the realm of stories that exemplify the power of these traits and explore how to harness them to fuel success and create lasting change.

Reflect for a moment on the impoverished streets of Kolkata, where Mother Teresa dedicated her life to aiding those in need. Despite the harsh conditions and constant challenges, her spirit remained untamed. Mother Teresa's relentless pursuit of service to humanity, irrespective of her hardships, is a testament to the extraordinary power of resilience and perseverance. Her leadership inspired millions and made a significant difference in the lives of countless individuals, proving that unyielding determination in the face of adversity can foster monumental change.

Now, shift your focus to the vibrant streets of Bengaluru, where a visionary named Nandan Nilekani dared to revolutionize the Indian IT sector and redefine the role of technology in societal development. His venture, Infosys, was met with skepticism and encountered numerous setbacks. However, Nilekani's resilience and perseverance enabled him to overcome these challenges and achieve remarkable milestones in the IT industry. His unyielding commitment to innovation is a potent example of how purpose-driven leadership can reshape industries and inspire future generations.

In the remote mountains of Pakistan, a young girl named Malala Yousafzai risked her life to advocate for girls' education, defying the oppressive regime of the Taliban. Despite being targeted and shot in the head, Malala's resilience and perseverance remained unwavering. She not only survived the attack but continued to fight for her cause, eventually becoming the youngest Nobel Peace Prize laureate in history. Her courageous leadership has galvanized a global movement for gender equality and education, illustrating the transformative power of resilience and perseverance in purpose-driven leadership.

As we delve into the intricacies of resilience and perseverance and their critical role in purpose-driven leadership, we will uncover the psychological and social mechanisms that underpin these traits. In addition, we will learn from the stories of remarkable leaders who have faced seemingly insurmountable challenges and yet have shaped the course of history through their resilience and perseverance. By examining the qualities that define these extraordinary individuals, we hope to inspire a new generation of purpose-driven leaders who will rise to meet the challenges of our time and usher in a brighter, more equitable future for all.

Numerous scientific studies have focused on Resilience and perseverance, particularly within psychology and organizational behavior. Resilience refers to an individual's ability to recover from adversity. At the same time, perseverance is the steadfast pursuit of a goal despite challenges or setbacks. These two traits are intrinsically linked, as a resilient leader is more likely to persevere through difficult times.

Research has demonstrated that resilient individuals possess specific psychological characteristics like optimism, self-efficacy, and emotional intelligence. These qualities help leaders maintain a positive outlook, believe in their ability to achieve their goals, and effectively manage their emotions in high-pressure situations.

Moreover, the "grit" concept, coined by psychologist Angela Duckworth, closely ties perseverance to it. Studies have demonstrated that individuals with grit, a combination of passion and perseverance for long-term goals, are more likely to succeed in various domains, including leadership.

In the context of purpose-driven leadership, resilience and perseverance are paramount. When a strong sense of purpose drives leaders, they are more likely to encounter obstacles and opposition as they challenge the status quo and strive for meaningful change. The ability to remain resilient and persevere in these challenges is essential for achieving the desired outcomes and sustaining long-term success.

Resilient and persevering leaders are more effective at inspiring and motivating their teams. By modeling these traits, leaders can demonstrate their unwavering commitment to the shared mission and instill a sense of confidence and determination within their team members. In addition, it fosters a culture of resilience and perseverance within the organization, helping propel the entire team toward their collective goals.

Developing certain mindsets and habits is essential to foster resilience and perseverance in one's leadership style. The following strategies can help leaders cultivate these traits and apply them in their pursuit of purpose-driven goals:

- **Embrace challenges**: Leaders must actively learn to view challenges as opportunities for growth rather than avoidable obstacles. This mindset can foster a greater willingness to take risks and bounce back from setbacks more quickly. Indra Nooyi, a former CEO of PepsiCo, consistently embraced challenges throughout her career, taking on complex projects and pushing for innovation. Nooyi championed the diversification of PepsiCo's product portfolio to include healthier options. This move initially faced resistance from investors and the market. By embracing this challenge, she transformed PepsiCo into a more sustainable and responsible company, with healthier products now accounting for nearly half its revenue.
- **Develop a growth mindset**: As defined by psychologist Carol Dweck, a growth mindset involves the belief that abilities and intelligence can be developed through dedication and hard work. By adopting this mindset, leaders are more likely to persevere in adversity, viewing setbacks as opportunities to gain experience and grow. For example, Howard Schultz, the former CEO of Starbucks, demonstrated a growth mindset by transforming Starbucks from a small coffee shop into a global brand. Despite initial setbacks, including the

failure of Starbucks' first foray into the international market, Schultz maintained his belief in the company's potential for growth. He learned from these setbacks, adjusted the company's strategy, and eventually led Starbucks to become one of the most recognized brands in the world.

- **Practice self-compassion**: Self-compassion involves being kind to oneself in times of failure or difficulty, recognizing that setbacks are a natural part of the human experience. Leaders can develop the emotional resilience necessary to persevere through challenging situations by cultivating self-compassion. For example, Arianna Huffington, the founder of The Huffington Post and Thrive Global, experienced a personal wake-up call when she collapsed from exhaustion in 2007. Instead of criticizing herself for her inability to "do it all," Huffington practiced self-compassion and used this experience to reevaluate her priorities. It led her to create Thrive Global, which promotes well-being and work-life balance for individuals and organizations.
- **Build a support network**: A strong support network of trusted colleagues, mentors, and friends can provide valuable encouragement and guidance during difficult times. In addition, leaders can bolster their resilience and determination by surrounding themselves with individuals who share their purpose and values. For example, Sheryl Sandberg, the COO of Facebook, has consistently emphasized the importance of building a solid support network in both personal and professional life. After the sudden death of her husband, Sandberg relied on her support network to help her navigate her grief and continue her work at Facebook. She has since become an advocate for the importance of resilience and support networks, sharing her experiences in her book "Option B: Facing Adversity, Building Resilience, and Finding Joy."

- **Reflect on past successes**: Regularly reflecting on past accomplishments can help leaders maintain a sense of self-efficacy and optimism in the face of challenges. In addition, this practice serves as a reminder of the leader's ability to overcome obstacles and succeed. For example, Oprah Winfrey, a media mogul and philanthropist, has faced numerous setbacks throughout her career, including being fired from her first television job. As a result, Winfrey has often spoken about the importance of reflecting on past successes to maintain a sense of self-worth and confidence in facing adversity. This practice has enabled her to persevere through numerous challenges, ultimately becoming one of the most influential and successful figures in the entertainment industry.

Resilience and perseverance are essential traits for purpose-driven leaders, enabling them to navigate the inevitable challenges and setbacks in pursuing meaningful change. By understanding the science behind these traits, recognizing their importance in leadership, and learning from real-world examples, leaders can develop the skills and mindsets necessary to cultivate resilience and perseverance within themselves and their teams. In doing so, they will be better equipped to inspire and motivate others, ultimately driving their organizations toward long-term success and realizing their shared purpose.

As we conclude this journey of exploring resilience and perseverance in purpose-driven leadership, let us take a moment to pause and reflect upon the powerful stories, insights, and strategies that we have shared. We have delved into the realms of psychology and organizational behavior to understand the scientific underpinnings of these traits, unpacked their critical role in driving meaningful change, and drawn inspiration from iconic leaders who have triumphed in the face of adversity.

There has never been a more pressing need for resilient and persevering leaders in a rapidly changing world of uncertainty and challenges. As global issues such as climate change, social inequality, and political unrest continue to escalate, leaders who can stand firm in their convictions and relentlessly pursue their purpose are crucial to navigating these tumultuous times.

So, as we embark on our respective journeys as leaders, let us carry with us the lessons and wisdom gleaned from these pages. Let us not shy away from the trials that await us but instead embrace them as opportunities for growth and transformation. Let us strive to be beacons of resilience and perseverance, inspiring those around us to persevere in their pursuits, even in the face of seemingly insurmountable obstacles.

These moments, when we face stacked odds and a path forward shrouded in darkness, reveal the true essence of leadership. During these challenging times, leaders shine and demonstrate their true abilities. We must call upon our inner strength, courage, and determination to forge ahead, even when the outcome is uncertain.

And as we do so, let us remember that we are not alone in this struggle. We are part of a lineage of purpose-driven leaders who have come before us, faced their share of trials and tribulations, and emerged victorious through their unwavering commitment to their cause.

May their stories serve as a guiding light for us as we chart our course through the complex and ever-changing leadership landscape. And as we continue to cultivate our resilience and perseverance, let us not forget the goal at the heart of our endeavors: to create a better world for ourselves, our teams, and future generations.

So, dear reader, as you close this book and return to your leadership journey, remember that the power to shape the world lies within you. Your resilience, perseverance, and unwavering commitment to your purpose have the potential to inspire and catalyze change on a scale that is both unimaginable and attainable. The choice is yours.

Let this chapter serve as a call to action, an invitation to accept the mantle of purpose-driven leadership with renewed vigor and determination. Through our collective efforts, our resilience in the face of adversity, and our unyielding commitment to our shared goals, we can change the course of history and leave an indelible mark on the world. Together, we can shape a future defined by progress, equality, and hope for future generations.

Techniques for Staying Committed to Purpose and Moving Forward

Staying committed to one's purpose and moving forward is more important than ever for leaders who aim to inspire and motivate their teams. This unwavering commitment sets exceptional leaders apart as they navigate the tumultuous waters of the modern business landscape with a steadfast resolve rooted in a deep sense of purpose. The power of such purpose-driven leadership can be transformative, not only for individuals and organizations but for entire industries and societies as well.

When long-distance runner is nearing the final stretch of a grueling marathon, exhausted and pushed to the brink, they feel their body and mind screaming for them to stop. Yet, they press on, driven by an unyielding desire to reach the finish line. In many ways, this scenario mirrors the journey of a purpose-driven leader. Like marathon runners, leaders face countless challenges and obstacles as they strive to achieve their goals, from external pressures and competition to internal doubts and setbacks. Yet, despite these adversities, their unwavering commitment to their purpose propels them forward, allowing them to forge ahead and make a lasting impact.

The story of Jack Ma, the visionary entrepreneur behind Alibaba Group, is a testament to staying committed to one's purpose and moving forward. When Ma first set out to revolutionize commerce and create a platform that could empower small businesses in China and beyond, many deemed his ambitions to be mere pipe dreams, unlikely to ever come to fruition. Yet, undeterred by the skepticism of others and the countless challenges ahead, Ma remained steadfast in his commitment to his vision. Today, as Alibaba continues to expand its reach and influence, shaping the course of e-commerce and technology, Ma's unwavering commitment to his purpose serves as a beacon of inspiration for leaders worldwide.

The story of Sir Ernest Shackleton, the renowned polar explorer, serves as a powerful example of staying committed to one's purpose and moving forward in the face of adversity. In 1914, Shackleton embarked on the ambitious Imperial Trans-Antarctic Expedition, aiming to cross the Antarctic continent for the first time. However, when his ship, the Endurance, became trapped and was eventually crushed by ice, Shackleton's primary purpose shifted from exploration to ensuring the survival of his crew. Through his unwavering commitment to his new purpose, Shackleton successfully led his crew through an incredible 22-month ordeal, ultimately bringing everyone home safely.

Jawaharlal Nehru, the first Prime Minister of independent India, exemplifies purpose-driven leadership in another compelling story. Despite facing significant opposition and enduring periods of imprisonment during the independence struggle, Nehru remained steadfast in his commitment to a secular, democratic, and united India. His unyielding dedication to his purpose inspired millions, ultimately leading to the establishment of the world's largest democracy and leaving a legacy that continues to influence India's political and social landscape.

These real-world examples demonstrate that we should not underestimate the power of staying committed to our purpose and moving forward. This indomitable spirit allows leaders to inspire and motivate their teams, driving them to achieve seemingly impossible feats and make a lasting impact in the world.

In the following, we will delve deeper into the techniques that leaders can employ to stay focused on their purpose and maintain their forward momentum. This chapter aims to provide a comprehensive and practical guide for those seeking to harness the transformative power of purpose-driven leadership, drawing on insights from psychology and organizational behavior and real-world examples of successful leaders. By understanding and applying these techniques, leaders can cultivate the resilience, motivation, and determination needed to navigate the complexities of the modern world and make a meaningful and lasting impact.

Research in psychology and organizational behavior has shed light on several factors that can help individuals maintain their commitment to a purpose and continue moving forward. These factors include intrinsic motivation, self-efficacy, self-regulation, and grit.

- **Intrinsic Motivation**: Intrinsic motivation refers to the internal drive to engage in activities for personal satisfaction or fulfillment rather than external rewards or pressures. Studies have shown that intrinsically motivated individuals are likelier to persist in their efforts and maintain their commitment to their goals.

- **Self-Efficacy**: Self-efficacy is the belief in one's ability to accomplish specific tasks or achieve desired outcomes. Research has demonstrated that individuals with high self-efficacy are more likely to persevere in facing challenges and maintain their commitment to their goals.
- **Self-Regulation**: Self-regulation involves monitoring and controlling one's thoughts, emotions, and behaviors to pursue a goal. Research has linked effective self-regulation to remarkable persistence, goal attainment, and well-being.
- **Grit**: As previously mentioned, determination combines passion and perseverance for long-term goals. Gritty individuals are likelier to stay committed to their purpose and continue progressing despite setbacks or obstacles.

The following techniques, grounded in psychological and organizational principles, can help leaders stay committed to their purpose and progress:

- **Reconnect with your "why":** Simon Sinek, a renowned leadership expert and author of "Start with Why," emphasizes the importance of understanding and continually revisiting one's core purpose. Sinek argues that by focusing on the "why" behind their actions, leaders can maintain a clear sense of direction and motivation, even when faced with challenges or setbacks.
- **Set SMART goals:** Paul Polman, the former CEO of Unilever, implemented the company's Sustainable Living Plan in 2010, which included a series of ambitious yet clearly defined and measurable goals for improving social and environmental outcomes. By setting SMART (Specific, Measurable, Achievable, Relevant, and Time-bound) goals, Polman maintained focus and commitment to Unilever's purpose, ultimately driving significant progress in sustainability.

- **Break goals into smaller milestones:** Jeff Bezos, the founder and former CEO of Amazon, is known for his commitment to long-term thinking and vision. To maintain momentum and commitment to Amazon's overarching purpose, Bezos breaks down the company's goals into smaller, more manageable milestones, which allows for more frequent progress assessments and adjustments.
- **Develop a growth mindset:** As previously discussed, Howard Schultz of Starbucks exemplified a growth mindset in his leadership, viewing setbacks as opportunities for learning and growth. By adopting a growth mindset, leaders can maintain their commitment to their purpose by focusing on continual improvement and learning from setbacks.
- **Foster a culture of accountability:** Mary Barra, CEO of General Motors, has fostered a culture of accountability by emphasizing the importance of transparency, open communication, and individual responsibility. In addition, Barra has encouraged commitment and persistence throughout the company by creating an environment where team members feel accountable for their actions and contributions to the organization's purpose.
- **Practice self-compassion:** As previously mentioned, Arianna Huffington used self-compassion to recover from burnout and refocus her priorities. Leaders who actively practice self-compassion embrace setbacks and failures as natural occurrences and utilize them as opportunities for growth and learning, thus maintaining their commitment to their purpose.
- **Seek feedback and support:** Bill Gates, the co-founder of Microsoft, has long advocated seeking feedback and mentorship from others. By actively seeking feedback and support, leaders can maintain their commitment to their purpose and ensure they are on the right track to achieve their goals.

- **Celebrate progress and achievements:** Richard Branson, the founder of the Virgin Group, is known for his ability to celebrate progress and achievements, both big and small. By acknowledging and celebrating successes, leaders can reinforce their commitment to their purpose and maintain motivation among their team members.

Staying committed to one's purpose and moving forward in the face of challenges is crucial for effective leadership. By understanding the psychological and organizational principles behind commitment and perseverance and employing techniques such as reconnecting with one's "why," setting SMART goals, breaking goals into smaller milestones, developing a growth mindset, fostering a culture of accountability, practicing self-compassion, seeking feedback and support, and celebrating progress, leaders can maintain their focus and determination.

Real-world examples of leaders such as Simon Sinek, Paul Polman, Jeff Bezos, Howard Schultz, Mary Barra, Arianna Huffington, Bill Gates, and Richard Branson demonstrate the effectiveness of these techniques in staying committed to the purpose and moving forward. By applying these strategies in their leadership, leaders can inspire and motivate their teams, drive meaningful change, and achieve long-term success.

In pursuing purpose, the path forward is often fraught with challenges and obstacles that may assess even the most determined leaders. Yet, as the sun sets on the horizon, casting shadows on the journey ahead, these techniques can be a beacon of light, guiding leaders and their teams through the darkest moments of doubt and uncertainty.

Picture a captain at the helm of a ship, navigating through treacherous waters with waves crashing and storms raging all around.

The wind howls, and the ship creaks under the strain of its weight, threatening to buckle and break. Yet the captain remains steadfast, committed to reaching their destination, a vision in their mind's eye.

In moments like these, it is not the raw power of the storm that defines a leader's success but rather the indomitable spirit and unwavering commitment to purpose that sets them apart from the rest. It is a story of perseverance, triumph over adversity, and the unyielding human nature that drives us ever forward in the face of overwhelming odds.

As the storm begins to subside, the captain and crew emerge from the darkness, battered but not broken, their commitment to their purpose stronger than ever. During these moments of trial and tribulation, true leaders emerge, forged and tempered by the fires of adversity, and become an unstoppable force that defies denial.

But what drives these leaders to press onward, embrace the storm, and persist in pushing forward, even when the path becomes obscured and the way uncertain? It is an unshakable belief in their purpose, a deep-rooted conviction that their cause is just and their goals are worth the struggle.

And so, we come to the crux of the matter, the very essence of what it means to lead with purpose. It is not merely about having a clearly defined goal or a grand vision for the future. Instead, it is about cultivating an unwavering commitment to that purpose, remaining resolute in adversity, and leading by example, inspiring others to follow in one's footsteps.

For the leaders who embrace these techniques and forge ahead with unyielding determination, there is no storm too great, no challenge too daunting, and no obstacle too insurmountable. On the contrary, the crucible of adversity reveals the true mettle of a leader, and their steadfast commitment to purpose ultimately leads them to prevail.

As you stand on the precipice of your journey, consider the lessons imparted by those who have come before you. Embrace the techniques that have served them well and allow their stories to inspire you to reach greater heights. For it is in the pursuit of purpose that we come alive, and through our unwavering commitment to that purpose, we leave an indelible mark upon the world.

So, as you embark upon your voyage of discovery, remember that the true power of purpose lies not in the destination itself but in the journey that takes you there. Embrace the challenges ahead and arm yourself with the techniques that will guide you through even the darkest storms. In doing so, you will find your path to success and inspire others to do the same, creating a legacy of purpose-driven leadership that will echo through the ages.

Ultimately, it is not the storm that defines us but the courage, determination, and unwavering commitment to purpose that we display in the face of adversity. As you continue your journey, remember this truth. Let it guide you as a beacon of light in the darkness, illuminating the path forward and propelling you to pursue your purpose.

VI. CONCLUSION

"Lead with purpose, transform with impact. Ignite, inspire, create - for this is the true essence of leadership."

AS THE SUN begins to set on our odyssey through the labyrinthine landscape of purpose-driven leadership, we are perched on the precipice of enlightenment, surveying the panorama of lessons, insights, and stories illuminating our path. Are we not awestruck by the indomitable spirit of those who have trodden this hallowed ground before us, who have harnessed the unbridled power of their purpose to light a beacon of inspiration for those who follow in their wake? Are we not compelled to ask ourselves, as we bear witness to the feats of these titans of leadership, whether we, too, can rise to the challenge and heed the clarion call of purpose?

Indeed, this question reverberates through the annals of history, echoing in the tales of leaders who have shaped the course of humanity through the sheer force of their resolve. From the soaring orations of Dr. Martin Luther King Jr., whose impassioned plea for equality and justice inspired a nation to confront the shackles of prejudice, to the visionary foresight of Steve Jobs, who ushered in a technological revolution with his unrelenting pursuit of innovation, these paragons of leadership have demonstrated the transformative power of purpose.

As we stand on the shoulders of these giants, we cannot help but ponder the essence of their greatness. What threads bind their stories together, weaving a tapestry of purposeful leadership that transcends the boundaries of time, culture, and circumstance? Can we unravel this enigmatic tapestry, distilling its essence into a blueprint that can guide us toward purposeful leadership?

My fellow travelers, this is the quest upon which we have embarked in this tome. Through the labyrinth of tales and insights, we have sought to unravel the mysteries of purpose-driven leadership, casting light upon the principles, practices, and qualities that define its essence. And now, as we prepare to close the final chapter of our journey, we must pause and reflect on the lessons we have gleaned, the stories we have shared, and the wisdom we have amassed.

In these reflections lies the key to our transformation. This spark can ignite the flame of purpose within our hearts and propel us into the ranks of those who have dared to dream, strive, and conquer. Let us, therefore, gather the fruits of our journey, savoring the nourishment they provide, and use their sustenance to fuel our ascent towards the summit of purposeful leadership.

In this concluding chapter, we shall revisit the most poignant moments of our odyssey, retracing the footsteps of those before us and distilling their wisdom into a potent elixir that can fortify our resolve and illuminate our path. We shall also contemplate the call to action that resounds from the annals of purpose-driven leadership, beckoning us to seize the mantle of greatness and forge a legacy that will echo through the ages.

As we embark on the final leg of our journey through purpose-driven leadership, we must pause for a moment and reflect on the lessons we have gleaned from the numerous examples, stories, and insights shared throughout this book. Have we not been inspired by the tales of resilience and perseverance of leaders who have braved the stormy seas of adversity, only to emerge stronger, wiser, and more resolute in pursuing a purposeful existence? Have we not marveled at the myriad ways in which they have harnessed the power of their purpose to galvanize their teams, creating a collective force that transcends the sum of its parts?

The answer, my fellow leaders and aspiring change-makers is an unequivocal yes. And so, in this closing chapter, we shall revisit the most poignant lessons from our journey, weaving them into a tapestry of purposeful leadership that will serve as a beacon of inspiration for those who dare to heed its call.

So, let us embark on this final leg of our journey armed with stories and insights. We draw strength from the valuable lessons that have shaped our understanding of purpose-driven leadership, empowering us to rise to the challenge and make our mark on the world.

Reflections on the Journey of Purposeful Leadership

As we journey through the labyrinthine world of purposeful leadership, we must pause and reflect on the various milestones we have encountered. This segment serves as a retrospective contemplation, a chance to re-examine the central themes and real-world examples that have emerged throughout our odyssey. Through these reflections, we can better appreciate the essence of purpose-driven leadership and embrace the lessons learned.

- **Discovering and Articulating Purpose** -Our journey began with exploring personal purpose and its significance in leadership. We witnessed leaders who have embarked on a voyage of self-discovery, unearthing their core purpose and using it as a compass to navigate their leadership journey. One example is Oprah Winfrey, who overcame a challenging upbringing to build a media empire grounded in her passion for empowering others. Her life's purpose, to uplift and inspire, has driven her success and impact on millions of lives.
- **Cultivating a Compelling Vision**- We then delved into the importance of developing a clear and inspiring vision that aligns with our core purpose. A purposeful idea is a beacon, guiding leaders and their teams toward realizing their shared aspirations. Elon Musk, the visionary behind Tesla and SpaceX, exemplifies this principle. His audacious goal of making life multi-planetary and transitioning the world to sustainable energy sources has galvanized countless individuals, inspiring them to join him in his quest to reshape the future.
- **Building a Purpose-Driven Culture** - Our journey also highlighted the significance of fostering a purpose-driven organizational culture that promotes shared values, empowers employees, and encourages collaboration. By cultivating

such a culture, leaders can inspire their teams to embrace the organization's purpose and work collectively to achieve its goals. For example, Howard Schultz, the former CEO of Starbucks, has been instrumental in nurturing a culture that emphasizes social responsibility, ethical sourcing, and employee well-being. Schultz's commitment to the company's purpose has created a loyal and engaged workforce and contributed to the brand's enduring success.

- **Navigating Challenges with Resilience and Perseverance** - The importance of resilience and perseverance emerged as a recurring theme throughout our exploration of purpose-driven leadership. Leaders who demonstrate unwavering resolve in the face of adversity are potent examples of the strength and tenacity required to stay true to one's purpose. Indra Nooyi, the former CEO of PepsiCo, exemplifies this quality. Throughout her tenure, Nooyi navigated numerous challenges while steadfastly pursuing her vision of a more sustainable and socially responsible company. Under her leadership, PepsiCo achieved significant milestones, such as reducing its environmental footprint and promoting healthier food options.
- **The Power of Authentic Communication** - Effective communication is essential to purpose-driven leadership. We have observed leaders who excel in articulating their purpose and vision, connecting with others through authenticity, empathy, and vulnerability. For example, Brené Brown, a renowned researcher and author, has transformed the conversation around vulnerability and courage. Her ability to communicate complex concepts relatable and engagingly has made her ideas accessible to a diverse audience, inspiring countless individuals to embrace vulnerability as a strength.
- **Staying Committed to Purpose and Moving Forward** - Lastly, we have examined various techniques leaders can employ to

maintain their commitment to their purpose and continue moving forward. By understanding and applying these strategies, leaders can inspire and motivate their teams to persevere in facing challenges and achieve their collective goals. Simon Sinek's "Golden Circle" concept emphasizes the importance of reconnecting with one's "why" to maintain focus and commitment. Mary Barra, the CEO of General Motors, has fostered a culture of accountability and dedication to her company's purpose by aligning its operations with her vision of a safer, cleaner, and more sustainable future. Richard Branson, the founder of Virgin Group, has demonstrated the power of celebrating progress and rewarding success to maintain momentum and enthusiasm among team members.

Our journey through purpose-driven leadership has been a testament to the transformative power of purpose, vision, culture, resilience, communication, and commitment. By embracing these principles and learning from the examples of real-world leaders, we can navigate the complexities of leadership and make a meaningful and lasting impact on the world.

The lessons and insights we have gained from our journey are not merely intellectual exercises but a call to action. As leaders, we must embrace our purpose and harness its power to create positive change. So let us heed this call and embark on a purposeful leadership journey to inspire and motivate those around us to realize our full potential.

The Importance of Continuous Learning and Improvement

In a world where change is the only constant, the quest for knowledge and growth becomes an indispensable part of an individual's journey. In the dynamic and ever-evolving landscape of modern business, leaders must embrace continuous learning and improvement to stay ahead of the curve. As we explore the crucial role continuous learning plays in purpose-driven leadership, we will delve into the stories of real-world leaders who have exemplified this commitment to growth and, in doing so, have inspired and motivated their teams to reach new heights of success.

Think of a majestic forest with a canopy of green leaves dancing in the breeze and sunlight filtering through the trees, creating a symphony of light and shadow. Just as the trees in the forest adapt to their environment, shedding old leaves and growing new ones, leaders must also adapt to the changing landscape of their respective industries. Continuous learning and improvement are akin to the forest's natural cycle of growth and renewal, enabling leaders to flourish and thrive in an ever-changing world.

One such leader who embodies this spirit of continuous learning is Mary Barra, CEO of General Motors (GM). Barra's dedication to learning and personal growth fueled her rise to the helm of one of the world's largest automakers. When faced with the challenge of leading GM through immense change and disruption in the automotive industry, Barra's commitment to continuous improvement empowered her to make bold decisions and transform the company's culture. By embracing electric vehicles, autonomous technology, and a renewed focus on innovation, Barra has not only navigated GM through turbulent times but also positioned the company as a leader in the future of mobility.

As we delve deeper into continuous learning and improvement, we will encounter stories of leaders from various industries who have harnessed the power of learning to inspire, motivate, and propel their organizations forward. From the political arena to the world of technology, we will see how leaders like New Zealand's Prime

Minister Jacinda Ardern and Microsoft CEO Satya Nadella have used continuous learning as a cornerstone of their leadership style.

In this journey, we will examine the scientific concepts underpinning continuous learning, such as neuroplasticity and growth mindset, and explore the practical strategies leaders can employ to foster a culture of learning and improvement within their organizations. Weaving these real-world leaders' experiences with scientific insights and practical strategies aims to provide a rich tapestry of knowledge and inspiration for leaders seeking to enhance their leadership capabilities and drive their organizations toward success.

As we explore the importance of continuous learning and improvement, we invite you to join us in discovering the transformative power of knowledge and growth in purpose-driven leadership. Through the stories of these exceptional leaders and the insights gleaned from their experiences, we hope to inspire you to embrace continuous learning as a fundamental aspect of your leadership journey and, in doing so, unlock the limitless potential that lies within you and your team.

Continuous learning and improvement have become essential components of modern leadership. In an ever-evolving business landscape, leaders must remain adaptable, innovative, and committed to expanding their knowledge and skill sets. This ongoing pursuit of growth ensures that leaders remain effective, agile, and capable of guiding their organizations through the complexities of today's global marketplace. In addition, by embracing continuous learning, leaders are committed to personal and professional development, inspiring their teams to do the same.

In an increasingly interconnected and rapidly changing world, the ability to learn and adapt has become a critical factor in determining an organization's success. The accelerating pace of technological advancements, shifts in consumer demands, and emerging global challenges necessitate leaders to stay informed and up to date to make informed decisions and effectively navigate their organizations through uncertainty.

Christine Lagarde, the former Managing Director of the International Monetary Fund and current President of the European Central Bank, is a leader who exemplifies the importance of continuous learning. Lagarde is known for her extensive knowledge of finance and economics, which has allowed her to make significant contributions to global economic stability and development. Her commitment to continuous learning and improvement has played a crucial role in her ability to drive policy and stay at the forefront of global economic discourse."

Purpose-driven leadership centers around the idea that organizations should actively strive to impact society positively while achieving their business objectives. Continuous learning plays a vital role in this approach to leadership, as it enables leaders to understand better the evolving needs of their stakeholders, the broader societal context in which they operate, and the emerging opportunities and challenges that can influence their organization's purpose.

A great example is Paul Polman, the former CEO of Unilever. Under Polman's leadership, Unilever embarked on an ambitious sustainability plan, the Unilever Sustainable Living Plan, which aimed to decouple the company's growth from its environmental footprint while increasing its positive social impact. In addition, Polman's dedication to continuous learning allowed him to identify new ways to drive sustainable growth, engage with stakeholders, and align the company's operations with its purpose.

The Science of Continuous Learning and Improvement

Neuroplasticity, a term coined in neuroscience, refers to the brain's ability to change and adapt throughout an individual's lifetime. This remarkable feature of the human brain enables us to learn new skills, adapt to new environments, and continuously evolve our thinking and behavior. Neuroplasticity refutes the traditional belief that the brain's structure and function remain static after a certain age. Instead, it suggests that the brain remains malleable and can form new neural connections in response to new experiences and learning.

This groundbreaking discovery has significant implications for leaders who wish to embrace continuous learning and improvement. By understanding the brain's capacity for change, leaders can cultivate a mindset that encourages ongoing personal and professional development. For instance, Warren Buffett, one of the most successful investors in history, is known for his voracious reading habits and relentless pursuit of knowledge. Buffett's dedication to continuous learning exemplifies how one can actively harness neuroplasticity to drive success and personal growth.

Feedback loops play a critical role in the learning process by providing information on the effectiveness of actions and decisions. In essence, a feedback loop operates as a system where individuals actively use the output of a process as input to modify or improve the process itself. Feedback loops can be either positive or negative, depending on whether they amplify or dampen the changes in the system.

In leadership and continuous learning, feedback loops enable leaders to assess the impact of their actions and decisions, identify areas for improvement, and make necessary adjustments. For example, Ray Dalio, the founder of Bridgewater Associates, attributes much of his success to the culture of radical transparency and open feedback that he has fostered within his organization. By encouraging employees to share their thoughts and opinions openly, Dalio has created a feedback-rich environment that drives continuous learning and improvement at both the individual and organizational levels.

Developed by psychologist Carol Dweck, the concept of a growth mindset revolves around the belief that one's abilities and intelligence can be developed and improved through dedication, hard work, and continuous learning. It contrasts with a fixed mindset, where individuals believe their skills and intelligence are static and cannot be changed. Instead, a growth mindset encourages individuals to embrace challenges, persevere despite setbacks, and view failures as opportunities to learn and grow.

Leaders who adopt a growth mindset are better equipped to inspire and motivate their teams to learn and develop continuously. Satya Nadella, CEO of Microsoft, is a prime example of a leader who has embraced a growth mindset. Under his leadership, Microsoft has shifted from a culture of "know-it-alls" to a culture of "learn-it-alls," resulting in increased innovation, collaboration, and overall success for the company.

The science of continuous learning and improvement is rooted in neuroplasticity, feedback loops, and a growth mindset. By understanding and applying these concepts, leaders can foster a culture of continuous learning within their organizations, driving personal and professional growth for themselves and their teams.

Strategies for Leaders to Foster Continuous Learning and Improvement

In today's world, the ability to learn, adapt, and grow has become a crucial determinant of success for individuals and organizations. As the landscape of knowledge and technology expands at an unprecedented pace, continuous learning and improvement have emerged as vital components of leadership. The leaders who truly embrace this notion and who seek to empower their teams to unlock their full potential are the ones who will carve a path to enduring success.

Imagine a world where curiosity thrives, where employees are encouraged to explore new ideas, challenge conventional wisdom, and push the boundaries of their knowledge. In this world, failure is not a stigma but a stepping stone, an opportunity for growth and understanding. It is a world where leaders cultivate an environment that fosters experimentation, embraces the unknown, and celebrates bold, innovative ideas.

It is not a fantasy but a reality in organizations led by visionary leaders like Elon Musk, Jeff Bezos, and Mary Barra. These trailblazers have recognized the transformative power of continuous learning and have made it an integral part of their leadership philosophy. Moreover, they understand that to create a lasting impact, they must invest in their growth and the development of those they lead.

The journey toward fostering continuous learning and improvement begins with the understanding that a leader's most potent weapon is a mindset of perpetual growth. It is the realization that pursuing knowledge and self-improvement is not a destination but a never-ending journey. This journey will enable leaders and their teams to adapt, innovate, and rise above the challenges that the future holds.

As we delve deeper into the strategies for leaders to foster continuous learning and improvement, let us not forget the inspiring examples of those who have come before us. Let their successes and failures serve as guideposts to unlocking the limitless potential of our organizations and ourselves.

- Creating a learning culture within the organization involves fostering an environment where employees are encouraged to expand their knowledge, skills, and abilities. In addition, it requires leaders to prioritize learning as a critical component of their organization's success. For instance, Google's "20% time" policy allows employees to dedicate some of their working hours to pursuing innovative projects and learning new skills. This approach has led to the development of some of Google's most successful products, such as Gmail and Google Maps.
- **Encouraging curiosity and embracing failure as learning opportunities** - To promote continuous learning and improvement, leaders must create a safe space where employees feel comfortable asking questions, exploring new ideas, and taking risks. Jeff Bezos, CEO of Amazon, has strongly advocated embracing failure as a necessary part of innovation and growth. By celebrating failures as learning opportunities, Bezos has cultivated a culture of experimentation and curiosity at Amazon, contributing to the company's unparalleled success.
- **Setting and pursuing challenging goals** - Challenging goals can inspire individuals and teams to push their boundaries, learn new skills, and continually strive for improvement. For example, Sir Richard Branson, the founder of the Virgin Group, is well-known for setting ambitious goals that drive his organizations to achieve remarkable feats, such as pioneering commercial space travel and operating successful businesses in highly competitive sectors like music and airlines. Likewise, leaders can foster a culture of continuous learning and growth by setting high expectations and encouraging employees to work toward these objectives.
- **Implementing regular feedback and reflection processes** - Regular feedback and reflection are essential for learning

and improvement. Leaders should create mechanisms for employees to receive constructive feedback on their performance and reflect on their experiences. For example, Eric Schmidt, former CEO of Google, implemented an "Objectives and Key Results" (OKRs) system that allowed employees to set goals, track progress, and receive feedback on their achievements. This approach has been widely adopted by other leading companies, such as LinkedIn and Twitter, to drive performance and promote a culture of continuous learning.

- **Investing in employee professional development** - Supporting employees' professional development is crucial for fostering continuous organizational learning and improvement. By offering resources, such as training programs, mentorship opportunities, and access to industry conferences, leaders can encourage employees to grow their skills and knowledge. Recognizing the rapid evolution of technology and the need for a skilled workforce to keep pace with it, Ravi Kumar S has launched significant upskilling initiatives. For example, he oversaw the creation of Infosys Wingspan, a cloud-first and mobile-first learning solution, designed to provide continuous learning and upskilling opportunities to Infosys employees, preparing them for the technologies and roles of the future.

Leaders can foster continuous learning and improvement within their organizations by creating a learning culture, encouraging curiosity, setting challenging goals, implementing regular feedback and reflection processes, and investing in employee professional development. By applying these strategies, leaders can empower their teams to embrace new challenges, learn from their experiences, and continually strive for growth and improvement.

The Role of Continuous Learning in Purpose-Driven Leadership

The winds of change and uncertainty constantly buffet the shores of our organizations; it has become increasingly evident that leaders who wish to succeed must possess a specific attribute - the ability to embrace continuous learning. Purpose-driven leadership, a paradigm that has gained significant traction in recent years, acknowledges the importance of this truth. It is a journey filled with ups and downs, twists and turns, and the commitment to continuous learning enables leaders to navigate these challenges with grace and resilience.

Envision a ship's captain steering a vessel through stormy waters, taking responsibility for the lives, the well-being of the crew, and the cargo aboard. As dark skies loom, waves crash, and winds howl, the captain relies on their experience, instincts, and knowledge to ensure the ship's safety. In treacherous conditions, the captain continually adapts and navigates the unpredictable seas. Similarly, purpose-driven leaders must learn to adapt to the constantly changing business environment.

A purpose-driven leader stands at the helm of their organization with a clear vision, a strong sense of purpose, and a deep commitment to the well-being and growth of their employees, customers, and communities. They understand that the success of their organization lies not only in the products or services they provide but also in how they conduct their business and their impact on the world around them.

As the landscape of the global economy shifts, industries transform, and new challenges emerge, purpose-driven leaders must be agile, adaptive, and forward-thinking. This commitment to continuous learning empowers them to steer their organizations through uncharted waters, embrace innovation and change, and cultivate a culture of growth and development that benefits all stakeholders.

Imagine a world where leaders are always learning, growing, and seeking new ways to improve themselves and their organizations. In this world, businesses thrive, employees are engaged and fulfilled, and communities benefit from the positive impact of successful and purpose-driven organizations. It is the world that purpose-driven leaders strive to create - a world where continuous learning is not just an aspiration but a fundamental pillar of leadership.

As we delve into the role of continuous learning in purpose-driven leadership, we will explore its many facets, from adapting to changes in the business environment and staying relevant to ensuring that the organization remains true to its purpose, learning from setbacks, and using them as opportunities for growth. We will also discuss the importance of inspiring and motivating team members through personal growth and development, fostering a culture of continuous learning that benefits the leader and the entire organization.

We will journey through the stories of real-world leaders who have embraced the power of continuous learning, navigated the treacherous waters of change and uncertainty, and emerged more robust and resilient. Through their experiences and insights, we will uncover the secrets to their success and learn valuable lessons that can be applied to our leadership journeys.

As we navigate the complex and often unpredictable seas of purpose-driven leadership, remember that our commitment to continuous learning will ultimately guide us to safe harbor. The North Star illuminates our path and the compass that keeps us on the course, empowering us to steer our organizations toward a brighter and more prosperous future.

So, dear reader, as we set sail on this journey through the world of purpose-driven leadership and continuous learning, I invite you to join me in exploring the depths of this powerful concept. Together, let us uncover the secrets of successful leaders, the lessons they have learned, and the insights they have gained. Let us know from their experiences and apply their wisdom to our own.

- **Adapting to changes in the business environment and staying relevant** - Continuous learning is essential for purpose-driven leaders to adapt to the ever-changing business environment and ensure their organizations remain relevant. As the market evolves, leaders must actively prepare themselves to acquire new knowledge, skills, and perspectives to stay ahead. For example, Jack Welch, former CEO of General Electric, emphasized the importance of continuous learning and adaptation to maintain competitiveness. Under Welch's leadership, General Electric saw massive restructuring, emphasizing reducing bureaucracy and increasing competitiveness. In addition, Welch's policies pivoted the company towards higher-margin, technology-based sectors. As a result, General Electric was able to maintain its industry leadership.
- **Ensuring the organization remains true to its purpose** - Purpose-driven leaders must continually learn and adapt to ensure their organizations stay aligned with their core mission and values. For instance, Howard Schultz, Starbucks's former CEO, and Chairman, has consistently prioritized the company's social and environmental responsibilities alongside its business objectives. By continually learning about and engaging with the issues that matter to Starbucks' stakeholders, Schultz has maintained its commitment to its purpose, even as it has grown into a global brand.
- **Learning from setbacks and using them as opportunities for growth** - Setbacks and failures are inevitable in any

organization. However, purpose-driven leaders recognize the value of learning from these experiences and using them as opportunities for growth. For example, Ursula Burns, former CEO of Xerox, led the company through a significant transformation as it faced increasing competition and declining demand for its core products. By learning from Xerox's challenges, Burns developed and executed a successful turnaround strategy that repositioned the company as a services-focused organization.

- **Inspiring and motivating team members through personal growth and development** - Purpose-driven leaders recognize that continuous learning is crucial for their success and the growth and development of their team members. By investing in the professional development of their employees and fostering a culture of continuous learning, leaders can inspire and motivate their teams to achieve their full potential. For example, Indra Nooyi, former CEO of PepsiCo, championed the importance of developing future leaders within the organization. Under her leadership, PepsiCo implemented various leadership development programs and initiatives that enabled employees to acquire new skills, knowledge, and experiences, ultimately driving the company's long-term success.

Continuous learning plays a critical role in purpose-driven leadership, enabling leaders to adapt to changes in the business environment, ensure their organizations remain true to their purpose, learn from setbacks, and inspire their teams through personal growth and development. By embracing continuous learning, purpose-driven leaders can cultivate a resilient, adaptable, and high-performing organization better equipped to navigate the challenges and opportunities of the modern business landscape.

In exploring the role of continuous learning in purpose-driven leadership, we have journeyed through the stories of exceptional leaders who have embraced the concept of perpetual growth, adaptation, and improvement. We have witnessed the transformative power of learning for the individual leader, the organization, and the world. In this dynamic and ever-evolving global landscape, the need for leaders to be agile, adaptive, and forward-thinking has never been more crucial.

Through the examples of these real-world leaders, we have seen how the commitment to continuous learning has allowed them to adapt to changes in the business environment, stay relevant, and ensure their organizations remain true to their purpose. We have examined how they have harnessed their experiences, learning from setbacks and using them as opportunities for growth. Moreover, we have delved into the importance of inspiring and motivating team members through personal growth and development, creating a culture of learning that benefits the entire organization.

The examples of the leaders we have discussed throughout this journey have demonstrated the undeniable impact of a commitment to learning on an organization's success and ability to fulfill its purpose. As purpose-driven leaders continually invest in their personal growth and development, they create a ripple effect that cascades through their organizations, fostering an environment of innovation, adaptability, and resilience.

For instance, Satya Nadella's emphasis on a growth mindset at Microsoft has reinvigorated company culture and renewed success in the technology industry. Similarly, Indra Nooyi's dedication to learning and ability to adapt during her tenure as CEO of PepsiCo resulted in the company's increased focus on sustainability and healthier product offerings, aligning the organization with its purpose of delivering long-term value to shareholders and society.

These examples testify to the power of continuous learning in purpose-driven leadership. When leaders commit to their growth and development, they improve themselves and create a culture of learning that empowers their teams to reach new heights of success, driving the organization toward fulfilling its purpose.

We cannot overstate the role of continuous learning in purpose-driven leadership. It is the driving force that enables leaders to navigate the ever-changing business landscape, to adapt and innovate, and to inspire and motivate their teams. As we reflect on the lessons learned and insights gained throughout this journey, let us remember the words of American author and educator Alvin Toffler: "The illiterate of the 21st century will not be those who cannot read and write, but those who cannot learn, unlearn, and relearn." Therefore, as purpose-driven leaders, let us commit ourselves to a lifetime of learning, ensuring that our organizations continue to grow, evolve, and fulfill their purpose in an ever-changing world.

Lessons Learned and Insights Gained

In the journey of purposeful leadership, navigating the complex landscape of human emotions, societal expectations, and ever-evolving challenges requires an unwavering commitment to growth and learning. As we traverse the winding path of leadership, we stumble, fall, and rise again, gathering invaluable insights and lessons. By synthesizing these experiences, we can unlock the full potential of our purpose, igniting the spark within ourselves and our teams to create lasting change and impact.

Imagine standing at the precipice of a new beginning, your heart pounding with anticipation as you prepare to embark on a voyage that will not only define your legacy but also shape the lives of countless individuals who look to you for guidance and inspiration. As you peer into the vast expanse of possibilities, the weight of your responsibility becomes palpable, urging you to seek wisdom from those who have come before you, those who have walked the tightrope between aspiration and reality and emerged triumphant.

The stories of extraordinary leaders from diverse backgrounds and industries paint a vivid tapestry of the intricate dance between failure and success, humility and ambition, vulnerability and strength. These tales of perseverance and courage, woven from the threads of human experience, offer us a glimpse into the minds and hearts of individuals who dared to believe in a purpose greater than themselves. This purpose transcended personal gain and left an indelible mark on the world.

Eleanor Roosevelt embarked on a remarkable journey, championing human rights and embodying an unwavering commitment to social justice. As she navigated the turbulent waters of a nation grappling with economic depression and war, she drew upon her profound lessons of resilience and empathy to advocate for the marginalized. Through tireless efforts in reforming society and promoting equality, Roosevelt demonstrated the transformative power of purposeful leadership, inspiring millions worldwide to embrace a higher calling.

The trailblazing path of Indra Nooyi, the former CEO of PepsiCo, shattered the glass ceiling in corporate America and redefined the role of business in society. As she navigated the treacherous waters of global markets and stakeholder expectations, she remained steadfast in her belief that companies could—and should—play a meaningful role in addressing the world's most pressing challenges. Under her visionary leadership, PepsiCo embarked on a bold journey to integrate purpose into its core, reshaping the industry's landscape and leaving a legacy for future generations.

These remarkable leaders, and countless others, serve as beacons of hope and wisdom for those of us who aspire to walk the path of purposeful leadership. In the following pages, we will delve into the captivating stories of leaders from various realms—business, politics, and beyond—to uncover the invaluable lessons and insights they have gleaned along their journeys. By exploring their experiences, we will distill the essence of purposeful leadership, offering guidance and inspiration for those who seek to lead with purpose and make a difference in the world.

As we embark on this enlightening voyage, let us remember that each of our journeys is unique, shaped by the contours of our personal experiences and the tapestry of our shared humanity. The lessons and insights gleaned from the lives of purpose-driven leaders are not prescriptive blueprints but signposts, pointing us toward a deeper understanding of ourselves and the world around us. It is our responsibility, as purposeful leaders, to embrace the wisdom of those who have come before us, and to forge our paths, guided by the light of our purpose and the unwavering belief in our ability to make a difference.

So, let us begin this journey with open hearts and minds as we explore the captivating stories of purpose-driven leaders and their invaluable lessons. Let us immerse ourselves in the world of these extraordinary individuals, allowing their experiences to shape our understanding of what it means to lead with purpose. And as we traverse this landscape of wisdom and inspiration, let us remain steadfast in our commitment to growth and learning, for it is through the continuous pursuit of knowledge and understanding that we can unlock the full potential of our purpose.

As we delve into the intricate tapestry of human experience, we will witness the transformative power of purposeful leadership as it transcends boundaries, unites diverse communities, and paves the way for a brighter, more equitable future. We will explore the delicate balance between aspiration and reality as leaders navigate the complex landscape of human emotions, societal expectations, and ever-evolving challenges. And we will learn from their triumphs and setbacks as they demonstrate the resilience, adaptability, and unwavering commitment to their purpose at the heart of authentic leadership.

Together, we will embark on a journey that takes us across the globe, from the boardrooms of Silicon Valley to the bustling streets of New Delhi and from the hallowed halls of political power to the grassroots movements reshaping the world. Along the way, we will witness the indomitable spirit of purpose-driven leaders as they strive to make a difference in the lives of those they serve and create a legacy of impact and change.

As we traverse this enlightening path, let us remember that the footsteps of others do not define our journeys. However, by the unique paths, we forge as we strive to lead with purpose. Therefore, the lessons and insights gained from these stories do not serve as a prescriptive blueprint but as guiding stars, illuminating our way as we actively navigate the challenges and opportunities.

So, let us step forward into this world of wisdom and inspiration, armed with the knowledge, insights, and experiences of those who have come before us. Let us embrace the opportunity to learn from their journeys as we strive to unlock the full potential of our purpose and create a lasting impact in the world.

May the stories and lessons of these 20 purpose-driven leaders serve as a testament to the transformative power of leading with purpose, inspiring us to rise above our limitations, overcome adversity, and create meaningful change in the world. So, with open hearts and minds, let us embark on this journey together, and may the lessons learned and insights gained serve as a beacon of hope, wisdom, and inspiration for generations to come.

Anand Mahindra, Chairman of Mahindra Group

Anand Mahindra, the chairman of the Mahindra Group, is one of the most admired and respected business leaders in India and globally today. Leading a multinational conglomerate that operates across several industries, including automotive, finance, IT, leisure, and hospitality, he has been instrumental in driving the group's transformation into a global powerhouse. His leadership style embodies purposeful leadership - driven by a clear, meaningful purpose and a deep commitment to positively impacting the world. He is known for his strategic thinking, customer-centric approach, commitment to sustainability, and focus on people and culture. But above all, he is known for his ability to inspire and motivate his team members to achieve their full potential and positively impact the world.

One of the most significant examples of purposeful leadership is transforming the Mahindra Group into a globally competitive and sustainable organization. When Anand took the company's reins, he knew he needed to make significant changes to ensure the company's future success. Moreover, he understood that the global business landscape was changing rapidly and that the company needed to adapt to these changes to remain competitive.

Anand's vision was to transform the company into a global leader in the automotive industry, and he knew that achieving this goal would require a clear strategic plan and a commitment to innovation and sustainability. In addition, he believed that the company's financial performance and impact on society and the environment would measure its success. Under his leadership, the company embarked on a strategic transformation journey. He led the company in developing innovative, high-quality products that meet the needs of customers around the world. He also made sustainability a key focus of the company's strategy, implementing initiatives to reduce its environmental footprint and contribute to the communities in which it operates.

The result of purposeful leadership has been the successful transformation of the Mahindra Group into a global leader in the automotive industry, with a strong commitment to sustainability and social responsibility. As a result, the company's revenues and profitability have experienced significant growth. Furthermore, the company has garnered industry recognition for its commitment to sustainability, innovation, and customer satisfaction. Key lessons or purposeful leadership traits from Anand Mahindra's leadership include:

- Clear Vision: Anand's vision for the company's future was critical to its successful transformation. He understood the changes happening in the global business landscape. He had a clear vision of how the company needed to adapt to remain competitive.
- Commitment to Sustainability: He understands that businesses are responsible for contributing to society and the environment, and he has made sustainability a key focus of the company's strategy.
- Focus on People and Culture: He strongly emphasizes people and culture. He believes that the company's success depends on its people's success, and he has created a culture that values innovation, collaboration, and mutual respect.

- Ability to Inspire and Motivate: Mahindra has a unique ability to inspire and motivate his team members. He leads by example and encourages his team members to strive for excellence and positively impact the world.
- Strategic Thinking - He has a deep understanding of the business landscape. As a result, he can develop clear, strategic plans to achieve the company's objectives.

Angela Merkel, Chancellor of Germany (2005-2021)

Angela Merkel, the first woman to ever hold the office of Chancellor in Germany and widely regarded as one of the world's most powerful women, has become a symbol of steady and purposeful leadership during her tenure. Merkel's often pragmatic, scientific, and methodical leadership style stems from her research scientist background.

One of the most significant examples of Merkel's purposeful leadership is her managing the European refugee crisis in 2015. During this period, hundreds of thousands of refugees from war-torn countries like Syria and Afghanistan sought asylum in Europe.

What Merkel did was a bold and, to some, a controversial move. First, she announced that Germany would keep its borders open, allowing more than one million refugees to enter the country. This decision was grounded in her commitment to the human rights principles that Germany and the European Union hold dear. Moreover, she saw a humanitarian crisis unfolding and felt responsible for acting. She famously said, "Wir schaffen das" or "We can handle it," displaying a sense of optimism and resilience in the face of a severe crisis.

The process was not straightforward. Merkel had to navigate complex political, social, and logistical challenges to implement her decision. There was significant opposition both domestically and from other European leaders. But she remained resolute, working with her team, NGOs, and local communities to ensure the refugees were received, registered, and integrated into German society. She also used her diplomatic skills to negotiate with other European leaders and push for a collective European response to the crisis.

The result of Merkel's decision was a mixed bag. While it led to a rise in right-wing nationalism and temporarily strained some of Germany's international relations, many applaud Merkel for her compassionate response to the crisis. She demonstrated that a country could uphold its humanitarian values under immense pressure. The integration process of refugees is ongoing, with notable successes in education and labor market participation.

Key lessons or purposeful leadership traits from Angela Merkel's leadership during the refugee crisis include:

- Humanitarian Principles: Merkel's decision to open Germany's borders was grounded in humanitarian principles. She demonstrated that upholding these principles, even in challenging situations, is critical to purposeful leadership.
- Resilience and Steadfastness: Merkel remained steadfast in her decision despite significant opposition and challenges. She showed resilience in the face of criticism, staying focused on the task.
- Diplomatic Negotiation: Merkel used her diplomatic skills to negotiate with other European leaders and advocate for a collective response to the crisis. It highlights the importance of negotiation and diplomacy in purposeful leadership.
- Forward-thinking: Merkel's "Wir schaffen das" statement displayed her forward-thinking approach. She showed

confidence in Germany's ability to handle the crisis, inspiring others to do the same.

- Inclusive Decision-making: Merkel worked closely with her team, NGOs, and local communities in managing the crisis. This inclusive approach guaranteed that decision-making considered diverse perspectives and expertise.

Angela Merkel's leadership during the European refugee crisis exemplifies purposeful leadership. Her commitment to humanitarian principles, resilience, diplomatic negotiation skills, forward-thinking approach, and inclusive decision-making have made her one of the most respected leaders globally, leaving a lasting impact on Germany and the world.

Aung San Suu Kyi, Myanmar's State Counsellor and Leader of the National League for Democracy (NLD)

Aung San Suu Kyi, the Nobel Peace Prize laureate, was recognized as the embodiment of stoic resistance in the face of oppression when she emerged as a national icon during Myanmar's struggle for democracy. As the leader of the National League for Democracy (NLD), she dedicated her life to establishing a democratic government in a nation stifled by military rule.

One defining moment of Suu Kyi's purposeful leadership unfolded in the late 1980s. As Myanmar underwent a major political upheaval, with widespread protests against the military regimes, Kyi found herself thrust into the limelight. Her father, Aung San, was a revered figure in Myanmar's fight for independence. With her eloquence and bravery, Suu Kyi seemed a fitting heir to his legacy.

In 1988, she delivered a powerful speech at the Shwedagon Pagoda in Yangon, calling for a democratic government. Her commitment to democracy and human rights, courage to speak against the authoritarian regime, and willingness to risk her freedom for the nation's cause resonated with millions of Burmese citizens. She mobilized the masses and used nonviolent means to resist the military junta, much like Mahatma Gandhi and Martin Luther King Jr.

Her actions were not without consequences. The military regime placed her under house arrest in 1989, where she would spend 15 of the next 21 years isolated from her family and supporters. However, she never wavered from her convictions, using her time under arrest to read extensively and write about freedom and human rights.

In 2010, the authorities finally released Suu Kyi from house arrest. In 2015, her party, the NLD, won a landslide victory in the general elections, marking a significant milestone in Myanmar's transition to democracy. However, controversies have marred her leadership since then, particularly due to her handling of the Rohingya crisis. Her actions in this regard have drawn international criticism and have caused damage to her reputation as a champion of human rights.

Key purposeful leadership traits from Aung San Suu Kyi's leadership include:

- Courage and Conviction: Suu Kyi stood up against the authoritarian regime, demonstrating immense courage and steadfast conviction in her fight for democracy.
- Resilience: Despite the personal sacrifices and the long years under house arrest, Suu Kyi remained resilient, using her time to educate herself further and plan for a democratic Myanmar.

- Nonviolent Resistance: Following leaders like Gandhi, Suu Kyi employed nonviolent resistance, emphasizing the power of peaceful means to achieve political ends.
- Eloquence and Communication: Suu Kyi effectively communicated her vision for a democratic Myanmar, mobilizing millions of Burmese citizens and gaining international support.
- Understanding of Human Rights: Her writings and speeches display a deep understanding of human rights, which she upheld as fundamental to her vision of a democratic Myanmar.

Suu Kyi's leadership journey presents a complex narrative. Her early leadership, marked by courage, resilience, and an unwavering commitment to democracy, is a testament to purposeful leadership. However, her recent leadership raises questions about the importance of ethical considerations in purposeful leadership, reminding us that a leader's purpose and actions must align with universally recognized human rights and justice principles.

Doug McMillon, CEO of Walmart

Doug McMillon, the CEO of Walmart, is a leader with a clear vision and purpose. Under his leadership, Walmart, the world's largest retailer by revenue, has seen substantial evolution and growth, with a focus on sustainability and technology.

One of McMillon's most significant leadership moments is his decision to increase wages for Walmart's lowest-paid workers. In 2015, he announced that Walmart would raise its minimum wage to $9 an hour, significantly above the federal minimum wage. This decision reflected McMillon's belief in investing in employees to increase productivity and reduce turnover. In addition, it was a strategic move to position Walmart as a responsible corporate citizen.

This decision did not come without scrutiny. Critics questioned the impact on Walmart's bottom line and the feasibility of such a wage increase across a workforce of more than 2 million employees. However, McMillon stood by his decision, seeing it as an investment in his employees, whom he often refers to as "associates," and the company's future.

His approach proved successful. The wage increase decreased employee turnover and increased customer satisfaction due to better-staffed and more motivated teams. It also improved the company's public image, positioning Walmart as a leader in corporate social responsibility.

Another defining moment in McMillon's leadership was his response to the El Paso shooting incident 2019. After a horrific mass shooting in a Walmart store in El Paso, Texas, McMillon stopped selling ammunition for handguns and short-barrel rifles in all Walmart stores. Given the company's history as a major firearms retailer, this is a significant move.

This decision, deeply rooted in McMillon's commitment to social responsibility, demonstrated his ability to balance the needs of multiple stakeholders – from customers, employees, and shareholders to the broader communities that Walmart serves. It also highlighted his willingness to make tough decisions that align with the company's purpose and values, even in the face of potential backlash.

Key purposeful leadership traits from Doug McMillon's leadership include:

- Employee-Centric Approach: McMillon's decision to raise wages demonstrates his belief in investing in employees. He recognized that satisfied, well-compensated employees lead to increased productivity and customer satisfaction.

- Social Responsibility: McMillon has shown a commitment to corporate social responsibility, demonstrated by the wage increase decision and the new policy on ammunition sales. He understands that as the leader of a global corporation, his decisions have far-reaching implications.
- Strategic Decision-Making: McMillon's decisions, although sometimes controversial, are strategic and focused on long-term sustainability. He is willing to make tough decisions that align with the company's purpose and values.
- Visionary Leadership: McMillon has a clear vision for Walmart's future. He has embraced technology, sustainability, and social responsibility, positioning Walmart as a leader in the evolving retail landscape.
- Communication: McMillon effectively communicates his vision and decisions to employees, shareholders, and the public, ensuring stakeholders understand and align with the company's direction.

Jensen Huang, co-founder, and CEO of Nvidia

Jensen Huang, co-founder, and CEO of Nvidia, is a visionary leader who has propelled his company to become a dominant force in computing, gaming, and artificial intelligence. He has exemplified purposeful leadership through strategic decisions, technological foresight, and an unwavering commitment to innovation.

One of the defining episodes of Huang's leadership took place during the mid-2000s when Nvidia was primarily known as a manufacturer of graphics processor units (GPUs) for gaming. Huang, however, envisioned a broader role for GPUs. He believed they could be repurposed as general computing processors capable of solving complex mathematical problems, thus paving the way for accelerated computing and advanced artificial intelligence applications.

This bold vision faced considerable resistance both within and outside the company. Critics argued that changing the direction of Nvidia's successful, gaming-focused business model was a risky move. But Huang stood firm, driven by his conviction that GPUs had the potential to revolutionize computing.

With this vision in mind, Huang led the development of CUDA, a parallel computing platform and application programming interface model created by Nvidia. CUDA allowed software developers to write programs that could harness the power of Nvidia's GPUs for computational tasks, thus transforming these graphics-focused processors into general-purpose GPUs (GPGPUs).

This strategic shift has been nothing short of transformative for Nvidia. By pioneering GPU-accelerated computing, Huang positioned Nvidia at the forefront of the AI revolution. Today, Nvidia's GPUs power some of the world's most advanced supercomputers and are used by researchers and industries worldwide to advance AI and machine learning.

Key purposeful leadership traits from Jensen Huang's leadership include:

- Visionary Thinking: Huang's foresight into the potential of GPUs for general-purpose computing set the stage for Nvidia's evolution and growth into new markets, including AI and data centers.
- Risk-taking and Resilience: Huang was willing to take calculated risks and face resistance to realize his vision for Nvidia.

His resilience in the face of skepticism and criticism played a crucial role in driving the company's strategic shift.

- Innovation and Adaptability: Huang's commitment to innovation and ability to adapt to changing technological landscapes has allowed Nvidia to remain a leading player in the tech industry.
- Strategic Decision-Making: Huang's strategic decision to develop CUDA and promote GPGPU computing has been instrumental in securing Nvidia's position as a dominant force in AI and high-performance computing.
- Communication: Huang effectively communicated his vision and strategic decisions to employees, shareholders, and the wider tech community, fostering understanding and buy-in for his innovative ideas.

Under Jensen Huang's purposeful leadership, Nvidia has transformed from a gaming-focused GPU manufacturer to a multifaceted tech giant at the forefront of AI, data center technology, and high-performance computing. His strategic vision, commitment to innovation, and resilient leadership offer valuable lessons for industry leaders.

Elon Musk, CEO of Tesla and SpaceX

Elon Musk, the CEO of Tesla and SpaceX, has become a poster child for purposeful leadership in the 21st century. His audacious vision and relentless drive have transformed industries and sparked a new age of technological advancement.

One of the most remarkable examples of Musk's leadership is his role in the founding and development of SpaceX. In 2002, when commercial space travel was considered a pipe dream, Musk set out to make it a reality. His goal: to make life multi-planetary and ensure the survival of humanity in the event of a terrestrial catastrophe.

This vision was ambitious. The barriers to entry in the aerospace industry were astronomical, with high costs, significant technological challenges, and a dominant presence of government-backed entities like NASA. Yet, Musk's determination remained unshaken. He invested his fortune in SpaceX and set out to build a privately funded, reusable rocket.

A series of failures marked SpaceX's early years. The first three launches of their Falcon 1 rocket ended in explosions, draining the company's resources and bringing it to the brink of bankruptcy. However, Musk's unwavering determination and resilience carried the company through these challenging times. He poured his remaining funds into one final launch attempt.

In September 2008, the fourth Falcon 1 launch successfully reached orbit, marking the first privately funded, liquid-fueled rocket to do so. This pivotal moment saved SpaceX from financial ruin and set the stage for remarkable achievements, including developing the Falcon 9 and Falcon Heavy rockets, the Dragon spacecraft, and the first private crewed spacecraft to dock with the International Space Station.

Key purposeful leadership traits from Elon Musk's journey with SpaceX include:

- Visionary Thinking: Musk's ambitious vision of making life multi-planetary has guided SpaceX's mission and strategy since its inception.
- Risk-Tolerance: Musk's willingness to risk his fortune and face potential failure demonstrates a risk-tolerance characteristic of purposeful leaders.

- Resilience: Musk's resilience has enabled him to persevere and lead SpaceX to incredible success despite numerous setbacks and challenges.
- Innovation: Musk's commitment to innovation and continuous improvement has driven SpaceX to develop groundbreaking technology and disrupt the aerospace industry.
- Communication: Musk's ability to communicate his ambitious vision and rally his team around it has been critical to SpaceX's success.

Under Musk's purposeful leadership, SpaceX has revolutionized space travel and brought humanity one step closer to becoming a spacefaring civilization. His bold vision, risk tolerance, resilience, and commitment to innovation offer valuable lessons for leaders across industries. Elon Musk's leadership journey is a testament to the power of purpose in driving transformative change and achieving what many believed impossible.

Hamdi Ulukaya, CEO of Chobani

Hamdi Ulukaya, the founder and CEO of Chobani, is a shining example of purposeful leadership. His journey from a Kurdish shepherd in Turkey to the head of one of America's most successful yogurt companies is inspiring and filled with invaluable leadership lessons.

Ulukaya's purposeful leadership was evident when he purchased a defunct Kraft Foods factory in upstate New York in 2005 to make high-quality, nutritious yogurt accessible to all. With no prior experience in yogurt production, he faced significant challenges. However, his purpose drove him to make better food for more people, and he was willing to go to great lengths to fulfill it.

One of the most striking instances of Ulukaya's purposeful leadership is his decision to institute the Chobani Shares program in 2016. He recognized his employees' hard work and dedication and gave them a 10% stake in the company. As a result, if Chobani were to be sold or go public, some employees would stand to make hundreds of thousands, if not millions, of dollars. Chobani's move was unconventional, especially given the company's size, and it garnered praise and skepticism.

Ulukaya's decision was rooted in his belief that his employees were instrumental in the company's success and they deserved to share in the rewards. He demonstrated an understanding that true leadership involves not just guiding a team but also recognizing their contribution to the company's success. His move fostered a sense of unity and loyalty among his workforce, boosting productivity.

Another noteworthy incident occurred in 2015 when Chobani faced a significant downturn. Instead of resorting to layoffs, Ulukaya took a personal pay cut and worked tirelessly to turn the company around, demonstrating his commitment to his employees and his purpose of providing better food for more people.

Ulukaya's leadership has transformed Chobani from a small startup into a billion-dollar business that has revolutionized the American yogurt industry. His purposeful approach to leadership has resulted in a highly successful company and positively impacted the lives of his employees and the broader community.

Key purposeful leadership traits from Hamdi Ulukaya's leadership include:

- Vision: Ulukaya envisioned a company that would produce healthy, delicious yogurt accessible to all. His clear vision guided every decision he made for Chobani.

- Empathy and Generosity: Ulukaya's decision to share 10% of the company's equity with employees demonstrated his empathy and generosity, fostering loyalty and motivation among his workforce.
- Resilience: Despite facing significant challenges, Ulukaya's resilience allowed him to navigate them successfully, maintaining his commitment to his employees and purpose.
- Innovation: Ulukaya's innovative approach to yogurt production and employee engagement has significantly disrupted the industry.
- Commitment: Ulukaya's unwavering commitment to his vision and his employees has been a driving force behind Chobani's success.

Ulukaya has redefined what success can look like in the corporate world through his purposeful leadership. This powerful story serves as a reminder that when leaders guide their actions with a clear purpose and demonstrate commitment to their employees, they can build successful companies and foster more equitable and compassionate workplaces.

Howard Schultz, Former CEO and Chairman of Starbucks

Howard Schultz, former CEO and Chairman of Starbucks is a paragon of purposeful leadership. From his humble beginnings in Brooklyn to his ascension to the helm of one of the world's most recognized brands, Schultz's leadership journey stands out for his steadfast commitment to his purpose – to inspire and nurture the human spirit, one person, one cup, one neighborhood at a time.

One of the most poignant instances of Schultz's purposeful leadership was his response to the economic downturn 2008. Amidst the turbulence, Starbucks suffered a severe blow, as it experienced a significant decline in sales. As a result, many were advocating for cost-cutting measures like store closures and layoffs. However, Schultz, who returned as CEO after an eight-year hiatus, had a different vision.

Understanding that the heart and soul of Starbucks was the connection between the baristas and the customers, Schultz made an unprecedented move. He decided to invest in his people. So in the middle of the crisis, Starbucks shut down all of its US stores for a day to retrain baristas to make espresso. The message was clear – Starbucks was committed to the quality of its product and the experience of its customers.

This move was a risk, both financially and reputationally. However, Schultz was unwavering in his belief that investing in people and product quality would pay off in the long run. His decision paid dividends, reinvigorating the company's culture and restoring customer trust. Today, Starbucks is one of the most admired companies in the world, a testament to Schultz's purposeful leadership.

Another example of Schultz's purposeful leadership is his commitment to social impact. Under his leadership, Starbucks launched comprehensive health coverage for eligible full- and part-time workers, a rarity in the retail sector, and the pioneering Starbucks College Achievement Plan. In addition, this program provides tuition-free online college education for eligible employees. Schultz drove these initiatives based on his belief that businesses should balance profitability with a social conscience.

Schultz's leadership has left an indelible mark on Starbucks and the broader business landscape. His purpose-driven approach has not only driven Starbucks to new heights of success. However, it has also redefined the role of a for-profit corporation.

Key purposeful leadership traits from Howard Schultz's leadership include:

- Vision: Schultz had a clear vision for Starbucks – to inspire and nurture the human spirit. This vision guided his leadership, especially during challenging times.
- Courage: Schultz demonstrated courage in making bold decisions, such as investing in employee training during the economic downturn and offering comprehensive benefits to employees.
- Empathy: Schultz's decision to provide health coverage and tuition-free college education reflects his empathy and belief in treating employees with dignity and respect.
- Commitment to Quality: Schultz's commitment to product quality and customer experience is a cornerstone of Starbucks' success.
- Social Responsibility: Schultz has shown that businesses can be profitable while positively impacting society.

Howard Schultz's leadership journey is a powerful example of purposeful leadership in action. His story underscores that a clear purpose, courage, empathy, a commitment to quality, and a sense of social responsibility, can drive both business success and positive social impact.

Indra Nooyi, Former CEO of PepsiCo

Indra Nooyi, the former CEO of PepsiCo, is widely recognized as a pioneer of purposeful leadership. During her 12-year tenure as

CEO, she transformed PepsiCo into a forward-thinking company, steadfastly guided by her ethos of "Performance with Purpose."

A seminal moment of Nooyi's purposeful leadership was in 2006, when she boldly repositioned PepsiCo's corporate strategy. With the rise of health consciousness among consumers and increasing criticisms of the food and beverage industry's role in public health issues, Nooyi recognized that the status quo was untenable for the company's long-term growth.

Against significant internal and external resistance, she launched the "Performance with Purpose" initiative. This bold strategy aimed to marry the company's financial performance with social responsibility. It encompassed transforming the product portfolio with healthier offerings, reducing the environmental footprint, and empowering associates and people in the communities PepsiCo served.

Pivoting a company synonymous with sugary beverages and snacks towards healthier products was no easy task. But Nooyi was steadfast in her belief that companies must "do well by doing good." So she integrated purpose into PepsiCo's business model. Moreover, she firmly believed that the company's success and societal impact were inherently linked.

The results of Nooyi's purposeful leadership and the "Performance with Purpose" initiative are tangible. PepsiCo significantly expanded its nutritious product offerings and reduced over 3 million tons of greenhouse gas emissions. It provided access to at least 3 billion servings of healthy foods and beverages to underserved communities and consumers. Under Nooyi's leadership, PepsiCo's net revenue grew from $35 billion in 2006 to $63.5 billion in 2017, proving that purpose and profitability coexist.

Moreover, Nooyi's commitment to diversity and inclusion was another hallmark of her purposeful leadership. She championed gender equality in the workplace and launched initiatives to develop women leaders within PepsiCo. As a result, Nooyi herself shattered the glass ceiling, serving as an inspiration to countless women around the world.

Key purposeful leadership traits from Indra Nooyi's leadership include:

- Visionary Thinking: Nooyi foresaw the shift in consumer preferences towards healthier products and sustainability. She had the foresight to pivot PepsiCo's strategy, ensuring its continued relevance and growth.
- Courage: Nooyi faced significant resistance when she launched "Performance with Purpose." But she dared to stand by her convictions and lead PepsiCo through this transformation.
- Resilience: The journey faced its share of obstacles, but Nooyi demonstrated remarkable strength in confronting challenges and staying the course until she realized her vision.
- Empathy: Nooyi's focus on diversity and inclusion and her commitment to improving societal health outcomes show her empathy and understanding of businesses' broader societal role.
- Long-term Orientation: Nooyi was willing to make short-term sacrifices for long-term benefits, a trait central to purposeful leadership.

Indra Nooyi's leadership at PepsiCo is a potent example of purposeful leadership in action. Her strategic foresight, resilience, and unwavering commitment to doing what's right have not only transformed PepsiCo but also redefined the role of businesses in the 21st century.

Jacinda Ardern, Former Prime Minister of New Zealand

Jacinda Ardern, Former Prime Minister of New Zealand, is widely recognized as an embodiment of purposeful leadership, consistently demonstrating empathy, decisiveness, and effective communication throughout her tenure. One of the most illustrative examples of her leadership style is her response to the COVID-19 pandemic.

When the pandemic first emerged in early 2020, Ardern quickly recognized its potential severity. From the outset, she was clear about her goal – eliminating the virus from New Zealand. It was a significant decision when many countries opted for a mitigation strategy to slow the spread rather than stop it.

Ardern based her approach on the understanding that protecting public health was a moral imperative and the most effective way to safeguard the economy in the long term. She communicated this strategy with clarity, empathy, and transparency, ensuring the public was well-informed and on board with the stringent measures required to achieve elimination.

Under Ardern's leadership, New Zealand implemented a swift and strict lockdown, going "hard and early," in her own words. These measures were undoubtedly disruptive, but Ardern's consistent communication, which blended scientific evidence with compassion, helped the public understand and accept them.

The result of Ardern's decisive and empathetic leadership was a successful elimination strategy that saw New Zealand return to normalcy. At the same time, many other countries continued to grapple with the virus. Moreover, her leadership throughout the crisis helped keep New Zealand's COVID-19 cases remarkably low and earned her high public approval ratings.

Ardern's leadership style also exemplifies her response to the Christchurch Mosque shootings in 2019. She displayed remarkable empathy and resolved, standing in solidarity with the Muslim community and swiftly advocating for stricter gun laws.

Key purposeful leadership traits gleaned from Jacinda Ardern's handling of these incidents include:

- Empathy: Ardern consistently leads with empathy, understanding, and addressing the emotional needs of her constituents. This empathy has been a hallmark of her leadership, helping to build trust and unity.
- Decisiveness: In times of crisis, Ardern has shown that she can make tough decisions quickly. Her swift actions in response to the COVID-19 pandemic and the Christchurch shootings have been crucial in mitigating their impact.
- Effective Communication: Ardern is an outstanding communicator who conveys complex information clearly and transparently. Her communication skills have been instrumental in securing public buy-in for challenging measures.
- Clarity of Purpose: Ardern effectively communicates her decisions guided by a clear purpose and values. This clarity helps provide direction and instill confidence in times of uncertainty.
- Resilience: Ardern's leadership demonstrates resilience, with her ability to guide her nation through multiple crises, maintain her composure, and focus on her nation's wellbeing.

Jacinda Ardern exemplifies purposeful leadership. Her empathy, decisiveness, outstanding communication skills, clarity of purpose, and resilience make her a role model for leaders worldwide. Her leadership during the COVID-19 pandemic and in the aftermath of the

Christchurch shootings demonstrates how purposeful leadership can guide nations through crisis and foster unity and resilience.

Kiran Mazumdar-Shaw, Founder of Biocon

Kiran Mazumdar-Shaw, the founder of Biocon, is a pioneering figure in the global biotechnology industry and one of the most successful businesswomen in India. Her extraordinary journey to the top of this traditionally male-dominated field provides a wealth of insights into the nature of purposeful leadership.

Mazumdar-Shaw started Biocon in 1978 in her garage in Bangalore, India, with a seed capital of just $500. Despite facing numerous challenges, including skepticism from banks and a lack of credence due to her gender and young age, she persisted, driven by her passion for biotechnology and a vision to make a difference in the world.

In the early 2000s, India, like many other low- and middle-income countries, grappled with a growing burden of chronic diseases, particularly diabetes. The cost of insulin, a critical drug for managing diabetes, was prohibitively high for many patients. Recognizing this, Mazumdar-Shaw embarked on a mission to make insulin affordable for patients in India and globally.

She spearheaded Biocon's efforts to produce human insulin using Pichia, a proprietary, yeast-based fermentation technology. This innovative and cost-effective approach allowed Biocon to produce high-quality insulin at a fraction of the cost of traditional methods. Despite the technical complexities and regulatory hurdles, Mazumdar-Shaw's steadfast commitment to her purpose ensured that Biocon persevered.

In 2004, Biocon launched Insugen, its recombinant human insulin, in India. The company priced the drug significantly lower than imported options, making it accessible to more patients. As a result, Biocon's insulin is now available in several emerging markets, improving access to this life-saving drug for millions of patients worldwide.

This accomplishment was a testament to Mazumdar-Shaw's purposeful leadership. She navigated numerous obstacles to create significant value for her company and society by focusing on a clear, socially relevant objective.

Kiran Mazumdar-Shaw's journey yields the following key lessons and purposeful leadership traits:

- Visionary: Mazumdar-Shaw had a clear vision for Biocon and the role it could play in addressing healthcare challenges. This vision guided her actions and helped her persevere in adversity.
- Resilience: Her journey was fraught with challenges, but she displayed remarkable resilience. She did not let setbacks deter her from her purpose.
- Innovative: Mazumdar-Shaw's approach to producing insulin was innovative, demonstrating her ability to think outside the box to achieve her goals.
- Socially Conscious: A defining characteristic of her leadership is her focus on creating social value. For example, she recognized the need for affordable insulin and made it her mission to address this gap.
- Determined: Despite the skepticism she faced as a young woman entrepreneur in a male-dominated industry, she remained determined and proved her detractors wrong.

Kiran Mazumdar-Shaw's leadership at Biocon exemplifies how purposeful leadership can drive innovation and create significant social impact. Her vision, resilience, innovation, social consciousness, and determination have built a successful global business and improved access to essential medicines for millions of patients worldwide. She continues to inspire leaders across sectors, demonstrating the power of purpose in driving transformative change.

Mary Barra, CEO of General Motors (GM)

Mary Barra, the CEO of General Motors (GM), is a shining example of a purposeful leader. She has navigated the company through significant challenges and championed a bold vision for its future. Her decisive actions in times of crisis and her forward-looking stance on electric vehicles (EVs) underscore her leadership prowess.

One of Barra's most significant leadership tests occurred in 2014, less than two months into her tenure as CEO when GM became engulfed in a recall crisis. The company recalled 2.6 million vehicles due to a faulty ignition switch linked to several fatalities. Barra's response to this crisis offers valuable lessons in purposeful leadership.

Rather than downplaying the issue or deflecting blame, Barra took full responsibility. She initiated an internal investigation, publicly acknowledged the company's mistakes, and apologized to the victims' families. Moreover, she made sweeping changes to GM's safety practices and established a compensation fund for the victims.

Barra's decisive and empathetic response helped GM navigate the crisis. It signaled a new era of transparency and accountability at the company. In addition, her actions demonstrated a commitment to putting customers' safety first, underscoring the purpose-driven nature of her leadership.

In addition to handling crises, Barra has shown purposeful leadership in steering GM toward a sustainable future. Recognizing the threat of climate change and the role of the automotive industry in addressing it, she has committed GM to an ambitious goal: to stop selling gasoline and diesel vehicles by 2035 and to become carbon neutral by 2040.

Achieving this goal involves a massive shift in GM's business model from internal combustion engines to EVs. Barra has backed this vision with significant investments, pledging $27 billion towards developing EVs and autonomous vehicles by 2025.

Given the current dominance of gasoline vehicles in the global market, this bold move is not without risks. However, Barra's commitment to sustainability underscores her willingness to make tough decisions for long-term value creation and societal impact.

Key lessons and purposeful leadership traits from Mary Barra's tenure at GM include:

- Accountability: Barra displayed high accountability during the recall crisis, taking responsibility for the company's mistakes and making necessary changes.
- Empathy: Her concern for the victims of the faulty ignition switch and her commitment to customer safety showed her empathy, a critical trait for purposeful leaders.
- Courage: Barra has shown remarkable courage in committing GM to a future dominated by EVs, despite the risks and uncertainties involved.

- Long-term orientation: Her focus on sustainability and long-term value creation, rather than short-term profits, clearly indicates her long-term orientation.
- Transparency: Barra has fostered a culture of transparency at the company by openly acknowledging GM's mistakes and communicating her plans.

Mary Barra's leadership at GM epitomizes purposeful leadership. Her handling of the recall crisis demonstrated her accountability, empathy, and transparency. At the same time, her commitment to sustainability reflects her courage and long-term orientation. As a result, her actions serve as a valuable guide for leaders seeking to navigate challenges and drive meaningful change in their organizations.

Narayana Murthy, Founder of Infosys

Narayana Murthy, the Founder of Infosys, is a prime example of purposeful leadership, demonstrating how a singular vision, integrity, and unyielding determination can lead to the creation of one of the world's leading technology companies.

Born into a modest family in India, Murthy faced financial constraints during his educational years. However, this did not deter him from pursuing his ambitions. Post-graduation, he worked with Patni Computer Systems in Pune, India, where he saw the enormous potential of the nascent IT industry. However, his vision of creating a world-class Indian IT company seemed far-fetched, given the country's limited access to technology and foreign investment.

In 1981, Murthy and six other software professionals co-founded Infosys with a paltry sum of INR 10,000 borrowed from his wife,

Sudha Murthy. The establishment of Infosys was motivated by Murthy's desire to create an Indian company that could compete with the best globally. In addition, he sought to disrupt the status quo and create a company emphasizing integrity, transparency, and fairness.

The early days were fraught with difficulties. Securing the required licenses and permissions was challenging due to the tight regulations in the Indian economy. Additionally, access to capital and technology was limited. However, Murthy's unwavering commitment and clarity of purpose saw Infosys through these challenges. He championed the global delivery model, which became a game-changer in the IT services sector.

One of Murthy's defining moments as a leader came in the early 2000s when corporate governance scandals rocked the global IT industry. Murthy, then the chairman of Infosys, was a strong advocate for corporate governance and transparency. He led Infosys in setting new standards in financial disclosure, even when it was not legally required.

Why did Murthy emphasize corporate governance? He believed in creating an organization based on fairness, transparency, and accountability. He recognized that to attract international clients and investors, Infosys needed to demonstrate an unwavering commitment to these principles.

How did he do it? By leading from the front. Infosys was among the first Indian companies to adopt US GAAP (Generally Accepted Accounting Principles), demonstrating its commitment to transparency. Infosys also became the first Indian company to list on NASDAQ, opening access to international capital.

The results were astonishing. Infosys grew exponentially, becoming a multi-billion-dollar company and one of the bellwethers of the

Indian IT industry. But, more importantly, it became a role model for corporate governance and transparency in India, setting the tone for other Indian companies.

From Murthy's purposeful leadership, we can glean several key traits:

- Visionary Thinking: Murthy saw the potential of the IT industry when it was in its infancy and dared to act on his vision.
- Resilience: Despite numerous challenges, Murthy remained committed to his vision, demonstrating the resilience required of a purposeful leader.
- Integrity and Transparency: Murthy emphasized the importance of corporate governance, transparency, and fairness and ingrained these values into the Infosys culture.
- Innovation: Murthy championed the global delivery model, which became a standard in the IT services sector, showcasing his ability to innovate.
- Lead by Example: Murthy's commitment to these principles inspired trust and confidence among stakeholders, demonstrating that purposeful leadership involves leading by example.

Narayana Murthy's story is a testament to the power of purposeful leadership. His leadership has shaped Infosys and influenced the broader IT industry and corporate culture in India, demonstrating the far-reaching impact of purposeful leadership.

Narendra Modi, Prime Minister of India

Narendra Modi, the Prime Minister of India, is a compelling figure who has redefined the landscape of Indian politics with purposeful leadership. From his humble beginnings as a tea seller to his ascendance as the country's Prime Minister, Modi's journey has been a testament to his determination, strategic acumen, and unwavering commitment to his vision for India.

Modi's tenure as the Chief Minister of Gujarat from 2001 to 2014 laid the groundwork for his leadership style. He was known for his administrative skills and was instrumental in transforming Gujarat into one of the most prosperous states in India. However, it was the 2002 Gujarat riots that truly tested his leadership. The riots were a critical turning point in his political career, bringing him under intense national scrutiny. Modi's response to this crisis, whether viewed as controversial or decisive, demonstrated his tenacity and resilience as a leader.

His vision to make the state a hub for investment and growth drove his initiatives for economic development in Gujarat. So why did he focus on this? Modi believed in the transformative power of economic development and saw it as the key to addressing the state's socio-economic challenges.

How did he achieve this? Modi adopted a proactive approach to governance, promoting policies that attracted investment, improved infrastructure, and fostered a culture of innovation. He initiated the Vibrant Gujarat Global Investors' Summit, a biennial event showcasing the state's investment opportunities. Under his leadership, Gujarat became known for its business-friendly policies and robust attracting significant domestic and international investment.

When Modi became Prime Minister in 2014, he brought this economic development vision to the national stage. One of his most significant initiatives has been the 'Make in India' campaign, aimed at transforming India into a global manufacturing hub. The campaign seeks to facilitate investment, foster innovation, and enhance skill development, among other objectives.

His focus on digital transformation has also characterized Modi's leadership. For example, he launched the 'Digital India' initiative to ensure government services are available to citizens electronically by improving online infrastructure and increasing internet connectivity. This initiative has been crucial in promoting digital literacy and inclusivity, especially in rural and semi-urban areas.

From these instances of Modi's leadership, several vital traits emerge:

- Vision: Modi's leadership exhibits a clear vision for economic development and modernization, evident in his initiatives in Gujarat and, later, as Prime Minister.
- Resilience: Despite adversity, Modi has demonstrated resilience, using challenges as stepping stones toward his goals.
- Proactivity: Modi's proactive approach to governance, seen in his initiatives like the Vibrant Gujarat Summit, 'Make in India,' and 'Digital India,' demonstrates his ability to anticipate and respond to the country's evolving needs.
- Inclusivity: His efforts towards digital literacy and inclusivity highlight his commitment to ensuring that the benefits of progress and development reach all sections of society.
- Strategic Acumen: Modi's strategic approach to economic development, through investment-friendly policies and a focus on infrastructure, reflects his adeptness at maneuvering complex political and economic landscapes.

Narendra Modi's leadership presents a case study of purposeful leadership. His leadership approach, characterized by a clear vision, resilience in the face of adversity, proactive governance, inclusivity, and strategic acumen, offers valuable insights into the traits that define purposeful leaders. Moreover, his tenure as Prime Minister underscores the transformative potential of such leadership.

Paul Polman, Former CEO of Unilever

Paul Polman, a former CEO of Unilever, has been a pioneering figure in the corporate world, embodying the essence of purposeful leadership. His tenure at Unilever, from 2009 to 2019, was marked by a radical shift towards sustainability, demonstrating his firm belief in the potential of businesses to be a force for good.

Polman's journey at Unilever began amid the global financial crisis. It was challenging, with businesses worldwide grappling with the economic fallout. At such a time, Polman took an unconventional and risky step. He did away with Unilever's practice of providing quarterly profit forecasts, arguing that it encouraged short-term thinking that was detrimental to the company's long-term success.

Why did Polman take this step? He believed in the importance of long-term strategic planning, and his vision went beyond mere profitability. He sought to transform Unilever into a sustainable and responsible business, contributing positively to society and the environment.

How did Polman achieve this? First, he introduced the Unilever Sustainable Living Plan, a comprehensive blueprint to decouple economic growth from environmental impact. The plan set ambitious targets, such as halving the environmental footprint of Unilever's products, improving health and well-being for billions of people, and enhancing the livelihoods of millions of people by 2020.

This shift was not without its challenges. Many were skeptical about the plan's feasibility and its potential impact on Unilever's profitability. However, Polman remained steadfast in his commitment to the plan, insisting that profitability and sustainability could go hand in hand.

The results were transformative. Not only did Unilever achieve a significant part of its sustainability goals, but it also saw consistent profit growth. Moreover, under Polman's leadership, Unilever's market capitalization doubled, proving that a purpose-driven business model can be profitable.

Reflecting on Polman's purposeful leadership, we can glean several key traits:

- Visionary Leadership: Polman demonstrated visionary leadership by aiming to integrate sustainability into Unilever's business model at a time when few companies saw it as a strategic priority.
- Courageous Decision-Making: Polman dared to do away with quarterly forecasts, a bold step that underscored his commitment to long-term, sustainable success.
- Resilience: Despite skepticism and resistance, Polman remained committed to his vision, demonstrating the resilience characteristic of purposeful leaders.
- Strategic Thinking: Polman's strategic approach to sustainability, encapsulated in the Unilever Sustainable Living Plan, exemplifies how purposeful leaders can balance profitability with social and environmental responsibility.
- Inspirational Leadership: By leading Unilever's sustainability journey, Polman inspired not just his employees but also the broader corporate world, highlighting the influential role of purposeful leadership.

Paul Polman's leadership at Unilever provides a compelling example of purposeful leadership. His unwavering commitment to sustainability, strategic thinking, and inspirational leadership has transformed Unilever and inspired a broader shift toward sustainability in the corporate world. His leadership underscores the power of purposeful leadership in driving meaningful change and creating lasting value.

Ratan Tata, Former Chairman of Tata Sons

Ratan Tata, former Chairman of Tata Sons, is a stalwart of the Indian business landscape and an exemplar of purposeful leadership. His tenure at the helm of the Tata Group, spanning from 1991 to 2012, was characterized by strategic growth, ethical business practices, and a commitment to social responsibility - hallmarks of a purposeful leader.

One of the defining moments of Ratan Tata's leadership came in the wake of the 2008 Mumbai terror attacks. The Taj Mahal Palace Hotel, a Tata Group property, was one of the primary targets. The response of the Tata Group under Ratan Tata's leadership was a testament to his humane and empathetic leadership style.

Why did Tata react the way he did? Tata believed in the fundamental tenet of the Tata Group – the commitment to the community, which is also the primary stakeholder. He saw his employees and the victims as his responsibility, and this sense of responsibility guided the Group's response.

How did he respond? Post the attacks; Tata personally visited the families of the 80 employees who had lost their lives or were injured. In addition, the Tata Group provided compensation and cared for the education of the victims' children and other welfare measures. Furthermore, Tata played a crucial role in the rebuilding and restoration of the hotel, demonstrating resilience in the face of adversity.

Another significant incident during Tata's tenure was the Singur controversy, which revolved around the Tata Nano plant in West

Bengal. With vehement protests over land acquisition, Tata relocated the plant to Sanand in Gujarat.

Why did he make this decision? Tata's commitment to the safety of his employees and the ethical standards that the Tata Group stood for guided his decision. He refused to compromise on these principles, even if it meant a considerable financial setback.

How did he manage the situation? First, the relocation was executed swiftly and efficiently, with minimal disruption to the project timeline. Despite the controversy and the financial impact, Tata Nano rolled out of the Sanand plant within a year of the relocation.

These incidents highlight several critical traits of Ratan Tata's purposeful leadership:

- Empathy and Compassion: Tata's response to the Mumbai terror attacks showed his deep empathy and compassion for the victims and their families.
- Resilience: The swift recovery and restoration of the Taj Hotel and the relocation of the Nano plant are a testament to Tata's resilience.
- Commitment to Ethical Practices: Tata's decision to relocate the Nano plant underscores its unwillingness to compromise on ethical business practices.
- Social Responsibility: Tata's leadership has been characterized by a solid commitment to social responsibility, as demonstrated by the Tata Group's various philanthropic initiatives.
- Visionary Leadership: Through acquisitions like Jaguar Land Rover and Corus, Tata's vision for the Group's strategic growth demonstrates his foresight and strategic acumen.

Ratan Tata's leadership of the Tata Group is a compelling example of purposeful leadership. His humane approach, resilience in adversity, commitment to ethical practices, and visionary leadership have shaped the Group's trajectory and reinforced its reputation as a socially responsible and ethical corporate entity. Moreover, his leadership underscores the transformative potential of purposeful leadership in creating lasting value for businesses and society.

Satya Nadella, CEO of Microsoft

Satya Nadella, the CEO of Microsoft, exemplifies the essence of purposeful leadership. Since assuming leadership in 2014, Nadella has revitalized Microsoft into a thriving, innovative, and collaborative organization.

Upon becoming CEO, one of the significant challenges Satya faced was reviving Microsoft's waning relevancy and competitive edge in the rapidly evolving tech industry. He needed to shift the company's focus from its legacy products and foster a culture of innovation and collaboration.

Why did he focus on this? Satya recognized that the technological landscape was changing, with emerging areas like cloud computing, AI, and machine learning becoming increasingly important. To ensure Microsoft's continued success, he understood the need for the company to adapt and innovate.

How did he do this? Satya embarked on a mission to change Microsoft's culture, moving from a siloed, competitive environment to a more collaborative and learning-focused one. He introduced the concept of a "growth mindset," encouraging employees to learn from failures and continuously innovate. Under Satya's leadership,

Microsoft became more customer-centric, focusing on building technology that empowers every person and organization to achieve more - a clear mission statement that Satya established.

He made strategic decisions to focus on emerging tech trends. For example, he steered Microsoft towards becoming a leader in cloud computing with Azure. In addition, he invested heavily in AI and machine learning. He also prioritized integrating Microsoft's products, creating a more cohesive and user-friendly ecosystem.

The result of Satya's purposeful leadership has been transformative. As a result, Microsoft has regained its position as a leading tech innovator, significantly increasing its market value. Moreover, Microsoft's culture has become more collaborative and innovative, leading to the development of successful products like Azure, Office 365, and Teams.

Key lessons learned, and purposeful leadership traits from Nadella's leadership are:

- Visionary Leadership: Nadella demonstrated visionary leadership by recognizing the changing tech landscape and strategically steering Microsoft toward growth areas like cloud computing and AI.
- Innovative Mindset: Nadella fostered a culture of innovation at Microsoft, emphasizing the importance of a growth mindset and continuous learning.
- Collaborative Leadership: Nadella transformed Microsoft's culture into more collaborative, breaking down silos and encouraging teamwork.
- Customer-Centric Approach: Under Nadella's leadership, Microsoft became more customer-centric, focusing on

creating technology that empowers every individual and organization.
- Resilience: Nadella showed strength in leading Microsoft through significant change and revitalizing its competitive edge.

Satya Nadella's leadership at Microsoft serves as a shining example of purposeful leadership. His visionary leadership, innovative mindset, emphasis on collaboration, customer-centric approach, and resilience have reestablished Microsoft as a leading tech innovator and created a culture that values learning and collaboration. Moreover, his leadership underscores the power of purposeful leadership in driving change and fostering innovation in a complex and rapidly evolving industry.

Sheryl Sandberg, Former COO of Facebook

Sheryl Sandberg, Facebook's former Chief Operating Officer (COO), is a powerful example of purposeful leadership in technology and beyond. Joining Facebook in 2008, she has been instrumental in scaling the social media giant's operations, managing its business strategy, and navigating various challenges.

One incident that stands out in her leadership journey is her advocacy for gender equality in the workplace. Sandberg noticed the glaring gender disparity in leadership roles across industries and decided to address this issue head-on.

Why did she do this? Sandberg recognized that gender diversity in leadership promotes equality and drives better business results. As a woman in a leadership position, she believed it was her responsibility to help break down the barriers women face in their professional journeys.

How did she do this? Sandberg launched the "Lean In" initiative in 2013, based on her bestselling book of the same name. The initiative aimed to empower women by offering support, education, and a like-minded community, helping them achieve their ambitions. Sandberg's approach was about advocating for change and providing practical tools and resources to effect that change.

Another significant aspect of Sandberg's leadership at Facebook was her driving the company's business strategy. When Sandberg joined Facebook, the company grew rapidly but lacked a sustainable business model. Instead, she saw the potential in leveraging Facebook's vast user base to generate advertising revenue.

Why did she focus on this? Sandberg knew that for Facebook to continue growing and innovating, it needed a robust and scalable business model. She identified advertising as a viable revenue stream that could capitalize on Facebook's strengths.

How did she achieve this? Sandberg led the development of Facebook's advertising platform, initially targeting small and medium businesses and then attracting larger corporations. Under her leadership, Facebook's ad business grew exponentially, transforming the company into a profitable enterprise.

These instances highlight vital lessons and purposeful leadership traits from Sandberg's journey:

- Advocacy for Equality: Sandberg's advocacy for gender equality in the workplace underscores the importance of leaders using their positions to drive positive social change.
- Practical Problem-Solving: Her approach to addressing gender disparity was about highlighting the problem and providing practical solutions through the Lean In initiative.

- Strategic Thinking: Sandberg's role in establishing Facebook's ad business demonstrates her strategic acumen, identifying opportunities that align with the company's strengths.
- Resilience: Despite facing criticism and challenges, both personally and professionally, Sandberg has shown resilience, a key trait of purposeful leaders.
- Empathetic Leadership: Sandberg's leadership style is marked by empathy and understanding, whether in supporting her team at Facebook or advocating for gender equality.

Sheryl Sandberg's leadership journey offers valuable insights into purposeful leadership. Her advocacy for gender equality, strategic thinking, resilience, and empathetic leadership has contributed to Facebook's growth and significantly impacted broader societal issues. Moreover, Sandberg's leadership underscores the influence and responsibility of leaders in shaping a more inclusive and equitable future.

Sundar Pichai, CEO of Alphabet

Sundar Pichai, the CEO of Alphabet, Google's parent company, is a remarkable example of purposeful leadership. Born in India, Pichai joined Google in 2004 and rose through the ranks due to his exceptional problem-solving skills and collaborative leadership style.

One pivotal moment in Pichai's leadership journey was his instrumental role in developing and launching Google Chrome. Pichai noticed that the browser space was not meeting the evolving needs of web users, and he envisioned a browser that was faster, more secure, and easier to use.

Why did he focus on this? First, Pichai recognized that a better browser would significantly improve the user experience on the web, aligning with Google's mission to organize the world's information and make it universally accessible and helpful.

How did he do this? First, despite initial skepticism, Pichai persuaded the leadership team to develop Google's browser. Next, he led a team that developed Google Chrome, launched in 2008. Thanks to its speed and simplicity, Chrome became the most popular web browser, demonstrating Pichai's vision and ability to execute.

Another significant aspect of Pichai's leadership is his commitment to ethical AI. With Google at the forefront of AI research and development, Pichai has been vocal about the importance of developing AI responsibly and ensuring it benefits everyone.

Why is he focusing on this? Pichai understands the transformative potential of AI, but he also acknowledges its potential pitfalls, such as bias in AI algorithms and privacy threats. Nevertheless, he believes everyone should benefit from AI, and conducting its development responsibly to avoid harm is essential. So how is he addressing this? Pichai initiated the development of AI principles at Google, guiding the ethical development and use of AI in their products. He has also emphasized the need for regulation in AI, demonstrating his commitment to responsible innovation.

Key lessons learned, and purposeful leadership traits from Pichai's leadership include:

- Visionary Leadership: Pichai's role in developing Google Chrome showcases his ability to envision and execute transformative ideas.
- Commitment to User-Centric Innovation: Pichai's focus on improving the user experience on the web aligns with

Google's mission and underscores the importance of user-centric innovation.

- Ethical Leadership: Pichai's commitment to ethical AI demonstrates his belief in responsible innovation and the ethical obligations of tech leaders.
- Inclusive Leadership: Pichai's belief in ensuring the benefits of AI reach everyone highlights his inclusive leadership style.
- Collaborative Leadership: Pichai is known for his collaborative leadership style, which fosters a culture of open dialogue and teamwork.

Sundar Pichai's leadership at Google and Alphabet exemplifies purposeful leadership. His visionary leadership, commitment to user-centric innovation, ethical leadership, and collaborative leadership have driven Google's growth and established it as a leader in various technology domains. Furthermore, his leadership in advocating for ethical AI reflects the broader responsibilities of tech leaders in shaping a future where technology serves the greater good. His leadership journey underscores the power of purposeful leadership in driving innovation, fostering a collaborative culture, and navigating ethical complexities in the rapidly evolving tech industry.

Yvon Chouinard, Founder of Patagonia

Yvon Chouinard, the founder of Patagonia, is an exemplar of purposeful leadership. Under Chouinard's direction, Patagonia has grown from a small company producing climbing gear into an international business renowned for its commitment to environmental activism and sustainable business practices.

One of the defining moments of Chouinard's leadership at Patagonia was the decision to switch to organic cotton in 1996. The company discovered that conventional cotton, used in their clothing line, was one of the most environmentally damaging crops.

Why did he do this? Chouinard has always been a passionate environmentalist, believing that his business should not contribute to environmental damage. However, he recognized that Patagonia was responsible for reducing its environmental impact as a company.

How did he do this? Despite the higher costs and risks associated with organic cotton, Chouinard switched. He worked closely with suppliers to secure organic cotton and retooled the manufacturing process. This decision marked a significant shift in the apparel industry, inspiring other companies to consider their environmental impact.

Another instance of Chouinard's purposeful leadership was implementing the "1% for the Planet" initiative. As a result, Patagonia pledged to donate 1% of its sales or 10% of its profit, whichever is greater, to environmental causes.

Why did he do this? Chouinard wanted to use the success of Patagonia to drive positive environmental change. He saw an opportunity to use the business to address environmental issues.

How did he achieve this? Since 1985, Patagonia has donated millions to grassroots environmental groups worldwide. This initiative has directly impacted environmental conservation and set a standard for corporate responsibility in the business world.

Key lessons and purposeful leadership traits from Chouinard's leadership include:

- Environmental Stewardship: Chouinard's decision to switch to organic cotton underscores businesses' role in environmental conservation.
- Courageous Leadership: Despite the risks and challenges, Chouinard made bold decisions that aligned with his values and the company's mission.
- Innovative Problem-Solving: Chouinard has consistently sought solutions to reduce Patagonia's environmental impact.
- Corporate Responsibility: Chouinard's belief in corporate responsibility and his commitment to using business success to drive positive change find reflection in the "1% for the Planet" initiative.
- Long-Term Thinking: Chouinard's decisions focus on long-term sustainability over short-term profits.

Yvon Chouinard's leadership at Patagonia exemplifies the power and potential of purposeful leadership. His environmental stewardship, courageous leadership, innovative problem-solving, commitment to corporate responsibility, and long-term thinking have contributed to Patagonia's success and positioned the company as a leader in sustainable business practices. Chouinard's leadership journey underscores the potential of businesses to drive positive change and the importance of aligning business practices with a larger purpose. In addition, his leadership serves as an inspiring example for leaders seeking to navigate the complexities of business while maintaining a commitment to social and environmental responsibilities.

Ursula Burns, Former CEO of Xerox

Ursula Burns, former CEO of Xerox, is a beacon of purposeful leadership. Born in a low-income neighborhood in New York City,

Burns rose at Xerox, breaking barriers to becoming the first African American woman to lead a Fortune 500 company.

One notable aspect of Burns' leadership was her instrumental role in transforming Xerox from a photocopying company into a services business. Upon becoming CEO during the 2008 financial crisis, Burns recognized that Xerox needed to pivot its business model to survive and thrive.

Why did she do this? Burns understood that the demand for traditional photocopying was declining, and there was a growing market for business services. This strategic shift was crucial to ensure Xerox's long-term sustainability and growth.

How did she do this? First, burns spearheaded the $6.4 billion acquisition of Affiliated Computer Services, which catapulted Xerox into the business services market. Under Burns, Xerox's services business grew to account for more than half of the company's revenue, demonstrating her strategic acumen and execution capabilities. Another significant aspect of Burns' leadership is her advocacy for diversity and inclusion. As a woman of color in a leadership position, Burns understood the importance of diverse representation in corporate leadership.

Why did she focus on this? Burns recognized that diversity brings different perspectives, ideas, and experiences, which drive innovation and better business outcomes. She also saw her role as an opportunity to pave the way for future leaders from diverse backgrounds.

How did she achieve this? Burns actively promoted diversity and inclusion initiatives at Xerox and advocated for greater representation in corporate America. She also mentored young professionals, particularly women, and people of color, in their professional journeys.

Key lessons and purposeful leadership traits from Burns' leadership include:

- Strategic Transformation: Burns' role in transforming Xerox's business model showcases her strategic foresight and execution capabilities.
- Resilience: Despite facing a challenging economic climate and internal resistance, Burns' resilience was crucial in driving the successful transformation of Xerox.
- Advocacy for Diversity and Inclusion: Burns' commitment to diversity and inclusion underscores the importance of diverse representation in leadership and its value to businesses.
- Role Modeling: As the first African American woman CEO of a Fortune 500 company, Burns was a role model, inspiring future leaders from diverse backgrounds.
- Mentorship: Burns' commitment to mentoring young professionals reflects her belief in nurturing the next generation of leaders.

Ursula Burns' leadership journey offers valuable insights into purposeful leadership. Her strategic transformation of Xerox, resilience, advocacy for diversity and inclusion, role modeling, and commitment to mentorship have contributed to Xerox's growth and significantly impacted corporate America. Burns' leadership underscores the influence and responsibility of leaders in driving business transformation, advocating for diversity and inclusion, and nurturing future leaders. In addition, her leadership is an inspiring example for future leaders navigating the complexities of business and societal expectations.

By understanding the principles that underpin purposeful leadership, such as adaptability, innovation, empathy, and social responsibility, leaders can better navigate the challenges and opportunities they encounter on their journey.

By reflecting on these real-world leaders' actions and decision-making processes, we can gain a deeper understanding of the complexities and nuances of purposeful leadership and apply these insights to our own lives and organizations. So, as we strive to inspire and motivate our teams, let us remember the importance of leading with purpose and the transformative impact it can have on individuals, organizations, and the world at large.

As we come to the end of exploring lessons learned and insights gained from the lives and careers of purpose-driven leaders, we must recognize the power and responsibility within each of us. The stories of these remarkable individuals, who have navigated complex challenges and embraced opportunities for growth and change, serve as a testament to the transformative impact of purposeful leadership. Moreover, their actions have left an indelible mark on the world, inspiring countless others to reflect upon their lives and consider the potential of purpose-driven leadership.

The tales we have shared evoke a sense of wonder and curiosity, prompting us to ponder the intricate tapestry of human experiences that define the journey of a purpose-driven leader. These stories are not merely about the individuals but the collective human experience, the shared aspirations, and dreams that unite us all in our pursuit of meaning and fulfillment.

As the sun sets on this chapter, it casts long shadows that dance and sway, mirroring the fluidity of leadership and the ever-changing landscape in which it unfolds. Yet, within these shadows, we find the subtle interplay of light and darkness, a reminder of the delicate balance that leaders must strike between their unwavering commitment to purpose and the pragmatic realities of the world in which they operate.

This balance is not static; it is a constant negotiation between competing forces, a reflection of the intricate web of relationships, decisions, and circumstances that shape the course of a leader's journey. And as we peer into this delicate dance, we are reminded of the importance of introspection and self-awareness and the need for leaders to engage in constant learning, reflection, and adaptation.

As we turn the final pages of this chapter, an irresistible call to action emerges, resonating deep within our hearts and minds, urging us to take immediate action. It is a call that implores us to recognize our potential for purposeful leadership and harness the power of our unique gifts and talents to serve something greater than ourselves.

This call is not a whisper or a fleeting thought; it is a resounding echo that reverberates through the very fabric of our existence, a clarion call that summons us to embrace the mantle of purposeful leadership and become the architects of a brighter, more equitable, and sustainable future.

And as we heed this call, we are reminded of the profound responsibility that accompanies purpose-driven leadership, the moral imperative to act with integrity, compassion, and humility in pursuing our goals. Through this unwavering commitment to purpose, we can inspire and motivate our teams, foster innovation and growth, and create lasting change.

We are faced with a choice as we stand on the precipice of this journey, gazing out at the vast expanse of possibilities that stretch out before us. We can choose to remain passive observers, to turn away from the call to action and allow the world to unfold around us, or we can choose to embrace the power of purposeful leadership, wield it as a force for good, and become active participants in the unfolding story of humanity.

The choice is ours, and the time for action is now. So let us choose to embark on this journey with courage and conviction, guided by the lessons learned and insights gained from the lives of those who have come before us. And as we step forth into the unknown, let us remember the words of the ancient Greek philosopher Heraclitus, who once said, "Big results require big ambitions."

So, dear reader, as we part ways and the curtain falls on this chapter, let us carry these stories and lessons etched upon our hearts and minds, a constant reminder of the power and potential of purpose-driven leadership. And let us step boldly into the future,

The Call to Action: Leading with Purpose and Making a Difference

"Answer the call to lead with purpose, for it's more than just leadership - it's a pledge to make a difference. Be the change you wish to see, for in that lies the power of transformational leadership."

In the pages of human history, a story unfolds—a narrative of leaders who have emerged from the shadows, driven by a higher purpose, and who have left an indelible mark on the world. What is it about these individuals that sets them apart from the rest? How have they harnessed the power of purpose to inspire and motivate their teams, create meaningful change, and, ultimately, make a difference? We shall explore this story as we embark on this journey together, delving into the heart of purpose-driven leadership and uncovering the secrets to its transformative power.

A sense of purpose drives every leader and organization, fueled by passion, innovation, and a commitment to positively impacting societyLeaders' focus goes beyond profit margins and quarterly reports; they are driven by a deeper calling to serve the greater good, uplift humanity, and leave a legacy for future generations. This world may seem like a utopia, a distant dream beyond the grasp of our reality. But what if we told you that such a world is possible, within our reach, and starting with you?

The power of a single individual, a single leader, who dares to challenge the status quo, break the chains of convention, and embrace a vision of a better tomorrow. What if that leader is you? What if you could be the spark that ignites a revolution, a catalyst for change that sends ripples through your organization, community, and the world? Are you ready to step up and take your place among the ranks of purpose-driven leaders who have come before you and forever altered the course of history?

Throughout this journey, we will traverse the landscape of purpose-driven leadership, drawing from the wisdom and experiences of those who have come before us. We will learn from the likes of Elon Musk, who has dared to push the boundaries of human ingenuity and re-shape our understanding of what is possible; from Jacinda Ardern, who has shown us the power of compassion and empathy in the face of adversity; and from Mary Barra, who has shattered glass ceilings and demonstrated the resilience and determination required to rise above the challenges that life throws our way.

But how do we begin? How do we unlock the secret to purposefully leading and making a difference? The answer lies not in the pages of a textbook nor the annals of academia but in the hearts and minds of those who dare to dream, aspire, and act. It begins with a single question: "What is my purpose?"

As we embark on this journey together, we invite you to join us in exploring the depths of purpose-driven leadership, delve into the stories of those who have dared to dream and make a difference, and discover the power within you to lead with purpose and create a lasting impact on the world. Are you ready to take the first step? Are you prepared to embark on the most incredible adventure of your life? This journey will forever change not only your destiny but the destiny of all those who follow in your footsteps. If so, it is time to heed the call to action, embrace purpose-driven leadership, and step boldly into the unknown, where your story awaits.

As we approach the culmination of our journey through the principles of purpose-driven leadership, reflecting upon the lessons learned, the insights gained, and the stories of remarkable leaders who have made a difference in the world is crucial. These leaders have demonstrated the power of leading purposefully, inspiring and motivating their teams to achieve extraordinary feats and bring about positive change. Now, it is time for you, the reader, to take up the mantle of purpose-driven leadership, apply these principles in your life and work, and make a difference in the world.

The Significance of Personal Purpose

The first step in embracing purpose-driven leadership is identifying and understanding your purpose. As we have learned from the stories of various leaders, having a strong sense of purpose is essential for driving success and making a meaningful impact. Your purpose serves as a guiding compass, helping you navigate the challenges and opportunities of leadership and aligning your decisions and actions with your core values and beliefs.

To understand your purpose clearly, you can engage in self-reflection, meditation, or journaling and seek feedback from trusted friends, family members, and mentors. Additionally, you can explore various techniques for identifying your purpose and values, such as the Ikigai framework, the Hedgehog Concept, or the Values in Action (VIA) Classification of Strengths.

Aligning Your Purpose with Your Organization's Purpose

Once you have a clear understanding of your purpose, the next step is to ensure that it aligns with the purpose of your organization. This alignment is crucial for maximizing your effectiveness as a leader and creating a shared purpose among your team members. When your purpose and your organization's purpose are in sync, you can harness the power of purpose-driven leadership to create a lasting impact on your team, your organization, and the world at large.

You can engage in open dialogues with your organization members, stakeholders, and fellow leaders to align your purpose with your organization's purpose. You can also review your organization's mission, vision, and values and assess whether they resonate with your purpose. Then, if necessary, you can work with your team to refine or redefine your organization's purpose, ensuring that it accurately reflects all stakeholders' shared aspirations and values.

Making a Difference Through Purpose-Driven Leadership

- Creating a Lasting Impact - As a purpose-driven leader, your goal is to make a difference in the world, whether that means improving your customers' lives, solving pressing societal issues, or contributing to the well-being of your employees and stakeholders. By leading with purpose and inspiring your team to strive for excellence, you can create a lasting impact on your organization and the world at large.
- Leaving a Legacy of Purpose-Driven Leadership - Finally, as you embark on your journey of purpose-driven leadership, remember that the difference you make in the lives of others will shape your legacy. By nurturing the next generation of leaders, fostering a culture of purpose and excellence within your organization, and contributing to the greater good, you can leave a legacy that inspires and motivates others to follow in your footsteps.

I hope you have gained valuable insights, inspiration, and tools to apply in your life and work. Embracing purpose-driven leadership can make a meaningful difference and inspire others to do the same.

We encourage you to seize this opportunity, take up the mantle of purpose-driven leadership, and make your mark on the world.

How to Apply Purposeful Leadership Principles in Your Own Life and Work

In today's rapidly changing world, we cannot overstate the importance of purposeful leadership. The ability to lead with purpose, passion, and conviction is a vital skill that can set you apart and help you navigate the complexities of modern business and personal life. As a purposeful leader, you must recognize that this transformation begins within yourself. By applying purposeful leadership principles in your life and work, you can achieve personal success and inspire those around you to reach their full potential.

Imagine for a moment the leaders who have left an indelible mark on history – visionaries such as Mahatma Gandhi, Martin Luther King Jr., and Nelson Mandela. These individuals, driven by a deep sense of purpose, transcended their circumstances and impacted the world. Closer to the business realm, figures like Steve Jobs, Elon Musk, and Indra Nooyi have harnessed the power of purpose to drive innovation, create industry-leading organizations, and redefine the status quo.

But how can you, as an aspiring purposeful leader, translate these principles into your life and work? How can you ignite the spark of purpose within yourself and, in turn, inspire others to follow suit?

The journey to purposeful leadership begins with introspection, self-awareness, and the willingness to embrace change. By understanding your values, passions, and motivations, you can cultivate a clear vision and purpose that guides your personal and professional life.

As you embark on this transformative journey, you'll discover that purposeful leadership is not a destination but a continuous growth, learning, and adaptation process. It requires resilience, empathy, and the ability to inspire and empower others to achieve their goals and aspirations.

Consider the extraordinary accomplishments of some of the world's most renowned purpose-driven leaders – from Jack Ma's meteoric rise as the founder of Alibaba to Oprah Winfrey's groundbreaking impact on media and philanthropy. These individuals exemplify the power of purposeful leadership to transcend obstacles, inspire others, and make a lasting difference in the world.

With these inspiring examples in mind, let us delve into the journey of applying purposeful leadership principles in your own life and work. Through this process, you will unlock the door to personal and professional fulfillment, empowering yourself and others to thrive in an increasingly complex and ever-changing world.

Join us as we explore the transformative power of purposeful leadership, and discover how you, too, can harness this potential to create a legacy of impact, inspiration, and lasting change. In the journey through the realm of purpose-driven leadership, we must not forget that this powerful force begins with each of us. Our sense of purpose fuels our passion, drives our determination, and shapes our destiny. So, how do we apply the principles of purposeful leadership in our own lives and work? How do we harness this potent energy and channel it towards the achievement of our goals, both personal and professional? We will explore the steps necessary to embrace purposeful leadership in our lives, drawing from the experiences of real-world leaders who have blazed the trail before us and learning from their triumphs and tribulations.

Discovering Your Purpose

The first step in applying purposeful leadership principles is discovering your unique purpose. It involves delving deep within yourself, asking the tough questions, and seeking out the innermost core of your being. What are your passions, your values, and your dreams? What legacy do you want to leave behind, and how can you positively impact the world?

- **Self-reflection:** Reflect on your beliefs, values, and aspirations. Consider writing in a journal or using other introspective tools to help you uncover your purpose.
- **Identify your passions:** Determine what truly excites and motivates you. Then, reflect on the activities and pursuits that bring you joy and fulfillment.
- **Align your values:** Align your values with your professional goals. Strive to integrate who you are and what you do seamlessly.
- **Seek guidance:** Consult mentors, colleagues, and loved ones for their insights and advice. They can often provide invaluable perspective and help you clarify your purpose.

Oprah Winfrey's purpose of empowering people and Tony Hsieh's (former CEO of Zappos) purpose to deliver happiness have guided their leadership styles and success.

Developing a Vision

Once you have discovered your purpose, the next step is to develop a clear and compelling vision that encapsulates your aspirations and provides a roadmap for your journey.

- **Craft a vision statement:** Create a succinct, inspiring statement that captures the essence of your purpose and the impact you want to make in the world.
- **Set clear objectives:** Define specific, measurable, achievable, relevant, and time-bound (SMART) objectives that align with your vision and purpose.
- **Engage stakeholders:** Involve your team, partners, and other stakeholders in developing and refining your vision. Their input can help strengthen your vision and increase your commitment to its realization.

Elon Musk's vision to "accelerate the advent of sustainable transport" guides Tesla's mission. In contrast, Satya Nadella's vision for Microsoft focuses on empowering people and organizations to achieve more.

Cultivating a Purpose-Driven Mindset

As you embark on your journey toward purposeful leadership, it is essential to cultivate a mindset that is attuned to your purpose and vision. This mindset will be the foundation for all your actions, decisions, and interactions.

- **Embrace a growth mindset:** Adopt the belief that your abilities, intelligence, and talents can be developed through dedication and hard work.
- **Foster resilience:** Develop the capacity to bounce back from setbacks and maintain a positive outlook in adversity.
- **Practice mindfulness:** Cultivate the habit of being present in the moment, fully engaged, and aware of your thoughts, emotions, and experiences.

- **Develop emotional intelligence:** Enhance your ability to recognize, understand, and manage your emotions and those of others.

Sheryl Sandberg, COO of Facebook, has demonstrated emotional intelligence and resilience in her leadership. At the same time, Indra Nooyi, former CEO of PepsiCo, has exhibited a growth mindset throughout her career, consistently pushing for innovation and embracing change.

Leading by Example

To effectively apply purposeful leadership principles in your own life and work, it is crucial to lead by example, modeling the behavior and values you wish to see in others.

- **Walk the Talk:** Ensure you align your actions and decisions with your purpose and vision. Consistently demonstrate the values you hold dear.
- **Be authentic:** Embrace your true self and be genuine in your interactions with others. Authenticity fosters trust and builds strong relationships.
- **Show empathy and compassion:** Develop the ability to put yourself in others' shoes and understand their feelings, needs, and perspectives.
- **Encourage collaboration:** Foster a collaborative environment where everyone's contributions are valued and encouraged.

Howard Schultz, former CEO and Chairman of Starbucks, has consistently demonstrated empathy and compassion. In contrast, Ratan Tata, the former Chairman of Tata Sons, is known for his humility and authentic leadership.

Empowering and Inspiring Others

A key aspect of purposeful leadership is empowering and inspiring others to pursue their dreams and aspirations.

- **Develop your team:** Invest in your team members' personal and professional growth, providing them with the tools and resources they need to succeed.
- **Delegate and trust:** Delegate tasks and responsibilities to your team, allowing them the autonomy to make decisions and learn from their experiences.
- **Communicate effectively:** Develop strong communication skills to articulate your vision and purpose clearly and persuasively, inspiring others to join you.
- **Recognize and celebrate achievements:** Acknowledge and reward your team's accomplishments, reinforcing the connection between their efforts and the organization's purpose.

Kiran Mazumdar-Shaw, the founder of Biocon, has empowered her employees through her commitment to their development. At the same time, Sundar Pichai, CEO of Alphabet, has consistently demonstrated the importance of recognizing and celebrating team achievements.

Continuously Assessing and Adapting

As a purpose-driven leader, it is essential to assess your progress and adapt your approach as needed continuously.

- **Seek feedback:** Solicit feedback from your team, peers, and other stakeholders to gain insights into your performance and identify areas for improvement.

- **Reflect and learn:** Regularly reflect on your experiences and learn from successes and failures. Use these insights to refine your approach and enhance your leadership effectiveness.
- **Stay informed:** Keep abreast of industry trends, technological advancements, and other factors that may impact your organization and its purpose.
- **Be agile:** Develop the ability to quickly adapt and pivot in response to changing circumstances, ensuring your organization remains agile and responsive.

Narayana Murthy, the Founder of Infosys, consistently sought feedback and embraced a learning mindset. At the same time, Hamdi Ulukaya, CEO of Chobani, has demonstrated adaptability in the face of industry disruptions.

Applying the principles of purposeful leadership in your own life and work is a powerful and transformative process. By discovering your purpose, developing a vision, cultivating a purpose-driven mindset, leading by example, empowering others, and continuously assessing and adapting, you can unleash your potential and impact your organization and the world. As you embark on this journey, let the stories and experiences of real-world leaders serve as a source of inspiration and guidance, propelling you toward a future of purpose, passion, and achievement.

Recognizing that the process is not finite but an ongoing evolution is essential. True purpose-driven leadership is a lifelong commitment to growth, learning, and adaptation, fueled by an unwavering sense of responsibility to make a meaningful difference in the lives of others and the world at large.

Imagine the possibilities if every leader embraced the principles we've discussed. The ripple effect would be felt far and wide, with profound implications for organizations, communities, and societies. As a purpose-driven leader, you can create this transformative impact, shaping the future for generations to come.

Consider the legendary leaders whose stories we have shared—those who have risen above adversity, challenged the status quo, and inspired countless others through their unwavering commitment to a purpose greater than themselves. Reflect upon their journeys and the incredible feats they have achieved. These leaders have demonstrated exceptional vision and tenacity and proven that purposeful leadership is an undeniable force for change.

Now, envision yourself at the helm of such a journey, standing on the precipice of greatness with an opportunity to leave an indelible mark on the world. The path before you may be fraught with challenges and uncertainty, but armed with the principles of purposeful leadership, you have the power to overcome these obstacles and emerge victorious.

So, what will your legacy be? How will your leadership shape the lives of those around you and contribute to improving the world? Of course, only you can answer these questions. However, one thing is sure—embracing purposeful leadership is not merely a choice but a calling.

As you venture into the world, bearing the mantle of purpose-driven leadership, remember the wise words of the great philosopher and poet Rumi: "Let the beauty of what you love be what you do." This powerful sentiment reminds us that when we actively guide our actions with a deep sense of purpose and passion, we can accomplish extraordinary feats and impact the world.

Let this be your clarion call to action, urging you to embrace the principles of purposeful leadership and forge a path that is not only personally fulfilling but also transformative for those you lead and the world at large. The journey may be long and arduous, but the rewards are boundless, and the legacy you leave will echo through the ages.

The world is waiting for you, ready to witness your greatness. So, take up the mantle of purposeful leadership and let your light shine brightly, illuminating the path to a brighter, more purpose-driven future for all.

The Power of Purposeful Leadership to Create Positive Change in the World

Uncertainty and chaos seem to be the order of the day; it is easy to feel overwhelmed and disheartened. The relentless barrage of news about economic downturns, social unrest, and environmental catastrophes can make it challenging to find hope and inspiration. Yet, amidst this cacophony, there are stories of extraordinary individuals who, through their unwavering commitment to a greater purpose, are transforming industries, organizations, and communities, creating a better future for all. These purposeful leaders stand as beacons of hope, demonstrating that each one of us has the potential to make a meaningful difference in the world.

For a moment, please think of the incredible perseverance of Elon Musk, who, in the face of skepticism and setbacks, has revolutionized the automotive and space industries with his companies, Tesla and SpaceX, demonstrating that sustainable energy and space exploration can be both economically viable and technologically advanced. Likewise, imagine the resilience of Mary Barra, who, as the first female CEO of General Motors, steered the company through turbulent times, taking bold decisions to reshape the organization and committing to an all-electric, zero-emissions future.

Envision the unwavering dedication of Dr. Paul Farmer, who co-founded Partners in Health and has devoted his life to fighting global health inequalities, providing healthcare to millions of people in impoverished communities worldwide. And consider the transformative leadership of Satya Nadella, who, as CEO of Microsoft, has reinvigorated the tech giant with a growth mindset, fostering innovation and collaboration that have led to groundbreaking advancements in fields such as artificial intelligence and cloud computing.

These real-world examples of purposeful leaders inspire admiration and challenge us to reflect on our potential to create positive change in the world. As we explore the power of purposeful leadership, let us be mindful of the lessons and insights we can glean from these extraordinary individuals. Taking such action can uncover an untapped potential within ourselves, ready to be unleashed for the greater good. So, let us begin our journey, and together, let us unlock the power of purposeful leadership to create a better world for all.

With a myriad of global challenges to confront, from climate change to social and economic inequality, leaders must step up and drive positive change through the power of purpose-driven decision-making.

Purposeful leadership catalyzes creating a lasting impact by inspiring and motivating teams to pursue a common goal that transcends short-term gains and focuses on a greater, long-term vision. Throughout history, some of the most transformative leaders have harnessed the power of purpose to revolutionize industries, reshape societies, and improve the lives of millions.

We will explore the power of purposeful leadership to create positive change in the world. We will delve into the stories of real-world leaders who have used their sense of purpose to make a significant difference, examining their strategies and outcomes. Through these examples, we will gain a deeper understanding of the transformative potential of purpose-driven leadership.

The Impact of Purposeful Leadership on Society

- **Economic Growth and Job Creation -** One of the most direct ways that purposeful leaders can create positive change is by fostering economic growth and job creation within their organizations and communities. These leaders can inspire innovation, encourage sustainable practices, and create new employment opportunities by pursuing a higher purpose beyond profit maximization. For example, Howard Schultz, the former CEO of Starbucks, pursued a purpose-driven mission to source coffee ethically and to create a third place between work and home for people. Under his leadership, Starbucks expanded globally and implemented comprehensive employee benefits and initiatives, including healthcare, stock ownership, and college tuition support. Schultz's efforts created numerous jobs worldwide while steadfastly committed to his overarching vision.
- **Social and Environmental Responsibility -** Purposeful leaders also recognize the importance of addressing social and environmental challenges, using their influence and resources to impact them positively. By prioritizing corporate social responsibility and sustainable practices, these leaders can create lasting change that benefits their organizations, the broader community, and the environment. One such leader is Paul Polman, the former CEO of Unilever. Polman's

purpose-driven leadership led to the creation of the Unilever Sustainable Living Plan, a comprehensive strategy to reduce the company's environmental footprint, improve health and well-being, and enhance livelihoods across its value chain. Under Polman's guidance, Unilever made significant progress toward its sustainability goals, setting a powerful example for other corporations.

- **Fostering Inclusivity and Diversity** - Inclusive and diverse organizations are more innovative, resilient, and successful. Purposeful leaders understand the value of fostering a culture that embraces diversity and promotes equality, ensuring everyone has an equal opportunity to contribute to the organization's success. For instance, Mary Barra, CEO of General Motors (GM), has advocated for gender equality and inclusivity in the male-dominated automotive industry. Under her leadership, GM has made significant strides towards achieving gender parity, with women now occupying key leadership positions within the company. In addition, Barra's commitment to inclusivity has created a more diverse workforce and contributed to GM's continued success and innovation.

Strategies for Purposeful Leadership to Drive Positive Change

- **Aligning Organizational Goals with a Greater Purpose** - To create positive change in the world, purposeful leaders must ensure that their goals align with a greater purpose. By establishing a clear and compelling vision, these leaders can inspire and motivate their teams to work towards a common objective that transcends short-term gains and focuses on creating lasting impact. For example, Yvon Chouinard, the founder of Patagonia, has built a company with a solid commitment to environmental conservation and sustainability. Patagonia's mission statement, "Build the best product, cause no unnecessary harm, use business to inspire and implement solutions to the environmental crisis," clearly communicates its purpose and guides its actions. This alignment of goals has allowed Patagonia to become a leader in sustainable business practices while also contributing to the fight against climate change.

- **Engaging Stakeholders and Building Partnerships -** Purposeful leaders recognize the importance of engaging with stakeholders and building partnerships to drive positive change. By collaborating with other organizations, governments, and individuals who share their purpose, leaders can leverage their collective resources and expertise to tackle complex challenges more effectively. One prime example is Dr. Paul Farmer, co-founder of Partners in Health (PIH). Dr. Farmer has dedicated his life to fighting global health inequalities and providing healthcare to impoverished communities. By partnering with governments, NGOs, and local communities, PIH has delivered high-quality healthcare services to millions of people in need, demonstrating the power of collaborative leadership to create a lasting impact.
- **Investing in Innovation and Continuous Improvement -** Purposeful leaders understand that to create positive change in the world, they must be willing to invest in innovation and continuous improvement. By fostering a culture of learning and experimentation within their organizations, these leaders can encourage the development of new ideas, products, and services that have the potential to transform industries and improve lives. Reed Hastings, CEO of Netflix, is a prime example of a leader who embraces innovation and continuous improvement. Under Hastings' leadership, Netflix transformed from a DVD rental service into a pioneering

> streaming platform and eventually a content production powerhouse. This commitment to innovation has driven Netflix's continued success and contributed to a paradigm shift in how people consume entertainment worldwide.

The power of purposeful leadership to create positive change in the world cannot be understated. By aligning organizational goals with a greater purpose, engaging stakeholders, building partnerships, and investing in innovation and continuous improvement, purposeful leaders can drive transformative change that benefits society.

In a world of turbulence and uncertainty, where societal challenges often seem insurmountable, one might wonder if any individual can make a genuine difference. Yet, as the tides of change swell around us, crashing against the shores of businesses, governments, and communities, a beacon of hope emerges, a force capable of navigating these treacherous waters to create lasting, positive change. This force is the power of purposeful leadership.

Picture a magnificent ship, once adrift in the stormy sea, now guided by a skilled and visionary captain with a clear destination. The wind fills its sails, and the vessel surges forward with every wave, driven by an unwavering purpose. The crew, once demoralized and disjointed, now works together in harmony, their morale lifted by their shared mission. It is the transformative power of purposeful leadership at work.

Yet, what does it indeed mean to be a purposeful leader, and how can we harness this power in our lives and work? Can we, as individuals, ignite the flame of change, and if so, how do we kindle that fire and fuel its growth? As we embark on this journey, let us consider the incredible potential within each of us when we align our personal and professional goals with a greater purpose that transcends profit and self-interest and instead focuses on the betterment of humanity.

Envision the possibilities that emerge when we embrace a shared vision of a better world. Imagine the impact we can create when we wield the power of purposeful leadership to overcome the challenges that confront us. The stories of real-world leaders who have harnessed this power serve as both a guide and an inspiration, illuminating the path forward and revealing the true potential of purposeful leadership to create positive change.

So, dear reader, as we delve into the depths of purposeful leadership and its capacity to create lasting impact, let us ask ourselves: Are we ready to embark on this voyage? Are we prepared to navigate the uncharted waters of our potential, discover our true purpose, and harness the power within us to create a better world? The time has come for us to step up, take the helm, and lead purposefully. The journey ahead may be challenging, but the rewards are immense. So, together, let us chart a course toward a brighter future for all.

MESSAGE TO THE READERS -

As we stand on the precipice of our exploration into purposeful leadership, we must pause momentarily and consider the magnitude of our journey together. This book has been a voyage through the leadership landscape, revealing the power and potential of purposeful leading. During our shared adventure, we have encountered inspiring examples of purpose-driven leaders who have left indelible marks on the world and their organizations. The stories we have shared and the lessons we have learned serve as invaluable guideposts, illuminating the path toward becoming purpose-driven leaders ourselves.

Now, as we reach the culmination of our journey, it is crucial to turn our gaze inward and reflect on the legacy we wish to leave behind. We must ask ourselves, what kind of leaders we aspire to become? What will be the lasting impact of our purpose-driven actions? How will our decisions and choices shape not only our own lives but also the lives of those around us?

Life, in all its complexity, is akin to an intricate tapestry, with each thread representing a decision, action, or choice that ultimately contributes to the emerging pattern. As leaders, our influence extends far beyond our immediate circle, weaving a complex web of connections that can touch the lives of countless individuals, communities, and even the world at large. As we pursue our purpose, we must remain acutely aware of our profound responsibility and the extraordinary potential within our grasp.

In an ideal world, every leader wholeheartedly embraces their purpose, using it as a guiding star to navigate the often-turbulent waters of life. In this world, businesses, governments, and communities work harmoniously, unified by a common goal – to create a better, more just, and sustainable existence for all. This vision may seem ambitious, even audacious. However, it is entirely within our reach if we dare to dream and commit to taking the necessary steps to make it a reality.

As you close the pages of this book, take the time to ponder the following questions: What kind of leader do I want to be? What is my purpose, and how can I harness my unique talents, passion, and influence to make a positive difference? Remember that the journey toward purposeful leadership is not a solitary endeavor but a collective effort, for we can improve the world through collaboration, unity, and a shared sense of purpose.

This book must catalyze your transformation, an invitation to embrace purposeful leadership and make a lasting impact. We have delved deeply into the power of leading with purpose, exploring the principles underpinning this approach and the potential for creating positive change in the world. Now, the time has come for you to assume the mantle of purposeful leadership and chart your course toward a brighter future, empowered by the knowledge and inspiration you have gained throughout this journey.

As you embark on this voyage, remember that the horizon stretches far beyond our sight, and the potential for growth and learning is boundless. So embrace the challenge, seize the opportunity, and lead with purpose, for the world is waiting for your unique contribution, and the time to act is now.

May the winds of change fill your sails, propelling you forward on your journey to inspire and motivate your team and ultimately leave a legacy of purposeful leadership. As you navigate the vast ocean of possibilities, remember that pursuing purpose is an ongoing process that demands constant growth, reflection, and adaptation.

In the face of adversity, draw upon the resilience, determination, and courage that have brought you this far. Learn from your setbacks and use them as stepping stones toward greater achievement and fulfillment. Cherish the large and small victories, and celebrate the milestones that mark your progress toward purposeful leadership.

Stay open to the insights and wisdom of others, for it is through collaboration and the exchange of ideas that we grow, evolves, and become better leaders. Encourage your team to share their perspectives, challenge your assumptions, and contribute their unique talents and abilities to the collective effort. Foster a culture of continuous learning and improvement, instilling in your team the values of curiosity, humility, and a shared commitment to excellence.

And, as you forge ahead on this path, never forget the power of empathy and compassion in leadership. Strive to understand the hopes, dreams, and fears of those you lead, and let that understanding inform your decisions and actions. By cultivating an authentic connection with your team, you will create an environment where they feel valued, inspired, and motivated to contribute their best.

The world needs purposeful leaders – individuals willing to rise above the status quo, challenge convention, and create lasting, positive change. By embracing the principles and practices outlined in this book, you have taken the first steps toward becoming one of these transformative leaders. Your journey may be difficult, but the personal and global rewards are immeasurable.

As we conclude this exploration of purposeful leadership, let the words, stories, and insights you have encountered serve as a beacon, guiding you toward a future of greater meaning, impact, and fulfillment. Remember that you possess the power to shape not only your destiny but also the destiny of countless others and that every action, no matter how small, can have a profound ripple effect.

So, as you close this book and step forward into the world, please take with you the knowledge, inspiration, and determination you have gained, and use them to create a legacy of purposeful leadership that will echo through the generations. The world is waiting for your unique contribution, and the time to act is now. So, embrace the challenge, seize the opportunity, and lead with purpose, for the journey toward a better future begins with you.

KEY PRINCIPLES OF PURPOSEFUL LEADERSHIP

In a world where change is the only constant, purposeful leadership has emerged as the compass that steers organizations toward their true north. At its core, purposeful leadership transcends the transactional nature of business operations to connect with the more profound aspirations of individuals and societies. It pivots on the belief that work is not merely a means to an end but an opportunity to contribute to a larger narrative, a more significant cause. Here are some fundamental principles of purposeful leadership:

i. Clear Vision and Mission: Purposeful leaders clearly understand their organization's vision and mission and are committed to achieving these goals.
ii. Inspirational Motivation: They can inspire and motivate their team members, encouraging them to give their best toward the shared mission.
iii. Empathy and Understanding: Purposeful leaders show empathy and understanding towards their team members, acknowledging their efforts and addressing their concerns.
iv. Ethical Behavior: They uphold high ethical standards, promoting a culture of integrity and honesty in the organization.
v. Accountability: They take responsibility for their actions and decisions and expect the same from their team members.
vi. Inclusiveness: Purposeful leaders value diversity and inclusiveness, ensuring that all team members feel valued and heard.

vii. Continuous Learning: They believe in continuous learning and improvement and encourage their team to develop new skills and knowledge.

viii. Adaptability: They are flexible and adaptable, able to navigate changes and challenges with resilience.

ix. Empowerment: Purposeful leaders empower their team members, providing them with the resources and support they need to succeed.

x. Service to Others: They prioritize the needs of others, serving their team members, stakeholders, and the community with dedication and commitment.

xi. Long-Term Thinking: They focus on long-term success rather than short-term gains, making strategic decisions that benefit the organization in the long run.

xii. Emphasis on Relationships: Purposeful leaders prioritize building and maintaining strong relationships within their team and with external stakeholders.

xiii. Communication: They communicate effectively, ensuring their team members are well-informed and aligned with the organization's goals.

xiv. Growth and Development: They foster an environment that encourages personal and professional growth, providing opportunities for their team members to develop and advance.

xv. Transparency: They are transparent in their actions and decisions, fostering a culture of trust and openness in the organization.

REFERENCES

These references provide a starting point for understanding the leaders' leadership qualities and accomplishments. By exploring these resources, you can gain deeper insights into their leadership styles, decision-making processes, and impact on their respective organizations and industries.

IKEA: "Inter IKEA Group Yearly Summary FY19" (https://www.inter.ikea.com/content/dam/inter-ikea-group/About%20IKEA/Yearly%20Summary/Yearly%20Summary%20FY19.pdf)

Tesla: "Tesla Motors: Master of Innovation" (https://www.investopedia.com/articles/investing/031815/tesla-motors-master-innovation.asp)

Salesforce: "Salesforce Named One of the 2020 World's Most Ethical Companies by Ethisphere for the 12th Year" (https://www.salesforce.com/news/press-releases/2020/02/200213/)

REI: "REI Co-op 2019 Annual Stewardship Report" (https://www.rei.com/content/dam/documents/Stewardship/2019-annual-stewardship-report.pdf)

TOMS: "Our Impact" (https://www.toms.com/our-impact)

Unilever. (2021). Our Purpose. https://www.unilever.com/about/who-we-are/our-vision/

Warby Parker. (2021). Our Story. https://www.warbyparker.com/story

Danone. (2021). Our Commitments. https://www.danone.com/sustainability/our-commitments/

Polman, P. (2019). Leadership Lessons From Purpose-Driven Companies. Harvard Business Review. https://hbr.org/2019/11/leadership-lessons-from-purpose-driven-companies

Eccles, R. G., & Serafeim, G. (2013). The Performance Frontier: Innovating for a Sustainable Strategy. Harvard Business Review Press.

Gostick, A., & Elton, C. (2018). The best teams have a purpose. Harvard Business Review. https://hbr.org/2018/05/the-best-teams-have-a-purpose

Grant, A. M. (2012). Leading with meaning: Beneficiary contact, prosocial impact, and the performance effects of transformational leadership. Academy of Management Journal, 55(2), 458-476. https://doi.org/10.5465/amj.2009.0470

Lencioni, P. (2012). The advantage: Why organizational health trumps everything else in the business. John Wiley & Sons.

Sinek, S. (2009). Start with why: How great leaders inspire everyone to act. Penguin.

Thompson, J. (2018). Why your team needs a shared sense of purpose. Harvard Business Review. https://hbr.org/2018/05/why-your-team-needs-a-shared-sense-of-purpose

Waddock, S. (2018). Purpose-led leadership: Insights from visionary leaders. Routledge.

Weick, K. E., & Sutcliffe, K. M. (2007). Managing the unexpected: Resilient performance in an age of uncertainty. John Wiley & Sons

"Elon Musk: Tesla, SpaceX, and the Quest for a Fantastic Future" by Ashlee Vance (2015)

"What We Can Learn from Elon Musk's Risk-Taking" by Carolyn Gregoire, Forbes (2018)

"Indra Nooyi: A Transcultural Leader" by Annette Ranft and Cynthia Ingols, Harvard Business Review (2018)

"Indra Nooyi's leadership at PepsiCo: Collaboration, diversity and inclusion" by Kellie Cummings, Know Your Value (2019)

"Jeff Bezos: The Founder of Amazon.com" by Ann Byers (2019)

"The Jeff Bezos School of Long-Term Thinking" by Kevin Maney, Wired (2011)

Sundar Pichai and resources for innovation:

"Sundar Pichai: The Inside Story of Google's New CEO" by Steven Levy, Wired (2016)

"Google's 20% Time: What the 'Innovation Time Off' Actually Accomplished" by Claire Cain Miller, The New York Times (2018)

"How LinkedIn's Reid Hoffman Started a Movement to Reinvent Silicon Valley's Relationship with Failure" by Dan Lyons, Business Insider (2012)

"Reid Hoffman: The Startup of You" by Kristin Leutwyler, Scientific American (2012)

"Mark Zuckerberg: A Biography of the Facebook Billionaire" by Michelle Grey (2014)

"Inside Facebook's 'Bootcamp' for New Hires" by Rachel King, Fortune (2017)

"The Road Ahead" by Bill Gates (1995)

"How Bill Gates Celebrates Innovative Ideas at Microsoft" by Kevin Purdy, Fast Company (2014)

"Microsoft's Nadella: 'Every organization now a software organization'" by Mary Jo Foley, ZDNet (2016)

"Why CEO Satya Nadella Believes the Future of Microsoft Is All About the Cloud" by Betsy Mikel, Inc. (2018)

"IBM's Ginni Rometty on Leadership, Tech and the Future" by Matthew Boyle, Bloomberg (2018)

"Ginni Rometty of IBM: Mastering the Art of Leadership" by Roger Trapp, Forbes (2016)

"What Amazon's 'Career Choice' Program Will Teach You About Leadership" by Daniel H. Pink, Forbes (2017)

"What Jeff Bezos Wants His Employees to Know About the Future" by Justin Bariso, Inc. (2018)

"What Jack Welch Taught Me About Leadership" by Daniel Goleman, Harvard Business Review (2018)

"The 7 Habits of Highly Effective People: A Book Review" by Jack Welch, LinkedIn (2018)

Immelt, J. R. (2017). How I Led GE Through the Great Recession. Harvard Business Review. https://hbr.org/2017/10/how-i-led-ge-through-the-great-recession

Barra, M. (2017). Sustainability at General Motors: An Interview with CEO Mary Barra. Harvard Business Review. https://hbr.org/2017/09/sustainability-at-general-motors-an-interview-with-ceo-mary-barra

Nadella, S. (2017). Hit Refresh: The Quest to Rediscover Microsoft's Soul and Imagine a Better Future for Everyone. HarperBusiness.

Mulally, A. (2012). Alan Mulally: The Man Who Saved Ford. Forbes. https://www.forbes.com/sites/brianakessler/2012/05/09/alan-mulally-the-man-who-saved-ford/?sh=1daa8dcb6ba7

Burns, U. (2016). How Xerox CEO Ursula Burns Keeps Innovating. Harvard Business Review. https://hbr.org/2016/09/how-xerox-ceo-ursula-burns-keeps-innovating

Mary Barra, CEO of General Motors:

Source: "Mary Barra's No. 1 Priority: Get GM's Culture Right," Fortune, November 13, 2018.

Link: https://fortune.com/2018/11/13/mary-barra-general-motors-culture/

Kevin Johnson, CEO of Starbucks:

Source: "Starbucks Announces New Partner Investments to Advance its Commitment to Opportunity, Sustainability and Resilience," Starbucks, September 22, 2020.

Link: https://stories.starbucks.com/press/2020/starbucks-announces-new-partner-investments-to-advance-its-commitment-to-opportunity-sustainability-and-resilience/

Doug Conant, former CEO of Campbell Soup Company:

Source: "CEO Doug Conant Discusses Campbell Soup Company's Leadership Development Program," Stanford Graduate School of Business, February 4, 2009.

Link: https://www.gsb.stanford.edu/insights/ceo-doug-conant-discusses-campbell-soup-companys-leadership-development-program

Tony Hsieh, former CEO of Zappos:

Source: "The Zappos Experience: 5 Principles to Inspire, Engage, and WOW," by Joseph A. Michelli (2012).

Link: https://www.amazon.com/Zappos-Experience-Principles-Inspire/-Engage/dp/0071749586

Shantanu Narayen, CEO of Adobe:

Source: "How Adobe Reinvented Its Performance Management System," Harvard Business Review, April 1, 2016.

Link: https://hbr.org/2016/04/how-adobe-reinvented-its-performance-management-system

David Novak, former CEO of Yum! Brands:

Source: "David Novak on Leadership Development," Chief Executive, March 7, 2013.

Link: https://chiefexecutive.net/david-novak-on-leadership-development/

Satya Nadella, CEO of Microsoft:

Source: "Microsoft's Satya Nadella on empathy and innovation," Financial Times, September 30, 2018.

Link: https://www.ft.com/content/79c7371a-b590-11e8-bbc3-ccd7de085ffe

James Whitehurst, former CEO of Red Hat:

Source: "How Red Hat Motivates its Employees Through Recognition," Forbes, April 11, 2016.

Link: https://www.forbes.com/sites/jacobmorgan/2016/04/11/how-red-hat-motivates-its-employees-through-recognition/?sh=1c9a1de44211

The Benefits of a Positive Workplace Culture. (2019, November 20). Retrieved from https://www.forbes.com/sites/alankohll/2019/11/20/the-benefits-of-a-positive-workplace-culture/?sh=557df6fb3db1.

Luthans, F., & Youssef, C. M. (2007). Emerging positive organizational behavior. Journal of Management, 33(3), 321-349.

Spreitzer, G., Sutcliffe, K., Dutton, J., Sonenshein, S., & Grant, A. M. (2005). A socially embedded model of thriving at work. Organization Science, 16(5), 537-549.

Cameron, K. S., & Dutton, J. E. (2003). Positive organizational scholarship: Foundations of a new discipline. Berrett-Koehler Publishers.

Coffman, C. (2018). The power of positivity in the workplace. Retrieved from https://www.gallup.com/workplace/236213/power-positivity-workplace.aspx.

Harvard Business Review Analytic Services. (2015). The impact of employee engagement on performance. https://hbr.org/resources/pdfs/comm/achievers/hbr_achievers_report_sep15.pdf

Goodwin, D. K. (2005). Team of Rivals: The Political Genius of Abraham Lincoln. Simon & Schuster.

Mandela, N. (1994). Long Walk to Freedom: The Autobiography of Nelson Mandela. Little, Brown & Co.

Lodge, T. (2006). Mandela: A Critical Life. Oxford University Press.

Nooyi, I. (2021). My Life in Full: Work, Family, and Our Future. Portfolio.

Useem, M. (2011). The Leadership Moment: Nine True Stories of Triumph and Disaster and Their Lessons for Us All. Three Rivers Press.

Quandt, W.B. (1986). Camp David: Peacemaking and Politics. Washington, D.C.: Brookings Institution.

Wright, L. (2014). Thirteen Days in September: Carter, Begin, and Sadat at Camp David. New York: Alfred A. Knopf.

Andersen, S.O., & Sarma, K.M. (2002). Protecting the Ozone Layer: The United Nations History. Earthscan.

Parson, E.A. (2003). Protecting the Ozone Layer: Science and Strategy. Oxford University Press.

Bower, J.L., & Hout, T.M. (2001). The DaimlerChrysler Merger: A New World Order? Harvard Business School Case Study.

Cole, R.E. (2003). From post-merger integration to corporate renewal: The DaimlerChrysler case. International Journal of Automotive Technology and Management, 3(1-2), 61-78.

Gandhi, M. K. (1993). An Autobiography or The Story of My Experiments with Truth. India: Navajivan Publishing House.

Erikson, E. H. (1969). Gandhi's Truth: On the Origins of Militant Nonviolence. New York: W. W. Norton & Company.

Mandela, N. (1994). Long Walk to Freedom: The Autobiography of Nelson Mandela. Boston: Little, Brown and Company.

Stengel, R. (2010). Mandela's Way: Lessons on Life, Love, and Courage. New York: Crown Publishers.

Welch, J., & Welch, S. (2005). Winning. New York: HarperCollins.

Slater, R. (1999). Jack Welch and the GE Way: Management Insights and Leadership Secrets of the Legendary CEO. New York: McGraw-Hill.

Mitchell, G. (1999). Making Peace. Berkeley: University of California Press.

O'Clery, C. (2010). The Greening of the White House: The Inside Story of How America Pulled Back from the Brink of Collapse in Northern Ireland. London: Gill & Macmillan.

Goodwin, D. K. (2005). Team of Rivals: The Political Genius of Abraham Lincoln. New York: Simon & Schuster.

McPherson, J. M. (1988). Battle Cry of Freedom: The Civil War Era. New York: Oxford University Press.

Jenkins, R. (2001). Churchill: A Biography. New York: Farrar, Straus, and Giroux.

Gilbert, M. (1991). Churchill: A Life. New York: Henry Holt and Company.

Nooyi, I. K. (2019). My Life in Full: Work, Family, and Our Future. New York: Portfolio.

Byrne, J. A. (2007). Indra Nooyi: What I've Learned. BusinessWeek, June 25, 2007.

Kahney, L. (2019). Tim Cook: The Genius Who Took Apple to the Next Level. New York: Portfolio.

Isaacson, W. (2011). Steve Jobs. New York: Simon & Schuster.

Schultz, H., & Gordon, J. (2011). Onward: How Starbucks Fought for Its Life without Losing Its Soul. Rodale Books.

Satya Nadella: "Hit Refresh: The Quest to Rediscover Microsoft's Soul and Imagine a Better Future for Everyone" by Satya Nadella (2017)

Microsoft's culture change: "How Microsoft's CEO has 'hit refresh' on company culture" by Mark Sullivan, Fast Company (2017)

Indra Nooyi: "Indra Nooyi Steps Down as PepsiCo's C.E.O." by Sapna Maheshwari, The New York Times (2018)

PepsiCo's diverse and inclusive workplace: "PepsiCo CEO Indra Nooyi is Stepping Down" by Maria Aspan, Fortune (2018)

Nelson Mandela: "Long Walk to Freedom" by Nelson Mandela (1994)

Truth and Reconciliation Commission: "The Truth and Reconciliation Commission" by The Nelson Mandela Foundation

Kofi Annan: "Interventions: A Life in War and Peace" by Kofi Annan (2012)

Kofi Annan's diplomatic skills: "The Art of Mediation: Kofi Annan's Diplomatic Legacy" by The Editorial Board, The New York Times (2018)

Bob Chapman: "Everybody Matters: The Extraordinary Power of Caring for Your People Like Family" by Bob Chapman and Raj Sisodia (2015)

Barry-Wehmiller's "truly human leadership" approach: "Truly Human Leadership" by Barry-Wehmiller

Abraham Lincoln: "Team of Rivals: The Political Genius of Abraham Lincoln" by Doris Kearns Goodwin (2005)

Lincoln's compromise approach: "Abraham Lincoln and the Politics of Compromise" by William E. Gienapp, Reviews in American History (1992)

Jacinda Ardern: "New Zealand passes historic zero carbon bill with near-unanimous bipartisan support" by Isabelle Gerretsen, CNN (2019)

New Zealand's zero-carbon bill: "New Zealand's new climate change law: a zero carbon future by 2050" by Charlie Mitchell, The Guardian (2019)

Angela Merkel: "Angela Merkel's leadership style: collaborative consensus, with a dash of calculation" by Josie Le Blond, The Conversation (2021)

Merkel's collaborative approach: "Angela Merkel: the pragmatic, modest chancellor who revamped Germany" by Kate Connolly, The Guardian (2021)

"Apple CEO Tim Cook on innovation, privacy and the environment" by Niall O'Dowd, IrishCentral (2019)

"Apple's Tim Cook: The Genius Who Took Over From Steve Jobs" by Miguel Helft, Forbes (2018)

"New Zealand PM Jacinda Ardern wins global praise for handling of Christchurch shootings" by Nicola Smith, The Telegraph (2019)

"New Zealand's Jacinda Ardern: the politics of kindness" by Eleanor Ainge Roy, The Guardian (2018)

Mandela, N. (1995). Long Walk to Freedom: The Autobiography of Nelson Mandela. Little, Brown, and Company.

Lain, B. (2018). Nelson Mandela: A Life From Beginning to End. Hourly History.

Vance, A. (2015). Elon Musk: Tesla, SpaceX, and the Quest for a Fantastic Future. Ecco.

Straubel, J. (2018). The Story of Tesla, SpaceX, and Elon Musk. Independently Published.

Malala Yousafzai:

Yousafzai, M., & Lamb, C. (2013). I Am Malala: The Girl Who Stood Up for Education and Was Shot by the Taliban. Little, Brown, and Company.

Guggenheim, D. (Director). (2015). He Named Me Malala [Documentary]. Fox Searchlight Pictures.

- John, D. L. (2015). How Indra Nooyi Turned Design Thinking into Strategy: An Interview with PepsiCo's CEO. Harvard Business Review. Retrieved from https://hbr.org/2015/11/how-indra-nooyi-turned-design-thinking-into-strategy-an-interview-with-pepsicos-ceo.

Koehn, N. F. (2005). Howard Schultz and Starbucks Coffee Company. Harvard Business School Case 801-361.

Schultz, H., & Yang, D. J. (1997). Pour Your Heart into It: How Starbucks Built a Company One Cup at a Time. Hyperion.

Huffington, A. (2014). Thrive is The Third Metric to Redefining Success and Creating a Life of Well-Being, Wisdom, and Wonder. Harmony.

Huffington, A. (2016). The Sleep Revolution: Transforming Your Life, One Night at a Time. Harmony.

Sandberg, S., & Grant, A. (2017). Option B: Facing Adversity, Building Resilience, and Finding Joy. Knopf.

Sandberg, S. (2013). Lean In: Women, Work, and the Will to Lead. Knopf.

O'Connor, L. (2013). 7 Times Oprah Winfrey Turned Failure into Success. Huffington Post. Retrieved from https://www.huffpost.com/entry/oprah-failures-success_n_4168591.

Mair, G. (1994). Oprah Winfrey: The Real Story. Carol Publishing Group.

Lansing, A. (1959). Endurance: Shackleton's Incredible Voyage. Basic Books.

Morrell, M., & Capparell, S. (2001). Shackleton's Way: Leadership Lessons from the Great Antarctic Explorer. Viking.

Gandhi, M. K. (1927). An Autobiography or The Story of My Experiments with Truth. Navajivan Publishing House.

Fischer, L. (1950). The Life of Mahatma Gandhi. Harper.

Simon Sinek: - Sinek, S. (2009). Start with Why: How Great Leaders Inspire Everyone to Take Action. Portfolio.

Paul Polman: - Unilever. (2010). Unilever Sustainable Living Plan. Retrieved from https://www.unilever.com/Images/slp_unilever-sustainable-living-plan_tcm244-424656_en.pdf.

Jeff Bezos: - Stone, B. (2013). The Everything Store: Jeff Bezos and the Age of Amazon. Little, Brown, and Company.

Howard Schultz: - Koehn, N. F. (2005). Howard Schultz and Starbucks Coffee Company. Harvard Business School Case 801-361.

Schultz, H., & Yang, D. J. (1997). Pour Your Heart into It: How Starbucks Built a Company One Cup at a Time. Hyperion.

Boudette, N. E. (2014). G.M. Chief Steps Up Effort to End 'Cobblestone' Culture. The New York Times. Retrieved from https://www.nytimes.com/2014/06/06/business/gm-chief-steps-up-effort-to-end-cobblestone-culture.html.

Huffington, A. (2014). Thrive is The Third Metric to Redefining Success and Creating a Life of Well-Being, Wisdom, and Wonder. Harmony

Huffington, A. (2016). The Sleep Revolution: Transforming Your Life, One Night at a Time. Harmony.

Isaacson, W. (2021). The Code Breaker: Jennifer Doudna, Gene Editing, and the Future of the Human Race. Simon & Schuster.

Richard Branson: - Branson, R. (2012). Like a Virgin: Secrets They Won't Teach You at Business School. Portfolio/Penguin.

"Anand Mahindra: A Leader with a Vision." (2018). Forbes India https://www.forbesindia.com/article/indias-greatest-leaders-2018/anand-mahindra-a-leader-with-a-vision/49917/1.

"How Walmart CEO Doug McMillon is Shaping the Future of Retail." (2019). Fortune. https://fortune.com/longform/walmart-ceo-doug-mcmillon/

"Hamdi Ulukaya: The Anti-CEO Playbook." (2019). TED Talk. https://www.ted.com/talks/hamdi_ulukaya_the_anti_ceo_playbook

"Kiran Mazumdar-Shaw: The Entrepreneur Who Pioneered India's Biotech Industry." (2016). https://www.forbes.com/sites/naazneenkarmali/2016/08/24/kiran-mazumdar-shaw-the-entrepreneur-who-pioneered-indias-biotech-industry/

"Narayana Murthy: A Lifetime of Lessons." (2019). Forbes India. https://www.forbesindia.com/article/leadership-awards-2019/narayana-murthy-a-lifetime-of-lessons/56441/1

"Ratan Tata: The Gentle Giant of the Tata Empire." (2020). https://www.bbc.com/news/business-51121273

"Sundar Pichai: Google's Rising Star Reaches the Top." (2019). https://www.bbc.com/news/business-50505254

"Narendra Modi: India's Economic Reformer." (2018). https://www.ft.com/content/5d62447c-5e5f-11e8-9334-2218e7146b04

"The Quiet Power of Angela Merkel." (2019). The Atlantic. https://www.theatlantic.com/magazine/archive/2019/04/angela-merkel-holding-the-center/583252/

"Elon Musk: The Architect of Tomorrow." (2017). https://www.rollingstone.com/culture/culture-features/elon-musk-the-architect-of-tomorrow-120850/

"Jacinda Ardern's Leadership Masterclass." (2019). https://www.ft.com/content/6b26d6c0-7828-11e9-be7d-6d846537acab

"From the Projects to CEO of Xerox: The Journey of Ursula Burns." (2018). https://www.forbes.com/sites/elanagross/2018/09/20/from-the-projects-to-ceo-of-xerox-the-journey-of-ursula-burns

"The Lady and the Generals." (2017). The Economist. https://www.economist.com/briefing/2017/06/24/aung-san-suu-kyi-is-the-darling-of-democrats-but-at-home-she-must-learn-to-govern

"Patagonia's Philosopher-King." (2016). The New Yorker. https://www.newyorker.com/magazine/2016/09/19/patagonias-philosopher-king

"Sheryl Sandberg: Facebook's Quiet Power." (2012). https://www.theguardian.com/technology/2012/apr/29/sheryl-sandberg-facebook-quiet-power

"The Good Doctor." (2011). The New Yorker.https://www.newyorker.com/magazine/2011/10/31/the-good-doctor-3

"The World's Most Powerful Women: GM's Mary Barra." (2017). Forbes. https://www.forbes.com/sites/moiraforbes/2017/11/29/the-worlds-most-powerful-women-gms-mary-barra/.

"The Conscience of the Coffee World." (2016). The Atlantic. https://www.theatlantic.com/business/archive/2016/12/howard-schultz-starbucks/509047/

The Unilever CEO Who Tried to Make the World a Better Place." (2019). https://www.ft.com/content/cd639282-1e7d-11e9-b126-46fc3ad87c65

"Indra Nooyi on Why PepsiCo is a 'Performance with Purpose' Company." (2015https://fortune.com/2015/09/29/indra-nooyi-pepsico-performance-with-purpose/

"Microsoft's Satya Nadella: The Man Who Remade the Company." (2019). https://www.ft.com/content/2b91c8d0-ccb7-11e9-a1f4-3669401ba76f

Neuroplasticity and Warren Buffett

"Warren Buffett's reading routine could make you smarter; science suggests." (2018). CNBC. https://www.cnbc.com/2018/08/17/warren-buffetts-reading-routine-could-make-you-smarter-says-science.html.

Feedback loops and Ray Dalio - "Ray Dalio: The Culture of Radical Transparency." (2017). TED. https://www.ted.com/talks/ray_dalio_the_culture_of_radical_transparency.

Growth mindset and Satya Nadella "Microsoft's Satya Nadella: The Man Who Remade the Company." (2019). The Financial Times. https://www.ft.com/content/2b91c8d0-ccb7-11e9-a1f4-3669401ba76f.

Google's "20% time" policy

"The Google Way: Give Engineers Room." (2007). The New York Times. https://www.nytimes.com/2007/10/21/jobs/21pre.html.

Jeff Bezos and embracing failure.

"Amazon CEO Jeff Bezos: This is how to make better decisions." (2018). CNBC. https://www.cnbc.com/2018/04/24/amazon-ceo-jeff-bezos-this-is-how-to-make-better-decisions.html.

Elon Musk's ambitious goals

"Elon Musk's Philosophy for Aspiring Entrepreneurs: Shoot for the Stars." (2016). Inc. https://www.inc.com/ilan-mochari/elon-musk-goals.html.

Eric Schmidt and the Objectives and Key Results (OKRs) system

"Measure What Matters: A Brief History of OKRs." (n.d.). What Matters. https://www.whatmatters.com/stories/a-brief-history-of-okrs/.

Mary Barra and General Motors' professional development initiatives

"GM's Mary Barra Talks Talent, Culture and Leadership." (2017). Forbes. https://www.forbes.com/sites/iese/2017/02/28/gms-mary-barra-talks-talent-culture-and-leadership/?sh=7f76d79c2609.

ENDNOTES

1 https://www2.deloitte.com/content/dam/Deloitte/us/Documents/leadership/us-cons-purposedriven-leadership.pdf

2 Nadella, S. (2017). Hit Refresh: The Quest to Rediscover Microsoft's Soul and Imagine a Better Future for Everyone. Harper Business.

Milton Keynes UK
Ingram Content Group UK Ltd.
UKHW020928181023
430840UK00013B/546